D0095335

Better Than Store-Bought

Better Than Store-Bought

A COOKBOOK

Helen Witty
Elizabeth Schneider Colchie

HARPER & ROW, PUBLISHERS

NEW YORK, HAGERSTOWN, SAN FRANCISCO, LONDON

Some of the recipes in this book have appeared, in slightly different form, in *Cooking, Gourmet, The International Review of Food and Wine,* and *Woman's Day.*

BETTER THAN STORE-BOUGHT. Copyright © 1979 by Helen Witty and Elizabeth Schneider Colchie. All rights reserved. Printed in the United States of America. No part of this book may be used or reproduced in any manner whatsoever without written permission except in the case of brief quotations embodied in critical articles and reviews. For information address Harper & Row, Publishers, Inc., 10 East 53rd Street, New York, N.Y. 10022. Published simultaneously in Canada by Fitzhenry & Whiteside Limited, Toronto.

Designer: C. Linda Dingler

Library of Congress Cataloging in Publication Data

Witty, Helen.
    Better than store-bought.

    Includes index.
    1. Cookery.   I. Colchie, Elizabeth Schneider, joint author.   II. Title.
TX715.W843 1979   641.5   78–20195
ISBN 0–06–014693–1

80 81 82 83 10 9 8 7 6 5

Contents

Preface

As food writers, cooks, and longtime experimenters with food, we have become increasingly intrigued with the idea of making at home the products that seem to have been born right on the market shelves, already prepared and prepackaged. What other kind of busybodies would examine in such detail the alternatives to store-bought bean curd, zwieback, breakfast sausage, or green-peppercorn mustard? Our culinary curiosity has resulted in this bookful—with who knows what more to come?

The recipes that have occupied our minds and our kitchens for what seems decades are for foods that are usually thought of as uniquely "store-bought," but that can be better and/or cheaper if you make them at home. Since factory-prepared food has been with us for a relatively short time, many foods that are now made commercially were, obviously, made at home before industrialization. There are, as well, foods that have been developed commercially that can be improved upon when homemade. So what we're proposing, in presenting the recipes in *Better Than Store-Bought,* is largely a revival of formulas and techniques that were once familiar to homemakers, in the form of recipes that can be used by cooks at all levels of skill. What we have gathered together here will, we hope, satisfy those who are less than happy with the state of store-bought:

- People who love good, *real* food and are sad to see it disappearing. Those, for instance, who might yearn to taste genuine sour cream again, not the thick, chalk-white stuff we usually find in the market. Or cream cheese without vegetable gums and preservatives. Or dill pickles innocent of garlic oil and other heartburners. Or hamburger buns with taste, texture, and substance. Nitrate-free liverwurst. Hot fudge that makes a sundae a celebration. And marshmallows worthy of the toasting fork.
- Cooks who prefer to make more cheaply a range of specialized foods

that normally wear grand-scale price tags. Our recipes for smoked chicken, preserved duck or goose *(confit)*, *caponata,* pickled Jerusalem artichokes, various mustards, crystallized mint leaves, bitter-orange marmalade, and *cornichons* might comfort the luxury-loving with limited budgets (and provide them with gifts for their luxury-loving friends).

• Curious and questing cooks, often with a nostalgia for particular foods, who enjoy the creation of intriguing edibles. We hope some others who love experimenting in the kitchen will be as pleased as we were to produce pastrami, crumpets, salt herring, old-fashioned dried sweet corn, bouillon cubes, pita, anise liqueur, and graham crackers.

• People who find it hard to buy certain delicacies or ethnic specialties that they might need or simply fancy—like *chorizos,* ricotta, bialys, *crème fraîche,* Jewish "corn" bread, spice Parisienne, tahini, sweet German mustard, bagels, and real Chinese almond cookies.

• Those who, like us, shudder at the array of chemicals added to so many foods to lengthen their shelf life and give them what some think is a more enticing appearance (they often look embalmed to us). Anyone who reads labels (or newspapers) knows that while the side effects of many additives are unknown, those of others, unfortunately, are— and they are pretty awful. Thus we offer additive-free recipes, which should be especially welcome in some of the realms that are worst abused: breads, sausages, corned meats, pickles and relishes (often a gruesome green), candied fruits (ordinarily dyed improbable colors), and pudding mixes.

• Shoppers who are overwhelmed by the sugar shoveled unnecessarily into all manner of food. Why must we accept such a staggering amount of sweetening in many peanut butters? Pickled herring? Almost all breads? Ketchup? Marinara sauce? Yogurt?

We have not attempted (books not being built like accordions) to include recipes for all those commercially packed foods (baked beans, for instance) for which directions are easily found in good cookbooks. We do, however, include some things—Marinara Sauce (page 179), Crisp Pickled Green Beans (page 136), Vanilla Ice Cream (page 70)— for which recipes are fairly easy to locate in one version or another, because we think it's refreshing to be reminded that such banal things are worth making, and because we believe our particular recipes are more reliable than most.

We have left some categories of food to the experts who have the proper equipment and, often, generations of experience behind them.

Aged country hams, for example, still made in several parts of the United States, are best when they come from the hands of people who in some firms have been curing them since colonial times; some air-dried and smoked sausages require a perfectly controlled atmosphere, as well as constant attention from people with years of know-how; the same can be said of cheeses that need ripening and/or aging. In addition, there are branches of confectionery and baking that call for highly complicated machinery and heat- and humidity-controlled environments, not to mention ingredients not available to the home cook.

Much to our regret, we have found that such personal favorites as really good hard pretzels, jelly beans, matzos, and halvah are in this category. So far, too, delectable home-cured green olives have eluded us (after forty pounds or so have passed through our crocks), although many claim to have success with them. (Raw, ripe black olives, easier to cure, are rarely marketed in the United States.) And Turkish delight refused to be predictably delightful, although we ate our way through a few luscious (and many not so luscious) batches.

A final word on what you *won't* find in *Better Than Store-Bought:* brand-name replicas. You won't find copies of Wick Fowler's Two-Alarm Chili, Heinz ketchup, or Philadelphia Brand cream cheese. You *will* find out how to make fragrant chili powder, fine homemade ketchup, and pure cream cheese.

Meat and Fish

SAUSAGES

OTHER MEATS AND FISH

Notes on Making Fresh Sausages

Considering the luscious rewards, making sausages at home is well worth the effort. With little specialized equipment, a bit of practice, and some reasonable recipes, you will soon feel free to disdain forever the composites of ambiguous origin that often pass themselves off as fresh sausages.

We have limited ourselves here to the production of "fresh sausages," that is, those made of fresh pork meat and fat which are not lengthily air-dried (although one kind is smoked) before being poached, pan-broiled, or baked. Air-dried sausages (such as salami and summer sausage) have not been included because it is difficult to maintain the cool, dry, airy atmosphere necessary to prevent spoilage. For similar safety reasons, we have not included sausages that require smoke-curing at temperatures that demand the accuracy of professional equipment.

What we *have* included is a range of fresh sausages that are free of sweeteners, artificial flavors and preservatives, cereal fillers, harsh garlic and onion powders, and the other questionable additions that find their way into commercial sausages. Nor do they contain saltpeter, one of the undesirable nitrates used to keep the meat pink. And you choose the meat that goes into the grinder yourself, so, although you pay serious prices to make your sausages, you know that you are getting a pure meat product—not cereal and sugar in place of protein.

ABOUT MEAT CUTS AND PREPARATION

To make succulent sausage, you must use a sufficient amount of chilled fresh pork fat—whether hard fatback (the easiest to handle), loin fat, belly fat, or leaf fat from around the kidneys. It must be clean and smooth and trimmed of any rind or membrane. The fat usually makes up about one-third of the total volume of the ingredients, if not more. Do not be tempted to use less fat than specified, or you will have a dry, sawdusty product.

For the lean part of the sausage meat, you may use cuts from the loin, shoulder, butt, or leg (fresh ham) of the pig—any or all. The meat should be cold when you cut it and grind it, both so it can be tidily trimmed and so it will blend more easily with the fat. Weights in the following recipes are for meat that has been completely trimmed of all membrane, connective tissue, and sinewy or gristly parts.

ABOUT SAUSAGE-MAKING PARAPHERNALIA

For cutting up the meat, we prefer the clean chop of a food processor to the results achieved with a grinder (although you must be careful to prevent overprocessing of medium- or coarse-textured sausages). But a good meat grinder—one with a sharp blade and plates with several sizes of openings—can do a fine job. If you do use a meat grinder, change the procedure in all the recipes as follows:

Instead of cubing the trimmed meat and fat, cut it into strips about 2 to 3 inches long and ½ to 1 inch wide; toss them in a bowl with the seasonings and push them through the grinder; then beat in any liquids called for.

Although you may make loose sausage meat, or tie the meat in cheesecloth to poach or smoke it, we prefer to make neat, smooth, plump sausages properly shaped in natural casings. To simplify matters, all our recipes that require casings make use of the same kind: natural hog casings, about 1¼ inches in diameter. (If your butcher cannot get them for you, see page 308 for speedy mail-order sources.) If you keep the casings packed in salt in the fridge, they will endure virtually forever. Any time you have a mad desire to create sausages, snip off the amount of casing needed, re-cover the remaining casing with coarse (kosher) salt, and refrigerate it until the urge strikes again.

SAUSAGE-STUFFING PROCEDURE

Although it is possible to stuff sausages using a funnel or a pastry bag, it is messy and overly time-consuming. We suggest using a sausage horn attached to a meat grinder or one of the all-purpose machines that have such attachments.

Cut off the amount of casing you think you might need (don't worry about wasting any—you can always return the unused part to its salt box if you've pulled out too much). Open one end of the casing, slip it onto a faucet, and begin, slowly, to run cold water through it. If you find any holes, snip out the damaged part of the tube and keep the remainder. Fill each length of casing with water, keeping it free of twists and knots while you do so; let the water run through for about a minute. Place the rinsed casing in a bowl of tepid water while you continue with the preparations.

Cut a sufficient number of 3-inch pieces of thin cotton string or strong thread for tying links or longer sausages.

Attach the sausage horn to the meat grinder (which should not have the cutting blade in place at this time). Turn on the grinder to fill the horn with the meat mixture until the meat is flush with the aperture, then slip the casing onto the sausage horn, pushing it on gently until only about 2 inches of the casing remain dangling; knot the dangling end. Begin extruding the meat mixture, holding the casing lightly to prevent it from slipping off the horn before it is filled. Fill the casing evenly, without overstuffing. Do not hesitate to mold the meat gently with your hands as you go, but do beware of fingernails. If air pockets form, poke a needle into the casing and squeeze to press out the air.

You may tie links of the desired length as you fill the casing, or you may stuff the entire casing to within 2 inches of the end, then stop the machine. Carefully remove the stuffed casing from the horn and tie a knot at the end of it. Lay the long sausage on a working surface and roll it gently back and forth with your hands until it is all the same thickness. Make indentations with the side of your hand in the filled casing to mark links of the required size, then, at each mark, tie a knot with the string. If an air pocket forms at this stage, prick the spot with a needle and push the casing against the meat to expel the air.

Most sausages are improved by a bit of curing time, so if the air is fairly dry and the temperature is less than 70 degrees, hang the sausage for several hours, preferably in a breezy spot. If the weather does not permit this, place the sausages, unwrapped, on a cake rack or a hook in the refrigerator and leave them to dry for about 24 hours before wrapping or cooking.

REFRIGERATOR AND FREEZER STORAGE

Fresh sausages may be stored in the refrigerator for about 2 to 3 days after their initial curing period, tightly wrapped in plastic or foil. If you prefer to freeze them, be sure that they are very thoroughly wrapped in freezer paper; or enclose them in plastic, then foil, and tape the seams closed. Frozen, the sausages keep their flavor for about 2 months, after which it diminishes noticeably.

SPICY COUNTRY-STYLE SAUSAGE MEAT

If you don't want to bother with stuffing sausage casings, this is a most useful all-purpose mixture—well seasoned enough to stand on its own as breakfast patties, but not too assertive to be used as an ingredient in poultry stuffing, pâtés, and meat loaves, or in combination with other meats and vegetables, as in a *cassoulet.*

Makes about 1½ pounds

2 ½ teaspoons coarse (kosher) salt
2 teaspoons dried leaf sage, crumbled
¾ teaspoon dried summer savory, crumbled
¼ teaspoon whole black peppercorns
1 to 2 tiny dried hot red peppers or ¼ to ½ teaspoon crushed dried
    red pepper flakes
1 pound lean, trimmed pork, cut into 1-inch cubes and chilled
½ pound fresh pork fat, cut into ¼- to ½-inch cubes and chilled

1. Combine the salt, sage, savory, peppercorns, and red pepper in a spice mill or mortar and grind to a powder.
2. Sprinkle the spices over the meat in a large bowl and mix well.
3. Put half the mixture in the container of a food processor and process to a medium-coarse texture (if you are using a meat grinder, follow the instructions on pages 4–5). Scrape into a bowl and repeat the processing with the remaining ingredients, then cover the bowl with plastic and chill for 24 hours to mellow and firm up.
4. Form the sausage meat into a cylinder about 8 inches long and wrap it in plastic. You may then use it, refrigerate it for 3 or 4 days, or freeze it for longer storage.

TO COOK: Cut the sausage into ¾-inch-thick slices and arrange them in a heavy skillet. Cook over moderate heat until well browned on both sides, turning often and pouring off the fat as necessary.

SMOKED COUNTRY SAUSAGE

A few hours in a box-type electric home smoker adds the tang of hickory smoke to the seasonings of the preceding recipe, Spicy Country-Style Sausage Meat. This is a firm, easily sliced cylinder, golden on the outside. Slice and cook this sausage just as you would the unsmoked sausage that is its base.

Makes about 1½ pounds

Spicy Country-Style Sausage Meat (page 6)
Cheesecloth for wrapping

1. Prepare and chill the sausage meat, formed into a cylinder 10 inches long and wrapped in plastic, for 24 hours.

2. Remove the plastic and roll the sausage in a piece of cheesecloth about 13 inches wide and long enough to wrap around the sausage at least twice. Fasten the ends of the cheesecloth with wire bag-closing twists or string.

3. Preheat a box-type electric smoker for 45 minutes. Optionally, soak about 1½ pounds of hickory chips, chunks, or sawdust for about 20 minutes, then drain the wood. (You will have good results from smoking the sausage with dry hardwood, too. See A Note on Home Smoking on page 28 and the recipe for Smoked Chicken or Turkey on page 30.)

4. Hang the sausage in the smoker and put a double handful of fuel into the smoker pan; close the door and watch for smoke to emerge from the vent. If it does not appear soon, adjust the draft to admit more air (usually done by opening the smoker door slightly—see the manufacturer's directions). Smoke the sausage for 4 to 5 hours, or until golden and firm, renewing the fuel as often as necessary to keep the flow of smoke steady.

5. Cool, wrap, and refrigerate the sausage. Use within about a week, removing the cheesecloth before slicing.

BREAKFAST SAUSAGE LINKS

"Little pig" sausages have appeared on American breakfast tables for generations. The seasoning in the recipe that follows is to our taste— rather light on the sage and onion, which so often overpower sausage mixtures. The texture is close-grained but tender, and the meat is succulent without tasting fatty.

Makes about 2¾ pounds

4 teaspoons coarse (kosher) salt
½ teaspoon dried thyme
2 teaspoons dried leaf sage, crumbled
¼ to ½ teaspoon whole white peppercorns, or to taste
1 very small onion, finely chopped
2 pounds lean, trimmed pork, cut into ½-inch dice and chilled
¾ pound fresh pork fat, cut into ½-inch dice and chilled

1. Combine the salt, thyme, sage, and peppercorns in a spice mill or mortar and grind to a powder.

2. Sprinkle the onion and spices over the meat and fat in a large bowl and mix well.

3. Put half the mixture in the container of a food processor and process to a very fine puree (if you are using a meat grinder, follow the instructions on page 4, and use the finest disc); the mixture should be a homogenized pink paste. Turn into a bowl and repeat the operation with the other half. Cover the bowl with plastic and refrigerate for at least 6 hours, or up to 24 hours.

4. Stuff the casings as directed in the general instructions on pages 4–5, tying the casings every 3 inches. Refrigerate the sausage for at least 12 hours, or for as long as 48 hours. For longer storage, freeze.

TO COOK: Prick the sausages all over with a needle. Arrange in a skillet and pour in ¼ inch of water. Cook over moderate heat, turning often, until the water has evaporated and the sausages are browned. Or broil the sausages in a pan about 4 inches from the broiling unit and brown lightly, turning often.

SWEET ITALIAN SAUSAGE

Unless you live near an Italian pork butcher who makes his own sausages with Old World dedication, you will never taste better sweet Italian sausages than you can make yourself. The reputation of this widely manufactured sausage has suffered from indifferent commercial production, so you may not be wholly captivated by the idea of making your own. But we are convinced that the flavors of fine fresh pork and aromatic fennel seed combine to make one of the most distinctive of the world's fresh sausages.

Makes about 2¾ pounds

    4 teaspoons coarse (kosher) salt
    Scant 1 tablespoon fennel seeds
¼ teaspoon whole black peppercorns
    1 small dried hot red pepper (about 1½ inches long), seeds removed
¼ teaspoon very finely minced garlic
¼ cup ice water
    2 pounds lean, trimmed pork, cut into 1-inch dice and chilled
¾ pound fresh pork fat, cut into ½-inch dice and chilled

1. Combine the salt, fennel, peppercorns, and red pepper in a spice mill or mortar and grind to a coarse texture; do not powder. Mix with the garlic.

2. Combine the spice mixture, water, meat, and fat in a large bowl.

3. Put half the mixture in the container of a food processor and grind to a medium texture (if you are using a meat grinder, follow the directions on page 4, using the medium disc). The meat and fat should be distinct from each other, but reduced to tiny pieces of about the same size; do not overprocess. Scrape into a bowl and repeat the operation with the remaining ingredients. Knead the batches together to mix thoroughly, then cover and refrigerate for about 12 hours.

4. Stuff into casings as indicated in the general sausage-making instructions on page 4–5, tying off in 5-inch links. If the room is cool, hang the sausages for a few hours, or until they are just dry to the touch, then refrigerate them. Or, if it's too hot or humid to hang the sausages, simply refrigerate them, uncovered, for a minimum of 12 hours. Store in the refrigerator for up to 3 days, or freeze them for longer storage.

(continued)

TO COOK: Prick the sausages with a needle and arrange them in a baking dish or pan. Bake at 425 degrees for about 25 minutes, or until they are evenly browned, turning several times. Or place the pricked sausages in a large skillet and add ¼ inch of water. Cook over moderate heat, turning often, until the water has evaporated and the sausages are well browned.

HOT ITALIAN SAUSAGE

For those who prefer a hotter, more complicated flavor, this is a worthy rival to our own favorite, Sweet Italian Sausage (see preceding recipe).

Makes about 2 pounds

2 ½ teaspoons coarse (kosher) salt
 ½ teaspoon whole black peppercorns
 3 to 6 dried hot red peppers (each about 1½ inches long), seeds removed, or 1 to 2 teaspoons crushed dried red pepper flakes
 1 tablespoon paprika
 ½ teaspoon dried thyme
 1 teaspoon fennel seeds
 ½ teaspoon very finely minced garlic
1 ½ to 1¾ pounds lean, trimmed pork, cut into 1-inch dice and chilled
 ½ pound fresh pork fat, cut into ½-inch dice and chilled

1. Combine the salt, peppercorns, hot peppers, paprika, thyme, and fennel in a spice mill or a mortar and grind to a coarse texture, not a powder. Mix in a small bowl with the garlic.
2. Combine the meat, fat, and spices in a large bowl.
3. Put half the mixture in the container of a food processor and process to a medium-coarse grind (if you are using a meat grinder, follow the directions on page 4, using the medium disc). The meat and fat should be distinct from each other, but reduced to pieces of about the same size; do not overprocess. Scrape into a bowl. Repeat with the remaining ingredients, then knead the batches together, cover the bowl, and refrigerate for 12 to 24 hours.
4. Stuff the casings as indicated in the general sausage-making instructions on pages 4–5, tying off the links at 4 to 5 inches. If weather is cool, hang the sausages for a few hours, until they are just dry to the touch. If it's too hot or humid to hang the sausages, simply refrigerate

them, uncovered, for a minimum of 12 hours. Store in the refrigerator for up to 3 days, or freeze for longer storage.

TO COOK: Prick the sausages with a needle and arrange in a single layer in a baking pan. Bake in a 425-degree oven for 25 minutes, or until browned, turning often. Or place the pricked sausages in a large skillet and add ¼ inch of water. Cook over moderate heat, turning often, until the water has evaporated and the sausages are well browned.

CHORIZOS (Fresh Hot Spanish Sausages)

There are countless versions of this hot, spicy Hispanic sausage. So many, in fact, that we are fully prepared for accusations of inauthenticity. This, like all our homemade sausages, is a fresh sausage. So do not expect the taste of the more commonly sold Spanish smoked *chorizo* or the air-dried Latin version.

Makes 1¾ to 2 pounds

    ¾ teaspoon cumin seeds
    5 to 8 small dried hot red peppers (each about 1½ inches long), seeds removed, or 1½ teaspoons dried hot red pepper flakes, or more to taste
1 ½ teaspoons coriander seeds
    3 or 4 whole cloves
    ½ teaspoon sugar
2 ½ teaspoons coarse (kosher) salt
    4 teaspoons paprika (medium-hot, if available)
    ¼ teaspoon whole black peppercorns
    ½ teaspoon finely minced garlic (or more, if you like a garlicky sausage)
1 ¼ pounds lean, trimmed pork, cut into 1-inch dice and chilled
    10 ounces fresh pork fat, cut into ½-inch dice and chilled
    ⅓ cup robust red wine

1. Combine the cumin seeds, hot peppers or flakes, coriander, and cloves in a small pan and shake over moderate heat until the peppers are slightly toasted and the seeds start to crackle—about 1 minute.

2. Combine the toasted seasonings with the sugar, salt, paprika, and peppercorns in a spice mill or mortar and grind to a coarse texture. Mix with the garlic in a bowl.

3. Combine the pork, fat, and seasonings in a large bowl.

4. Put half the mixture in the container of a food processor, add half the wine, and process to a fairly coarse grind (if you are using a meat

grinder, follow the directions on page 4, using a medium-coarse disc). Scrape into a bowl and repeat with the remaining meat mixture and wine, then combine the batches thoroughly. Chill thoroughly.

5. Stuff the sausage casings as directed in the general sausage-making instructions on pages 4–5, tying off the links at 3 to 4 inches. Hang the *chorizos* in a cool, airy place for 8 to 12 hours, or until they are firm, smooth, and dry to the touch. If the weather is hot or very humid, instead of hanging the sausages, refrigerate them, uncovered, for at least 12 hours. To store, refrigerate for up to 3 days, or freeze for longer storage.

TO COOK: Prick the sausages all over with a needle. Place them in a heavy skillet with ¼ inch of water. Cook over moderate heat until the water evaporates and the sausages are browned, turning them often.

GARLIC SAUSAGE

One of the most straightforward and delicious sausages in the world is also one of the most difficult to find in this country. It is a mainstay of the French *cuisine bourgeoise,* but has close cousins in sausage shops throughout Europe. If you add garlic sparingly (as we prefer), the resulting sausage is, to our mind, one of the most versatile. Serve it plain with a French oil-dressed potato salad, or cook it with sauerkraut, or use it in a *cassoulet* or in any other bean or cabbage dish.

Hanging fresh sausages to dry is often optional, as we mention in the introduction, but with this sausage it's essential. So plan to make garlic sausage during cool weather.

Makes about 2 pounds

    4 teaspoons coarse (kosher) salt
    1 teaspoon Spice Parisienne (page 198)
    ¼ teaspoon ground white pepper
    ½ teaspoon sugar
    ½ to 1½ teaspoons finely minced garlic, according to taste
1 ¼ pounds lean, trimmed pork, cut into 1-inch cubes and chilled
    10 ounces pork fat, cut into ½-inch cubes and chilled
    ⅓ cup dry red or white wine, dry Madeira, or port

1. Combine salt, spice Parisienne, pepper, sugar, and garlic.
2. Combine the spice mixture with the meat and fat in a large bowl.
3. Put half the mixture in the container of a food processor (if you

are using a meat grinder, follow the directions on page 4, using the medium disc). Add half of the wine and process to a medium grind. Scrape into a bowl and repeat with the remaining meat mixture and wine. Combine the batches and mix very well. Chill, covered, for 30 minutes or more.

4. Stuff into casings as directed in the general sausage-making instructions on pages 4–5, tying off at 5-inch intervals. Hang for 1 to 2 days in a cool, slightly breezy place (45 to 70 degrees). Refrigerate or freeze.

TO COOK: Poach gently in broth or equal parts of wine and water for 15 to 20 minutes, having first pricked the sausage in several places with a needle. Or add to bean or cabbage stews or soups for the last 30 minutes of cooking. Or prick the sausage, place in a skillet with ¼ inch of water, and cook it over moderate heat, turning often, until the water evaporates and the sausage is lightly browned.

POLISH SAUSAGE (Kielbasa)

This sausage has many guises: smoked, raw, and precooked are the most common forms. Well known in Central Europe and parts of the Soviet Union, it has become associated most often with Poland (several versions hail from that country) and is therefore referred to in market nomenclature as "Polish sausage." The ingredients of kielbasa (as of practically all sausages) are remarkably variable, changing from town to town and even from house to house, but garlic does appear to be a constant. Hearty and rustic, this hefty sausage can be used in all recipes that call for garlic sausage.

Makes about 2¾ pounds

    4 teaspoons coarse (kosher) salt
1 ¾ teaspoons ground black pepper
    3 tablespoons sweet Hungarian paprika
    1 teaspoon dried marjoram, crumbled
    ½ teaspoon dried savory, crumbled
    2 teaspoons finely minced garlic
    10 ounces trimmed beef shin, cut into ½-inch dice and chilled
    14 to 16 ounces fresh pork fat, cut into ½-inch dice and chilled
    ⅓ cup ice water
1 ¼ pounds lean, trimmed pork, cut into 1-inch dice and chilled

1. Mix together in a small bowl the salt, pepper, paprika, marjoram, savory, and garlic.

(continued)

2. In the container of a food processor combine the beef, half the pork fat, half the ice water, and half the mixed seasonings (see step 1) and process to a very fine grind (if you are using a meat grinder, follow the directions on page 4). Scrape into a mixing bowl.

3. In a bowl combine the remaining seasonings, the pork, remaining pork fat, and remaining water. Process half of the mixture at a time to a coarse grind and add to the beef. Mix together very thoroughly, cover, and chill for 24 hours.

4. Stuff the sausage into casings as indicated in the general sausage-making directions on pages 4–5, tying links from 10 to 30 inches long, depending upon your preference. Both sizes (and everything in between) are considered traditional. Hang the sausages in a cool, airy place for several hours at least, or until the skin is smooth, dry, and crackly. If it's too hot or humid to hang the sausages, refrigerate them, uncovered, for at least 12 hours. To store, refrigerate for up to 3 days, or freeze for longer keeping.

TO COOK: Place one or more sausages in a large skillet with water to come halfway up them. Bring to a simmer and cook for about 8 minutes, then turn and cook for about 8 minutes on the other side. Pour off the water, prick the sausages, and cook them over moderate heat until browned on both sides.

FRANKFURTERS

As any hot-dog lover knows, there is no such thing as a standardized frankfurter. They come in all shapes and sizes, qualities, and shades of unbelievable pink (thanks to preservatives), and they range in flavor from sweet and mild to grossly garlic-powdered.

As our sausages contain neither nitrates nor nitrites (both controversial preservatives that keep meat pink), they are a pale grey-beige—the color of cooked meat—which takes a bit of getting used to.

If you like smoky sausages, hang them in a small home smoker containing smoldering hardwood chips for a few hours, until the color and flavor please you. (See the recipe for Smoked Chicken or Turkey on page 30, and A Note on Home Smoking on page 28.) Although it's possible to make frankfurter sausages with a meat grinder, you can achieve the familiar fine texture only by working the ingredients to a paste in a food processor.

Makes about 1½ pounds

¼ cup coarsely diced onion
½ teaspoon finely minced garlic
1 ½ tablespoons coarse (kosher) salt
  1 tablespoon ground coriander
½ teaspoon ground mace
½ teaspoon ground white pepper
½ teaspoon caraway seeds, measured, then ground in a spice mill or
    mortar
⅓ cup cold milk
  1 egg white
¼ cup very fine (virtually powdered), dry bread crumbs
  2 teaspoons light corn syrup
1 ½ pounds lean, trimmed pork, cut into 1-inch cubes and chilled
¾ pound fresh pork fat, cut into ½-inch cubes and chilled

1. Puree the onion, garlic, and salt in the container of a food processor. Add the coriander, mace, pepper, and caraway and process until well blended. Add the milk, egg white, bread crumbs, and corn syrup and again process until mixed. Scrape half the mixture into a bowl and set aside.

2. To the mixture remaining in the processor container, add half the chilled meat and fat cubes and process to a very fine puree. Scrape into a large bowl. Repeat with the remaining half of the seasoning mixture, meat, and fat. Mix the two batches well, then chill, covered, for several hours or overnight.

3. Fill casings as described in the general sausage-making directions on page 4. The sausage mixture will be squishier than most, so filling the casings is a bit tricky at first. Tie casings to make plump frankfurters about 8 inches long (they will shrink during cooking).

4. Place the sausages in a large pot and add cold water to cover them by about 2 inches. Weight the sausages with a plate to hold them under the surface, heat the water to a bare simmer, and simmer for 15 minutes.

5. Drain and set under cold running water until cooled. Hang the sausages briefly (you can loop them over a wire coat hanger), just until the casings are dry. Refrigerate (unlike many sausages, these will keep for up to a week) or freeze them.

TO COOK: Briefly simmer the frankfurters until just heated through, or pan-grill them.

LIVERWURST

If you lust for liverwurst but have held your passion in check because of the dubious array of additives, sweeteners, and synthetics that have weaseled their way into the commercial product, rejoice. You can make it yourself.

Gently pink, both sliceable and spreadable, our liverwurst is a reminder that this sausage is, in fact, a subtly spiced liver pâté. The recipe that follows requires a food processor, which makes a formerly arduous task quite simple, producing a creamy-smooth pâté. The hardest part may be locating a source of pork liver. (Frozen liver, incidentally, is fine for this sausage. If you find a supply of the fresh liver—it is highly perishable—you may want to freeze a quantity for future use.)

For our liverwurst you don't need special large casings, as we have devised a method of poaching the cheesecloth-wrapped sausage inside a plastic bag of the type sold for oven-roasting meats and poultry.

Makes one 1 1/2-pound sausage

¾ pound pork liver, fresh or frozen, cut into 1-inch cubes and chilled
½ pound lean, trimmed pork, cut into 1-inch cubes and chilled
¼ pound fresh pork fat, cut into ½-inch cubes and chilled
½ cup coarsely diced onion
  1 tablespoon nonfat dry milk
½ teaspoon ground white pepper
    Scant ½ teaspoon ground cardamom
    Scant ½ teaspoon ground ginger
⅛ teaspoon ground mace
½ teaspoon ground coriander
⅛ teaspoon dried marjoram, crumbled
1 ½ teaspoons salt
¾ teaspoon sugar
  2 ice cubes, broken up

1. Toss together the cubed meats, fat, and the onion.

2. Combine in a small bowl the dry milk, pepper, cardamom, ginger, mace, coriander, marjoram, salt, and sugar and sprinkle the mixture over the meat. Mix everything together.

3. In the container of a food processor, puree the seasoned meat in

several batches, running the machine as long as necessary to make as smooth a puree as possible. Combine all batches of the puree and mix them well in the processor, adding the ice and running the machine until the ice melts.

4. Using a food mill fitted with the finest disc, force the liverwurst mixture through. (This will eliminate any bits of stringy membrane not dealt with by the pureeing process.) Chill the mixture for an hour or two.

5. In a large pot bring enough water to a boil to cover by at least 2 inches a sausage 3 inches in diameter.

6. Double a piece of cheesecloth into a 12-inch square. Have at hand a needle and thread and either string or the wire twists used for closing plastic bags. (You'll also need a 10 × 15-inch plastic bag of the kind used for oven roasting.) Lay the doubled cheesecloth flat and spoon the sausage mixture into the center. Lift opposite edges of the cloth and roll the mixture back and forth a few times to form a cylinder about 3 inches in diameter, then tighten the cloth and fold one side over the other around the sausage roll, patting and smoothing it into an even cylinder. With a few long, slanting stitches, sew the overlapping edges of the cheesecloth together (you can run the needle right into the filling and out again—this is a quick job). Now gather and twist the ends of the cheesecloth to compress the sausage further and to give it rounded ends. Tie each end with string or fasten it with a wire twist.

7. Put the sausage into the oven-roasting bag, easing it carefully into the bottom; it should just fill the horizontal space (if it's a bit too long, compress the ends). Lay the bag flat on the table and use your hands to expel all possible air, beginning at the top of the sausage. Use string or a wire twist to close the neck of the bag, close to the top.

8. Ease the bag into the simmering water, making sure that the tied end is not immersed. Put a small, heavy plate over the sausage to keep it under the surface. Check the temperature of the water a few times as cooking begins and adjust the heat so that the liquid is kept between 170 and 175 degrees. Poach the sausage for about 2 hours, or until any juice collected in the bag looks clear, not pink. When you think the sausage is done, lift out the bag, open the top, and test the center of the sausage with an instant-reading thermometer, which will give a reading of at least 170 degrees when the sausage is done.

9. Pour the hot water out of the cooking pot and fill it with cold water. Refasten the bag containing the sausage and plunge it into the cold water, again with the neck of the bag above the surface. Let cold

water run slowly into the pot for about 20 minutes, or until the sausage has cooled completely.

10. Refrigerate the sausage, still in the cooking bag, for 24 hours before serving it (during this time it will reabsorb any juice in the bag). Remove the sausage from the bag, cut off the cheesecloth, and wrap and refrigerate the sausage. Plan to consume it within about a week to retain its full savor. (It can be frozen, but freezing makes it soggy, so we recommend making only the amount you can use within that time.) If you can use two liverwursts, double the recipe and make two rolls; they can be poached together in a single bag.

CORNED BEEF

Corning meat (curing it in brine) is a simple operation, requiring little work and no special equipment—only refrigerator space. Beef is the meat most commonly "pickled" in this fashion, although cuts of pork— see Home-Brined Pork (page 22), for instance—or mutton, ducks, tongues, assorted piggy parts, and sheeps' trotters are regularly found in the curing crocks of kitchens all over the world.

The following is a completely basic recipe for corned beef: the salt cures the meat, and the sugar (by complicated chemical transformations) develops in it both flavor and tenderness. Here, as in our other meat recipes, we have avoided using saltpeter (one of the nitrates, hence questionable), which is used merely to intensify the pinkness of meat. If you like spicy corned beef, see the recipe following this one. It starts with ready-to-cook plain corned beef.

Serves at least 6

A thin (or front) cut of beef brisket, weighing 4 to 5 pounds
Coarse (kosher) salt as needed
1 egg, in its shell (to test the brine)
½ cup (packed) brown sugar
Water as needed

1. Find a ceramic, glass, or enameled vessel large enough to hold both the beef and enough brine to cover the beef by 2 or more inches.

Be sure the crock or container will fit into your refrigerator.

2. To determine the brine quantity needed, enclose the beef in a plastic bag, put it into the container (no need to close the bag—just hold the open end above the water level), and run cold water into the container to cover the bag of meat by 2 to 3 inches. Remove the meat.

3. Stir coarse salt into the water, letting each addition dissolve before adding more, until an egg will float in the solution. (You'll probably need about 1½ cups salt). Remove the egg once it has served its purpose. Stir in the brown sugar.

4. Pour the brine into a pot and simmer it for 15 minutes, then let it cool completely and pour it back into the crock or container. Lower the meat, minus bag, into the brine and weight it down with a heavy plate or a round of heavy wood that has been sterilized by boiling. If necessary, add more weight—a nonmetallic object such as a canning jar full of water—to hold the meat under the brine. Set the container in the refrigerator and let the beef cure for at least 2 weeks, turning it every day or two. Don't plan to cure it for more than a month.

TO COOK: Rinse the corned beef and place it in a roomy pot. Add water to cover by 2 inches. Cook the meat at a barely perceptible simmer, partly covered, until it is very tender when tested with a long fork; count on at least 3 hours, perhaps as long as 5 for a large or thick piece of beef. Turn the beef occasionally and add boiling water, if needed, to keep the meat covered. Let the beef cool partially, uncovered, in the broth. Serve it warm; or cool, drain, and refrigerate it, wrapped. To rewarm, slice and steam the beef briefly; or wrap the piece in foil and steam until warmed through.

SPICED CORNED BEEF, DELICATESSEN STYLE

Starting with a well-cured piece of corned brisket (see the preceding recipe), lovers of deli-style corned beef ("on rye with mustard, pickle on the side") can now enjoy it in the quiet of their own homes. Once the beef has been rubbed with a collection of pungent seasonings, a stay in the refrigerator, followed by unsupervised gentle simmering, does the rest.

(continued)

Serves at least 6

A 4- to 5-pound piece of Corned Beef (page 18), drained
8 bay leaves, coarsely crumbled
5 large cloves garlic, coarsely chopped
1 tablespoon mustard seeds, bruised
2 teaspoons cracked black peppercorns
1 tablespoon coarse (kosher) salt
3 dried hot red peppers (each about 1½ inches long), seeds removed,
    crumbled; or 1 teaspoon crushed dried red pepper flakes
½ teaspoon ground coriander

1. Tear off a piece of heavy aluminum foil large enough to wrap the corned beef completely and lay the meat on it. Combine the bay leaves, garlic, mustard seeds, peppercorns, salt, red peppers, and coriander in a bowl.

2. Rub the seasonings hard into the corned beef, covering all surfaces. Wrap the meat closely and enclose the package in a plastic bag. Tie the bag securely at the neck, then refrigerate the meat for 3 to 5 days, turning it daily.

TO COOK: Leaving the coating of seasonings on the meat, place the corned beef in a large pot and cover it to a depth of 2 inches with cold water. Cook the meat at a *barely* perceptible simmer, partly covered, until it is very tender when pierced with a long fork. (Cooking will take from 3 to 5 hours if it is done at the correct rate.) Turn the meat now and then and add boiling water, if needed, to keep the meat covered.

Let the corned beef partially cool, uncovered, in the broth. It can be served warm (not hot), or it can be cooled completely, drained, wrapped, and refrigerated. It will keep well for a week or more. If you want to reheat the corned beef for sandwiches, slice it thin and steam the slices just until they are hot through.

CORNED BEEF OR VEAL TONGUE

Tongue takes particularly well to spicing, but if you prefer a plain cure, omit the spices from the brine. If calves' tongues are available, be sure to try them; they are very lean and delicate-flavored. Home-cured tongue does not have the excessive saltiness or the deep-rose hue of commercially brined tongues, which are cured with saltpeter.

Serves at least 6

1 fresh (or frozen and thawed) beef tongue (3 to 4 pounds), well
   trimmed, or 3 or 4 calves' tongues (about ¾ pound each),
   trimmed
Water as needed
Coarse (kosher) salt as needed
1 egg, in its shell (to test the brine)
½ cup (packed) dark brown sugar
2 bay leaves, crumbled
½ teaspoon whole allspice berries, bruised
½ teaspoon whole black peppercorns, bruised
2 teaspoons coriander seeds, bruised
1 teaspoon mustard seeds, bruised
2 cloves garlic, peeled but left whole

1. Select a ceramic, glass, or enameled crock or bowl large enough
to hold both the tongue and enough brine to cover the tongue by 2 or
more inches. Be sure the container will fit into your refrigerator.

2. To determine the brine quantity needed, enclose the tongue in
a plastic bag (no need to close the bag—just hold the open end above
the water level), and run cold water into the container to cover the
bagged meat by 2 to 3 inches. Remove the tongue.

3. Stir coarse salt into the water, letting each addition dissolve before
adding more, until an egg will float in the solution. (You'll probably need
about 1½ cups salt.) Remove the egg once it has served its purpose and
pour the brine into a pot.

4. Stir into the brine the sugar, bay leaves, allspice berries, peppercorns, coriander seeds, mustard seeds, and garlic. Bring to a boil and
simmer, covered, for 15 minutes, then let cool completely.

5. Remove the tongue from the bag and prick it well all over with
a skewer or a larding needle. Return it to the crock or bowl.

6. When the brine is cool, pour it over the tongue. Cover with plastic
wrap, then add a plate (with a weight on it, if necessary) that will hold
the meat well under the surface. Cover the crock with plastic wrap and
refrigerate for 10 days to 2½ weeks for beef tongue, 3 to 10 days for
calves' tongues. (Figure a minimum of 3 days' curing per pound of any
single piece of meat.) Turn the meat every few days and be sure it is
always immersed in the brine.

TO COOK: Put the tongue or tongues in a pot with water to cover by
several inches, 2 or 3 carrots, coarsely cut up, a peeled whole onion or

two, and a few tablespoons of vinegar and simmer, partly covered, until the meat is very tender. (The time will vary with the size of the tongue and its original tenderness.) Remove from the cooking liquid, then slit the skin and peel it off neatly. Serve hot as a main course, or cold and thinly sliced for lunch or in sandwiches.

HOME-BRINED PORK

This is not exactly your most popular store-bought item, but we feel it has a place here as a substitute for the often synthetically flavored, water-filled hams and shoulders that one encounters too frequently in today's markets.

This time-honored method of pickling meat makes a new animal of the pig. It acquires a totally different flavor and texture from fresh pork —as different as Canadian bacon is from fresh pork loin. As with the other recipes for meats cured in brine, there is virtually no labor involved for the cook; nature does the work.

A variety of pork cuts can be used for an interesting array of cooking possibilities. As a matter of fact, you can cure as few or as many pieces at a time as you wish; just be sure the meat is submerged in the brine and that you can keep track of the different pieces. To gauge the time needed to cure *each* piece of meat, figure on a minimum of 3 days per pound. Do not work out the time needed to cure the pork pieces collectively, but for each piece separately.

Try not to overcure the pork, or it will be too salty. If you suspect that it might be, simmer the pork, when you cook it, for 15 minutes in water to cover, taste the water, and start afresh if need be.

When you home-brine any meat, it should always be boned, or salt will not penetrate the flesh uniformly.

    4 to 5 pounds boned fresh pork (shoulder, loin, or leg)
    Water as needed
    Coarse (kosher) salt as needed
    1 egg, in its shell (to test the brine)
    2 bay leaves
  1 ½ teaspoons dried thyme
  1 ½ teaspoons whole black peppercorns

1 ½ teaspoons juniper berries
1 teaspoon whole allspice berries
⅔ cup (packed) light or dark brown sugar

1. Select a ceramic, glass, or enameled crock or bowl large enough to hold both the pork pieces and enough brine to cover them by 2 or more inches. Be sure the container will fit into your refrigerator.

2. To determine the brine quantity needed, enclose the pork pieces in a plastic bag (no need to close the bag—just hold the open end above the water level), and run cold water into the container to cover the bagged meat by 2 to 3 inches. Remove the meat.

3. Stir coarse salt into the water, letting each addition dissolve before adding more, until an egg will float in the solution. (You'll probably need about 1 to 1½ cups salt.) Remove the egg once it has served its purpose and pour the brine into an enameled, stainless-steel, or flameproof glass saucepan.

4. In a mortar, crush the bay leaves, thyme, peppercorns, juniper berries, and allspice berries to a fairly coarse texture. Add, along with the sugar, to the brine in the saucepan and bring to a boil, stirring to disolve the sugar; simmer, covered, for 15 minutes, then let cool completely.

5. Remove the pork pieces from the bag and prick the meat all the way through with a skewer or larding needle every 2 inches or so. Return the meat to the crock or bowl.

6. Pour the cooled brine over the pork, cover with a sheet of plastic with enough "give" to support a plate (with a weight on it, if necessary) to keep the meat under the surface of the liquid, then another layer of plastic. Refrigerate for at least 12 to 15 days for a single piece of meat (or 3 days per pound). Turn the meat every 3 or 4 days and check to be sure that it is always totally submerged. If the brine gets too low, boil water and kosher salt (¼ cup per 2 cups water), cool completely, and add to the crock.

TO COOK: Tie the meat with a string to make a neat package. Place it in a deep kettle with 2 to 3 carrots, coarsely cut up, an onion or two, and water to cover by several inches. Cook at a bare simmer until tender, about 25 minutes per pound. Serve as is, or glaze the meat as follows.

TO GLAZE THE MEAT: Preheat the oven to 375 degrees. Place the meat on a rack and smear all over with 3 tablespoons each sharp mustard and orange or ginger marmalade, combined. Roast for about 30 minutes, or until the meat is nicely browned and shiny. Serve the meat hot; at room temperature; or cold, cut small in a salad.

SALT PORK

Whether you yearn for a New England clam chowder, an authentic *coq au vin,* or cracklin' bread, there are times when you will need a piece of salt pork—and your neighborhood market has none. For this reason we suggest making a batch of this easily cured meat when you find a supply of fresh fatback.

We experimented with the traditional dry-cure and found that it did not preserve the pure fat. Instead, we recommend this brining method.

Fresh pork fatback
Coarse (kosher) salt as needed
Water as needed

1. Cut the fatback into pieces about 1 inch wide and 3 or 4 inches long. Put the pieces into a plastic bag, set the bag upright in a crock or a glass, ceramic, or stainless-steel bowl, and pour water around (not into) the bag to determine how much water will be needed for enough brine to cover the pork by at least 1 inch. Lift out the bag and measure the water into a stainless-steel or enameled pot. Return the fat, without the bag, to the crock or bowl.

2. For each 6 cups of water, add 1½ cups salt. Bring to a boil, simmer for 5 minutes, and cool completely.

3. Pour the cold brine over the fat in the crock or bowl to cover by at least 1 inch. Place a saucer over the fat to hold the pieces under the liquid, then cover the crock or bowl and refrigerate. Stir the fat pieces about once a week, making sure they are all resubmerged when you return the crock to the refrigerator. Use the pieces after a week, or for up to a month.

TO STORE: For longer storage, dry the pieces, roll them in salt to coat heavily, wrap, and freeze.

PRESERVED DUCK OR GOOSE *(Confit)*

Perhaps best known as part of the French *cassoulet,* preserved duck or goose is salty, rich, and intensely flavored. Even a small piece, with a little of the preserving fat, will make an inspiring difference in a bean soup or a vegetable stew. Or you can warm sections of your bird gently in their fat in a skillet and serve them with hot mashed potatoes.

When the preserved bird is all gone, don't discard the remaining fat —it keeps almost indefinitely and can be used to make more *confit,* or in cooking. The preserved poultry will keep, refrigerated, for up to a year, and its flavor improves in that period. This particular preparation maintains its interior pinkness, although it does not include the saltpeter often used in *confit.*

As with most other recipes that have developed over generations, there is no "true" *confit;* in French goose-raising country each region, or even each housewife, has the "definitive" version. We don't raise poultry, but this is our way to preserve a goose (or two ducks) in an American house that has no cool cellar.

About 8½ pounds fresh duck (approximate weight after necks,
  giblets, and extra fat have been removed from two 5½-pound
  ducklings) or a goose of about the same net weight
All fat removed from duck or goose, plus 1 to 1½ pounds extra duck
  or goose fat, if available
1 pound pork fat
1 cup coarse (kosher) salt
3 bay leaves, coarsely broken
1 tablespoon dried thyme
½ teaspoon whole white peppercorns
1 teaspoon Quatre Épices (page 197)
½ head of garlic, each clove peeled

1. Cut up the ducks or goose: remove and disjoint the legs (cut the goose thighs into two parts); remove wing tips for the stock pot and cut wings off with a section of the breast attached; cut backs into two pieces; cut breasts into two pieces each. Pull off and reserve all fat.

2. Cut up the reserved fat, plus any extra duck or goose fat available, and put it into a heavy pot with ½ cup water. Cook slowly, stirring once

in a while, until the water has evaporated and all fat has rendered out of the scraps. Strain off and reserve all the fat.

3. Chop the fresh pork fat and render, strain, and reserve it as described in step 2.

4. Grind the salt, bay leaves, thyme, peppercorns, and *quatre épices* in a blender or spice mill.

5. Rub the duck or goose with the spiced salt, using the entire amount. Put the pieces into a heavy plastic bag, close it tightly, and refrigerate for 48 hours, turning the bag occasionally.

6. Remelt the duck fat in a large, heavy pot, adding enough rendered pork fat, if necessary, to cover the pieces of poultry.

7. Wipe the duck or goose pieces dry. Put them into the fat, add the garlic, and weight the meat down with a heavy plate to keep it well under the surface. Regulate the heat to cook the meat very slowly—a bubble should rise to the surface only every few seconds—for 1 hour or more, or until the thick pieces are tender. Test by pricking a thigh: the juice should be clear or only faintly pink; don't overcook. Remove from the heat.

8. Pour about 1 inch of the cooking fat into a scalded, dry crock, or a large, scalded, dry wide-mouthed jar, and let it solidify. Pack the partly cooled pieces of duck or goose into the crock, then strain the fat from the pot over them. There should be no air spaces, and a thick layer of fat should seal the top. Cool completely, cover closely with foil, and refrigerate. The *confit* will keep for up to a year.

TO USE: Set the crock or jar in warm (not hot) water just long enough to let the fat soften to the point where you can remove the pieces required, then smooth the fat closely over the remaining pieces. Re-cover and refrigerate.

CONFIT IN A SLOW-COOKER

If you have a slow-cooker with a capacity of more than 4 quarts, the long, gentle (and relatively odor-free) cooking process is ideal for a *confit*. The procedure in the recipe above should then be changed as follows:

While the meat is marinating, render the duck or goose fat in the cooker (which will take about 6 hours at the "low" setting). Strain the fat, wash the cooker, and return the fat to it to store. When the poultry has cured long enough, remelt the fat in the cooker and proceed to cook the *confit* with the cover in place (no weighting is needed). Cooking will take about 5 hours at the "low" heat setting.

DEVILED HAM

When you have collected a batch of bits and pieces of ham, why not make spicy *real* deviled ham? It is unexpectedly delicious. But have you ever tried to track down a recipe for this familiar American sandwich filling? Strangely enough, we've never encountered a version anywhere among our thousands of cookbooks. Our recipe suits our taste buds, but it is not sacrosanct. Try it this way, then adjust it to desired spiciness or hotness.

Makes about 1½ cups

1 ½ cups cubed, cooked ham, trimmed of all membranes
 ¼ cup cubed firm fat from the cooked ham
1 ½ teaspoons (or to taste) Horseradish Mustard (page 193) or other hot
       prepared mustard
 2 teaspoons white wine vinegar
   Big pinch of grated nutmeg
   Small pinch of ground cloves
 4 or 5 drops of Pepper Sherry (page 183) or bottled hot pepper sauce
 ¼ teaspoon anchovy paste
 ⅛ teaspoon very finely minced garlic, or to taste
   Big pinch of ground pepper
   Big pinch of ground ginger
   Big pinch of ground dried thyme or finely crumbled dried leaf thyme

1. Grind the ham and fat fairly fine, either in a food processor or, in two batches, in an electric blender.

2. If using a processor, add the mustard, wine vinegar, nutmeg, cloves, pepper sherry, anchovy paste, garlic, pepper, ginger, and thyme to the ham at once and process until the mixture is rather like a coarse pâté. If using a blender, scrape the first batch of ground ham into a bowl, add the seasonings, process the rest of the ham, and combine with the mixture in the bowl. If too coarse, process again in two batches.

3. Taste for seasoning, then pack into a jar, cover, and refrigerate overnight or longer to let the flavors mingle. The spread will keep for up to 2 weeks.

A Note on Home Smoking

For smoking chicken, turkey, or fish we use a box-type electric smoker equipped with two shelves, a hanging bar with hooks, and a drip pan. It also has an electric element over which sits a small pan to hold the wood that produces the flavorful smoke. You can use hickory or any other hardwood such as oak, applewood, or sassafras—or you can use corncobs. Hickory chunks, chips, or sawdust are sold in bags where smokers are sold.

Don't try to use a box smoker indoors, even under a strongly vented range hood or in a fireplace, unless you want your premises to be redolent of hardwood smoke for a long time. Instead, smoke outdoors, in a spot sheltered from chilling winds. Plan to check the rate at which the fuel is burning about every hour, until you learn how fast your smoker consumes a panful of chunks, chips, or sawdust. (Sawdust burns the fastest.)

Smokers such as ours don't produce a lot of heat—a thermometer hung inside usually registers somewhere between 100 and 120 degrees on a cool day—so they do *not* "smoke-cook" foods from the raw state, except for small fish (see page 32), which are ready to eat after smoking.

PASTRAMI

"Spiced and smoked beef of a succulent cut" comes as close as possible to a general definition of pastrami, which can be seasoned in various regional fashions, reflecting the tastes of many Eastern European communities.

Our pastrami is cured in the refrigerator, with the flavors of garlic, pepper, and coriander predominating. As all pastramis, the best and the worst, seem to have become uniquely the province of Jewish delicatessens, this recipe is modeled upon the delicatessen style we like the best. It need hardly be said, to anyone who has ever tasted a pastrami on rye, that the meat should be steamed to rewarm it before it is sliced for serving, either on a plate or in a sandwich.

A word about the beef: Beef flanken—not always easy to come by —indisputably makes the best pastrami. In the absence of flanken, use brisket. The first (or straight) cut tends to be dry, so look for a well-marbled piece; or take the thicker second cut.

    About 4 pounds beef flanken or brisket
½ cup coarse (kosher) salt
  2 tablespoons (packed) dark brown sugar
  1 tablespoon ground ginger
  1 tablespoon coarsely cracked black peppercorns
  4 cloves garlic, finely chopped
  2 tablespoons coriander seeds, coarsely cracked

    1. With a trussing needle or a large darning needle threaded with twine, take a stitch through the narrow end of the meat. Bring out both ends of the string and make a loop about 3 inches long for hanging.

    2. Mix together thoroughly the salt, brown sugar, ginger, pepper, garlic, and coriander. Rub the mixture into every part of the meat's surface, massaging it well and coating it evenly. Wrap the meat in aluminum foil and then enclose it in a plastic bag. Refrigerate for 8 to 12 days, turning the package daily or as often as you think of it.

    3. Remove the seasoned meat from the package, patting onto it any seasonings that may have fallen off. Hang it by its cord loop in a cool, breezy spot (70 degrees or less is ideal) or in front of an electric fan; let dry for 24 hours.

    4. Remove the shelves from the smoker, hang an oven thermometer in it, and preheat it following the manufacturer's instructions (or, lacking instructions, preheat for 45 minutes), adding a panful of presoaked hickory or other hardwood chips (see page 31) after about 30 minutes. When smoke begins to emerge from the vent, hang the pastrami in the smoker, close the door, and smoke steadily for from 2 to 4 hours, depending on the heat your smoker produces (2 hours will be enough if the temperature is as high as 150 degrees) and the degree of smokiness you like; smoke the longer time if the temperature inside the smoker is in the 100- to 120-degree range.

    5. Cool the pastrami, then wrap and refrigerate overnight or for up to 2 or 3 days before cooking.

TO COOK: Cover the pastrami with a generous amount of cold water and simmer very gently until completely tender, at least 2 hours; the exact time will depend on the thickness of the meat. Cool partially in the cooking water, then either serve at once or drain, cool, and refrigerate, wrapped. To reheat cooked pastrami, slice thin (cut on the bias slightly, as you would flank steak) and steam briefly until hot through.

SMOKED CHICKEN OR TURKEY

Smoked poultry is not cured in the way a long-smoked country ham is, so it should be considered as perishable as a plain roasted bird. Refrigerate it as soon as it has cooled and use it within a few days. Frozen and thawed, smoked poultry is good but perhaps a bit damper than a bird that hasn't been frozen. We find that wrapping thawed smoked poultry in foil and warming it for half an hour in a 325-degree oven freshens it. Let it cool to room temperature to serve.

The directions that follow are for first brining the poultry, then roasting it before cold-smoking it.

NOTE: If you should possess a hooded barbecue that can be used for smoking, consult the manufacturer's instructions for using it. These units can almost all be used for hot smoking, and the preliminary roasting may not be necessary. And, of course, look at the instructions accompanying your box smoker. If they're sketchy, you can rely on the method given here.

> **1 tender roasting chicken (4 to 5 pounds), a turkey breast (bone in; weighing about 5 to 6 pounds), or a small whole turkey (6 pounds or less)**
> **4 to 6 quarts water, or as needed**

> *Ingredients <u>per quart</u> of water used for the brine:*

> **½ cup coarse (kosher) salt**
> **2 tablespoons (packed) dark brown sugar**
> **1 tablespoon granulated sugar**
> **⅛ teaspoon ground black pepper**
> **½ bay leaf**

> **A little vegetable oil for oiling the bird**

1. Pull off any surplus fat or loose internal tissue and rinse the chicken or turkey well. Place it in a crock or a ceramic, stainless-steel, or enameled container and pour in cold water to cover it by at least 2 inches. Measure the water and stir into it the appropriate amounts of salt, sugar, pepper, and bay leaves.

2. When the salt and sugar have dissolved, pour the brine into the crock. Put a small, heavy plate on top of the bird to keep it well submerged, adding, if necessary, a nonmetallic weight, such as a jar of water, to keep the plate under the surface. Refrigerate for 18 to 24 hours.

3. Preheat the oven to 325 degrees.

4. Remove the bird from the brine, rinse it quickly, and dry well, especially inside the cavity of a whole bird. Rub the skin with a little vegetable oil. Skewer the neck skin to the back to cover the neck opening; fasten the wing tips behind the back, "arms akimbo" fashion; tie the ends of the drumsticks loosely together. (If you are smoking a turkey breast, simply wipe it dry and oil all surfaces lightly.)

5. Put the bird on a rack in a roasting pan and roast for 20 to 30 minutes per pound, or until a meat thermometer registers 170 degrees when inserted into the thickest part.

6. Meanwhile, preheat an electric box smoker for 45 minutes (or follow the manufacturer's directions) and soak for 20 minutes in water to cover about 1½ pounds of hardwood pieces or sawdust. Drain the fuel and set it near the smoker. If you want to observe the smoking temperature, hang an oven thermometer near the top of the smoker; put a shelf in place near the center.

7. Shortly before the oven roasting is completed, put a double handful of dampened fuel into the smoker pan and close the door. When smoke is emerging from the smoker vent and the oven cooking is done, transfer the bird to the smoker shelf. Close the door and let smoking proceed for a few minutes. Smoke should soon emerge from the vent or vents; if it does not, check the manufacturer's instructions for increasing the air draft (usually accomplished by opening the door slightly). What you want is a steady but gentle flow of smoke through the chamber, not a stagnant cloud.

8. After an hour's smoking (or whenever the vent stops emitting smoke), check the fuel pan and add more hardwood if needed, first moving the hot material from the sides of the pan toward the burned-down ashes in the center. Refuel hourly, or as necessary for your particular smoker. Count on a minimum of 4 hours' smoking: at a smoker temperature between 100 and 120 degrees, your bird or turkey breast should be light golden brown and fairly lightly smoked after 4 hours. If you want a smokier flavor and deeper color, continue smoking for as long as 6 hours for a chicken, or up to 8 hours for a 6-pound turkey. (Note that cold or windy weather may force down the temperature in the smoker to as low as 80 to 90 degrees. This is okay, but smoking will take longer.)

(continued)

9. Cool the smoked bird at room temperature, then serve it thinly sliced. Wrap it and refrigerate it if you will use it within 3 days.

TO STORE: For longer storage, wrap securely for freezing and freeze for up to 3 months. Thaw in the refrigerator.

SMOKED TROUT OR OTHER SMALL FISH

Either freshwater or saltwater fish weighing from 4 to 8 ounces can be smoked and totally cooked by this simple process. (We use an electric box smoker—see A Note on Home Smoking, page 28.) Smoked trout— or other fish—are, needless to say, a delicacy that commands a hefty price. If you buy fish, make sure that they are spanking fresh. If you catch them, you know they are. Frozen fish will do surprisingly well, but be sure to brine them just as soon as they are thawed.

    2 quarts water
    ½ cup coarse (kosher) salt
    ¼ teaspoon coarsely cracked black peppercorns
    4 whole allspice berries, crushed
    2 or 3 bay leaves, crumbled
    6 small trout or other fish (whiting, butterfish, small porgies, snapper,
        bluefish, and so on, weighing from 4 to 8 ounces each), cleaned but
        with heads left on

1. Boil together the water, salt, peppercorns, allspice, and bay leaves. Cool, then chill.

2. With a sharp knife cut through the "collar" of each fish at the base of the gill openings. Inside the cavity, slit along one side of the backbone so the fish will spread open. If your smoker has hooks for hanging the fish, thread a needle with coarse thread and draw a length of thread through each fish just above the tail. Tie the thread in a loop an inch or so in diameter.

3. Put the fish into a ceramic, glass, or stainless-steel bowl and cover them with the cold brine. If the fish float, weight them with a saucer. Let the fish soak for 45 minutes.

4. Rinse each fish quickly under cold running water and hang by the string loops in a cool, preferably breezy spot to dry for an hour or two, until the surface, inside and out, is dry to the touch.

5. Meanwhile, preheat a box smoker for 45 minutes (or according to manufacturer's instructions). Put hardwood chips, chunks, or sawdust

(presoaked, if you like—see page 31) in the pan over the heating element and hang the fish in the smoker. (If your smoker lacks hooks, don't attach the string to the fish; just lay them on the smoker shelves, which should be lightly oiled.)

6. Smoke until the fish are golden-brown, renewing fuel as often as necessary. Check for doneness by squeezing the thickest part of a fish; it should yield. Time will be 3 hours, more or less, depending on the size of the fish and how smoky you like them.

7. Cool the fish and wrap closely in foil or enclose in heavy plastic bags; refrigerate and use within about a week.

TO STORE: The fish may also be frozen for up to a month. Thaw in the refrigerator.

SMOKED SALMON

It is impractical—nearly impossible—to home-cure and smoke a whole side of salmon in the Scottish (or even the Nova Scotian) manner. You can, however, create succulent smoked salmon that can be used in the same ways as the magnificent (and magnificently expensive) imported kinds.

The finished fish will be lightly salted and as lightly or assertively smoke-flavored as you wish. It will be more fibrous and without the translucence of the Scottish salmon. It is, in fact, a kind of kippered fish, a homespun version of a caviar-class delicacy.

When you choose salmon for smoking, buy only very firm, very fresh fillets or you'll end up with a woolly-textured mouthful. For this short cure, fillets should be no more than about 1 inch thick.

Bear in mind that the fish is not cured for long keeping. Consider it almost as perishable as fresh fish, and serve it with appropriate promptness.

Makes about 1 pound

1½ pounds salmon fillets, skin and scales left on
  6 cups water, or enough to cover fish
  1 cup coarse (kosher) salt
  ⅓ cup (packed) dark brown sugar

1. Wipe the fillets with a paper towel. Thread a trussing needle or a large darning needle with kitchen twine and take a stitch crosswise

through the smaller end of each fillet, tying the string into a 2- or 3-inch loop. Put the fish into a ceramic or stainless-steel bowl.

2. Stir together the water, salt, and sugar until the salt and sugar dissolve. Pour the brine over the fish and cover the fillets with a saucer, adding a weight, if necessary, so they are kept under the surface. Let stand for 1 hour.

3. Remove the fish from the brine and rinse very briefly under cold running water. Hang the fillets by their loops to cupboard knobs or a coat hanger and turn on them the air stream from an electric fan. (Or, if it's a cool, breezy day, let them hang in an airy spot.) Let the fish hang until the "pellicle," or glossy, nonsticky surface, forms: there should be no trace of dampness when you touch the flesh side.

4. Preheat a box smoker, shelves removed, for 45 minutes (or follow the manufacturer's suggestions for preheating). After 30 minutes or so, add a panful of hickory or other hardwood chips, chunks, or sawdust. Presoak the fuel, if you like (see page 31). When smoke emerges, hang the fillets in the smoker.

5. Smoke the salmon for 4 to 6 hours, keeping up a steady smoke by renewing the fuel as often as necessary. About 4 hours' smoking in the average smoker at a fairly low temperature (about 120 degrees) will produce a rather moist fish; if you like smokier, firmer salmon, smoke for up to 6 hours or even longer. (It's a good idea to hang an oven thermometer in the smoker—you may find that the temperature rises considerably after several hours; if this happens, you may want to shorten the overall smoking time.)

6. Remove the salmon, let cool (preferably hanging up), wrap, and refrigerate. To enjoy it at its best, serve it within 4 days, slicing it thin, on the bias, freeing each slice from the skin as you cut it.

TO STORE: The salmon may be frozen, but the texture will be altered somewhat. Don't plan on freezer storage for more than about a month.

BEEF ESSENCE OR EXTRACT

To cook a heap of bones, beef, and vegetables in a big pot for many hours and have to show for it a small jar or two of meat essence is truly making a molehill out of a mountain—but such a molehill! Possessing a batch of this essence—*glace de viande,* in the language of the un-known chef who devised it—is like having 8 quarts of strong beef stock miraculously confined in a small container in your refrigerator. Use it any time you like and keep it as long as you care to—it is virtually immortal if frozen and keeps several weeks refrigerated.

Add a tablespoonful of the essence to a cup of boiling water and you have better and beefier broth than any you can buy canned, cubed, or powdered.

A little of this concentrate, stirred into any meat-flavored preparation, adds both body and savor. *Glace de viande* can rescue a pallid soup, a vapid sauce, or a lackluster gravy, or it can be a sauce base on its own. The extract is unsalted, for greater versatility when added to sauces and such, so add ¼ teaspoon of salt to the cup if you're drinking the broth.

Try making this once and you'll find yourself wondering how you ever cooked without it. (A slow-cooker simplifies the making of basic stock—see the note after Chicken Extract on page 37). If you'd like to make bouillon cubes from this essence, see the recipe on page 39.

*Makes 2 cups (reconstituted, about 8 quarts of stock,
or 1 cup of broth per tablespoon of essence)*

**6 pounds (or more, if available) beef and veal bones, sawed into pieces
  by the butcher (try to have the pieces cut no more than 2 to 3
  inches long or wide, if possible)**
3 ½ to 4 pounds boneless shin of beef, cut into 1-inch cubes
2 large, unpeeled onions, one sliced, the other left whole
2 large carrots, scrubbed and cut up coarsely
  Water as needed
2 ribs celery, with leaves, cut up
½ teaspoon dried thyme, crumbled
1 medium bay leaf
1 whole clove
2 ripe tomatoes, coarsely chunked
1 unpeeled clove garlic, left whole
2 or 3 sprigs parsley

1. Preheat the oven to 450 degrees.

2. In one or two large, shallow roasting pans spread all the bones and half of the shin beef, reserving the other half in the refrigerator. Add the sliced onion and the cut-up carrots. Put the pan or pans into the oven and brown the ingredients for 40 to 50 minutes, stirring and turning them from time to time; you want a good brown color.

3. Pour off any fat and put the bones, meat, and vegetables into a very large stock pot. Pour 2 or 3 cups of water into the roasting pan(s),

then set over direct heat and stir and scrape to dissolve all the brown bits. Pour the deglazing liquid into the stock pot. Add enough water to cover everything by about 2 inches. Add the celery, thyme, bay leaf, the second onion (stuck with the single clove), tomatoes, garlic, and parsley.

4. Bring the liquid to a boil, then adjust the heat so that the pot, partially covered, maintains a gentle simmer, with only an occasional bubble. Skim off any foam at the beginning and cook everything for 7 or 8 hours, skimming occasionally (this is to achieve clarity in the finished essence). The simmering can be interrupted for several hours, or overnight; let the pot sit, uncovered, for up to 8 hours at room temperature, then resume cooking when convenient. (Refrigerate the stock if held for a longer period, or if the weather is warm.)

5. After you judge all possible flavor has been extracted from the solids in the pot, strain them all out, pressing on them with a spoon to extract all the juices. Skim all fat from the strained broth, which by now will amount to about 4 or 5 quarts. Strain the broth through a cheese-cloth-lined strainer into the washed-out pot (or into a smaller one) and add the remaining beef, which you have meanwhile chopped or ground to the fineness of hamburger.

6. Resume simmering, skimming off fat and scum about every half hour. After cooking the stock with the beef for 1½ hours, strain out the meat, pressing it to extract all possible flavor.

7. Strain the broth through the cheesecloth again and begin the final reduction. Resume simmering the stock, cooking the ever-strengthening essence gently as long as necessary for it to become a syrupy substance that will coat a cool metal spoon; this may take up to 2 hours. (For the clearest essence, skim frequently. However, the flavor of the finished product will be fine if you aren't too fussy about the skimming; just be sure to skim off any fat that appears.)

8. The essence is finished when it passes the metal-spoon test. Strain it through a fine-meshed metal strainer into small jars or pots and let it cool, uncovered. Cover it closely and store in the refrigerator, or freeze it. If frozen, scoop out with a hot spoon as needed.

NOTE: The exact yield will depend on how much collagen was contained in the bones and meat—the more collagen, the sooner the jellying stage is reached. The cooled essence will be firm, almost rubbery, and highly concentrated in flavor. If any surface mold should eventually develop, remove it—it's harmless.

CHICKEN EXTRACT

With a flavor derived entirely from chicken, seasoning vegetables, and an herb or two, this extract is light-years removed from commercial extracts, which are flavored mainly by hydrolyzed vegetable protein and a bit of chicken fat.

If you've never made your own extract, you may be surprised to see that it is a very deep brown in color and bouncy-firm in texture when cooled. You may also be surprised to know that this superior stock is comparatively cheap. As you use your extract, you can bask in a sense of virtuous economy, as chicken backs cost very little, like the few other ingredients. So your fine extract costs a fraction of what you would pay for canned broth (or an extract of good quality—if you can get your hands on one.)

You can keep chicken extract almost indefinitely in the freezer. Refrigerated, it will keep for a long time, but check now and then for mold (if any appears, cut it away with a hot spoon or knife blade).

When you need extract for stock, dilute it (the stock will be pale golden brown) and use as you would chicken broth. The extract is deliberately left unsalted so that it can be used to enrich seasoned sauces or soups. If you wish to sip it neat, dissolve 1 tablespoon of extract with ¼ teaspoon salt in a cup of boiling water. Like Beef Essence or Extract (page 34), this can be made into Bouillon Cubes (page 39).

Makes about 1¾ cups (reconstituted, about 7 quarts of stock, or 1 cup of stock per tablespoon of extract)

6 to 6½ pounds chicken necks and backs, with any loose fat removed
7 quarts water, or enough to cover the chicken by 2 inches
3 medium carrots, scrubbed and sliced
1 medium-large onion, stuck with 2 cloves
1 rib celery, with leaves, sliced
1 leek, roots and any discolored tops removed, split lengthwise and
    washed thoroughly
3 sprigs parsley
1 bay leaf
¼ teaspoon dried thyme
    Optional (for serving separately): 1 whole chicken (3 pounds)

1. Rinse and drain the chicken parts and put them into a stock pot. Add enough water to cover them by 2 inches. Bring to a boil and boil

briskly, skimming off the foam as it rises, for 5 minutes, or until no more scum appears.

2. Add the carrots, onion, celery, leek, parsley, bay leaf, and thyme and regulate the heat until the liquid simmers gently, with the pot partly covered. Cook the chicken and vegetables 3 to 4 hours, or until they are very soft. Do not allow the pot to boil.

3. Strain off the broth, pressing down the debris in the sieve to extract all possible juices. Discard the solids. Skim the fat from the broth and return the broth to the rinsed-out pot.

4. Bring the stock to a simmer and let it simmer, uncovered, until it has reduced by one-half. (If you wish to cook the extra whole chicken in the broth, add it at this point and poach it until it is done, about 45 minutes. Remove the chicken and set it aside for another use.)

5. Strain the broth again, this time through a sieve lined with dampened cheesecloth. Rinse out the pot, return the broth, and continue the reduction at a simmer, with the pot uncovered, skimming from time to time. (Note that the cooking and reduction needn't be a continuous process—at any point you may stop, let the stock cool, uncovered, and resume the cooking when it is convenient. Refrigerate the stock in warm weather or, in cool weather, if you're holding it for more than 8 hours.)

6. When the stock has been reduced to about 1 quart, strain it again —either through a very fine sieve or a coarser sieve lined with dampened doubled cheesecloth. Put it into a smaller pan (a wide, shallow one is best). Resume the reduction, still at a steady simmer. This is the point at which you must begin to watch the cooking and stir the extract occasionally; don't let it scorch. Skim frequently to remove scum and fat from the top.

7. When the extract is thick enough to coat a metal spoon, pour it into clean, dry jars. Cool it at room temperature, uncovered, then cover the containers and refrigerate or freeze the extract. If frozen, scoop out with a hot spoon as needed.

STOCK IN A SLOW-COOKER

We think that making stock in a slow-cooker is a great time- and fuss-saver whenever the supply of bones and meat or poultry trimmings in the freezer reaches crockpot size. It's virtually impossible to achieve anything but a fine stock with a cooker set on "low."

BOUILLON CUBES

They're not exactly cubes—they are, rather, thinnish squares—but these dried morsels of concentrated beef or chicken essence pack a lot of flavor. Although it's long been known that our ancestors, both in the New World and in England, made something similar—called "pocket soup," because travelers could carry the makings of broth in dried form —it hadn't occurred to us to reproduce it until our friend Barbara Kafka pointed out the feasibility of further dehydrating beef essence (or chicken extract, for that matter) to make "cubes" with a minimum of further labor.

To dry the cubed essence, we used a portable convection oven set at barely warm, but any food dehydrator or other means of drying food will work, so long as the temperature is low (around 100 degrees is ideal) and there is air circulation. Drying may take several days. (If you're using the oven to dry the cubes, tape a warning to the door lest you preheat the oven for another use and unwittingly melt the bouillon squares.)

Make either Beef Essence (page 34) or Chicken Extract (page 37), reducing it to as dense a consistency as possible (cook it beyond the point where it coats the spoon, so that it would be even more rubbery than you would want it to be if stored in a jar). Pour it into a foil-lined loaf pan—no more than ½ inch deep—and let it set. Turn out the cake of extract, cube it with a serrated knife, and spread the cubes on a cake rack covered with cheesecloth. Leave them in your drying oven or dehydrator as long as necessary to become very firm (they will never become completely dry), then store them in a plastic bag or a lidded jar. A half-inch square has approximately the same flavoring power as a tablespoonful of the original essence. No need to refrigerate the "cubes."

FISH ESSENCE OR EXTRACT

Many recipes for preparing seafood call for fish stock or, as an (unsatisfactory) alternative, for bottled clam juice—there being no such thing as fish bouillon cubes on the market. For times when it is inconvenient (which is almost always) to prepare fish stock, having this professional type of essence *(glace de poisson)* in the freezer or refrigerator provides you with the means to create dishes that you might not normally undertake. For the recipe, we are indebted to chef Richard Sax.

Use the essence to enrich sauces, make seafood poaching liquid, and to serve as a base for fish soups. Get the necessary fish bones and heads at the market or, in an even more frugal vein, save the bones each time you have a fish filleted and store them in the freezer until you have the needed amount to make the essence. (Be sure to use only nonoily fish —no salmon or bluefish, for example.) Similarly, you can save mushroom trimmings to use in the stock.

Makes about 1½ cups (reconstituted, about 4 to 6 quarts,
or ½ to 1 cup stock per tablespoon of essence,
depending on strength desired)

2 tablespoons unsalted butter, softened
4 pounds (or more) fish bones, trimmings, and heads (gills removed)
    from lean (nonoily) fish
2 medium onions, roughly diced
3 ribs celery, roughly diced
1 cup (moderately packed) parsley stems
½ cup diced mushroom trimmings or stems
1 bay leaf
    Pinch of dried thyme
3 or 4 whole black peppercorns
2 cups dry white wine
    Water as needed

1. Spread the softened butter on the bottom of a large stainless-steel or enameled saucepan. Add the fish bones and trimmings, onion, and celery, and cook, stirring occasionally, over moderate heat for about 5 minutes, or until the onion pieces are translucent.

2. Add the parsley stems, mushroom trimmings, bay leaf, thyme, peppercorns, and white wine. Cover the pot and bring to a boil, then lower the heat and simmer the ingredients slowly for 10 minutes, to release their juices.

3. Add enough water to cover everything in the pot. Again bring to a boil, lower the heat to a simmer, and cook, partially covered, for 20 minutes.

4. Strain through a sieve lined with several layers of damp cheesecloth. Rinse the pot well, discarding all the solids.

5. Return the broth to the pot and boil vigorously, uncovered, over high heat until it has reduced to about half. Then lower the heat to

moderate and continue to cook, reducing the stock until it has become a thick, syrupy glaze—it should coat a metal spoon—and has decreased in volume to about 1 to 2 cups. Skim occasionally during reduction.

6. Pour into a storage jar, cool, and either refrigerate (it will keep for 2 weeks or so) or freeze it. Richard Sax likes to freeze the essence in an ice-cube tray, then unmold the cubes and store them, plastic-bagged, in the freezer. (Frozen essence can be scooped from its container with a hot spoon.)

NOTE: The essence is unsalted; this makes it more versatile to use. Salt finished dishes accordingly.

SEASONED CHICKEN FAT AND CRACKLINGS

We think chicken fat (and duck or goose fat, while we're on the subject —see the recipe for Preserved Duck or Goose on page 25) deserves serious attention from cooks who have never experienced its flavorsome virtues.

Just as you save (or should save) wing tips and necks for making stock when you prepare a chicken for cooking, pull from the bird all loose fat and store it in a covered container in the freezer. When your hoard is large enough—you should have at least a cupful (about half a pound)—try this recipe.

Use your seasoned chicken fat—rather sparingly, as it is rich—to sauté chicken pieces, to fry potato pancakes, or to make hashed-browns. And don't discard the cracklings (the crispy bits left when the fat has been extracted from the tissues). They are a flavorsome addition to potatoes, beans, or other vegetables.

Makes 1 1/3 to 1 1/2 cups of seasoned fat
and about 1/2 cup of cracklings

1 pound chicken fat (including some chicken skin if you like), thawed,
if frozen
1/2 cup water
1/2 cup chopped onion

1. Rinse the chicken fat and skin, drain it thoroughly, and cut it into pieces measuring about 1/4 inch square.

2. Combine the fat and water in a skillet and cook at a simmer

until the water has evaporated, stirring occasionally. When the fat begins to run from the tissues, lower the heat and watch the pan, stirring occasionally.

3. When most of the fat has been rendered from the cracklings, add the onions and cook the mixture over medium-low heat, stirring as necessary, until it is a very light brown and the cracklings are crisp.

4. Strain the seasoned fat into a clean, dry jar and let it cool, then cover and refrigerate it. Refrigerate the cracklings separately and use them within a week or so. The fat keeps indefinitely.

SALT HERRING

Herring dishes of endless variety begin with salt herring. If you can't get a good supply of the salted fish in some ethnic hideaway, make your own. For this you obviously will need fresh herring (or frozen herring, if you can find them), which you may have to order in advance unless you live in a herring-loving community, either Scandinavian or Central or Eastern European.

You may use salt herring in recipes for cooked dishes (many are in Scandinavian cookbooks), as well as in the pickled and creamed versions for which we give recipes.

Herrings, heads removed, well cleaned
Coarse (kosher) salt as needed
Water as needed

1. Weigh the herrings. For every 2½ pounds of fish measure out ½ pound (1½ cups) of coarse salt and set it aside.

2. Split each fish up the belly, lay it flat, and remove the spine; the little bones can be removed later. Rinse the fish and put them to soak in a solution of ½ cup of additional salt per gallon of water for about 30 minutes.

3. Drain the fish and rinse them; drain again.

4. Sprinkle a layer of salt in a ceramic or glass dish that is deep enough to hold all the fish. Place a layer of fish on the salt, skin side down. Sprinkle with salt, covering the fish completely, and add another layer of fish, again skin side down, lying at right angles to the fish below. Salt as before and repeat the layering. Put the last layer skin side up and cover with a layer of salt.

5. Cover the container with plastic wrap and then with foil. Refriger-

ate the fish for at least 2 days (if you are using frozen herring) or for at least 10 days (for fresh fish) before using them for pickling; or keep them almost indefinitely in the brine that will form. The fish will shrink, so rearrange them occasionally to make sure they are covered with the brine.

PICKLED HERRING

This is a more-or-less-classical version, one you might encounter in a delicatessen that prepares its own pickled herring—plump, spicy fish pieces and crisp onion rings, considerably less sweetened than mass-produced pickled herring in jars.

Makes 2 pints

1 ½ to 2 pounds Salt Herring (page 42), drained
  ¾ cup water
  ¾ cup white wine vinegar
  2 teaspoons Pickling Spice (page 201)
  ⅓ cup sugar
  1 medium red onion, peeled, sliced, and divided into rings

1. Soak the drained herrings in plenty of water in the refrigerator for 12 to 24 hours, changing the water twice.

2. To make the pickling solution, bring to a boil the water, vinegar, pickling spice, and sugar in an enameled, stainless-steel, or glass saucepan. Let cool.

3. Rinse the soaked herrings and pat them dry. Halve each lengthwise, remove tails and back fins, and pull out as many of the small bones as will come out easily. Cut the fish crosswise into 1-inch slices.

4. Spoon some of the spices from the pickling solution into 2 clean pint jars. Make layers of the herring slices and onion rings, placing the skin side of the fish (for looks only) against the glass and packing tightly. Fill the jars almost to the top with pickling liquid and slip a stainless-steel knife blade gently into each jar, flat against the glass, to release any air bubbles.

5. Cap the jars and refrigerate the herring for at least 3 days before serving. Plan to use the herring within 3 weeks.

CREAMED HERRING

This takes off where pickled herring ends. Plan to make this pretty much as you need it, as the sauce loses its creaminess if kept for several days. Allow the herring, seasonings, and cream to mellow for at least 8 hours before serving.

Makes 2 pints

2 pints Pickled Herring (see preceding recipe)
1 cup light Sour Cream (page 63) or ½ cup of the sour cream plus
   ½ cup heavy cream

1. Empty the jars of herring into a strainer over a bowl. Reserve about one-fourth of the liquid and everything solid in the strainer.
2. Mix the reserved pickling liquid with the sour cream (or use the sour cream–heavy cream combination if you prefer a sweeter but more liquid sauce). Add the herring, onions, and spices, then return the mixture to the jars, cover, and refrigerate for 8 to 12 hours before serving.

GRAVAD LAX (Salmon Cured with Dill)

Salmon cured in the Scandinavian fashion is definitely not bargain fare, but it might be considered downright cheap when its cost is compared with today's prices for smoked salmon. If you make this with an impeccably fresh chunk of fish, you will wind up with quick-cured salmon of a glorious color, flavor, and texture, while smoked salmon from even the best purveyors has been known to be unpredictable in quality.

If you haven't had the pleasure of serving this, try it with butter on thin slivers of Westphalian Pumpernickel (page 114), or arranged on a platter in rosy, thin-sliced petals surrounded with lemon slices.

Makes about 1 pound

1½ pounds salmon, in one piece, cut from near the tail
   2 teaspoons crushed white peppercorns
   1 tablespoon sugar
2 ½ tablespoons coarse (kosher) salt
   2 teaspoons crushed coriander seeds
1 ½ tablespoons vodka
   Small bunch of fresh dill, rinsed and shaken dry

1. Remove the backbone from the salmon and separate the halves (or have the fish seller do the job).

2. Combine the peppercorns, sugar, salt, coriander, and vodka and rub evenly all over the fish. Spread a single layer of dill sprays in the bottom of a small glass, enamel, or ceramic dish. Place half of the fish, skin side down, on the dill and cover it with half of the remaining dill. Cover with the other half of the fish, skin side up, and top with the rest of the dill.

3. Cover the dish with plastic wrap, draping it loosely over the sides. Place a plate or bowl with weights—such as a can or two of food—on top of the plastic-covered fish and refrigerate, basting and turning the fish over every 12 hours or so, for 3 days.

4. Remove the weights and scrape off the dill and spices and either serve the *gravad lax,* or wrap it tightly and store in the refrigerator for as long as 3 or 4 more days. For longer storage, place fish in a small container—just large enough to hold it—sprinkle it with a little more chopped dill and a little vinegar, and cover with olive oil; it will keep in this fashion for up to 2 weeks.

TO SERVE: Place the fish, skin side down, on a carving board and slice across the grain in translucent thin slices, cut on a slant and freed from the skin at the base of each slice.

CAVIAR

Cross our hearts and hope to die, we *have* made caviar, but not lately: the vagaries of the market in our region of the country have been such that we have been unable, for the years we have been developing these recipes, to lay our hands on a supply of fresh salmon roe.

But we're telling you how to do it, anyway, in case you should have an angler kinsman or friend who is able to present you with fish eggs. Salmon roe is to be preferred for making caviar (unless, even less likely, you can obtain sturgeon roe), but there are those who like caviar made from the eggs of cod, tuna, whitefish, and even herring.

Fresh fish roe, preferably salmon

Ingredients <u>per 1 cup</u> fish roe:

2 cups cold water
½ cup coarse (kosher) salt

1. Assemble your equipment. You'll need a sturdy piece of wire netting with quarter-inch mesh, a fine sieve, and some patience.

(*continued*)

2. Spread the piece of coarse-mesh wire netting over a bowl. Break up the roe and rub the pieces over the mesh so that the eggs, loosened from the membrane that holds them, drop into the bowl. Be fairly gentle in this operation—you don't want to break the eggs, nor do you want to force bits of membrane through the mesh (you'll just have to pick them out later). Sometimes you can use your fingers to help free the eggs. However you do it, get them into the bowl.

3. Measure the eggs. For every cupful, make a brine of 2 cups of cold water and ½ cup of coarse salt. Stir until the salt has dissolved, then add the eggs and stir gently. Let the eggs stand in the brine for 15 to 20 minutes, swirling the mixture gently once in a while and picking out any bits of the membrane that have slipped through the mesh.

4. Dip the eggs into a fine-meshed sieve (ideally of nylon or stainless steel) and let them drain over a bowl in the refrigerator for about an hour.

5. Pack the caviar into a jar, cover closely, and refrigerate for about 12 hours before serving. (If the caviar seems too salty for your taste, rinse it quickly with ice-cold water and drain it.)

TO STORE: The caviar will keep, tightly covered, in the refrigerator for about a month. There are those who say it freezes well, but we haven't tried it—we'd rather consume it fresh.

TARAMOSALATA (Creamy Fish Roe Spread)

Taramosalata is a smooth, intensely fish-flavored creamy spread commonly served in Greece and Turkey. It has become a familiar appetizer in the Middle Eastern restaurants in this country, where it is often served as a dip with pita (for which see our recipe on page 90). The dish is based on mullet roe in its land of provenance, but other fish eggs—including those of carp, mackerel, and cod—are also used, either preserved or fresh. *Tarama,* the necessary base for the *salata,* is found in jars in specialty food shops, as is the commercially prepared *taramosalata*—which is often sweetened and always more expensive than the one you make yourself.

Makes about 1½ cups

⅔ cup *tarama* (or use your own Caviar, page 45)
1 cup crumbled white bread, crusts removed

¼ teaspoon minced garlic
2 teaspoons grated onion
2 tablespoons lemon juice, more as desired
⅛ teaspoon sugar
½ cup olive oil
   Pepper Sherry (page 185) or bottled hot pepper sauce to taste

1. Place the *tarama* in a sieve lined with two layers of cheesecloth and hold under a gentle stream of cold running water. Let drain.
2. In a dish soak the bread for a few minutes in water to cover. Squeeze the bread dry and combine in the container of a food processor or blender with the garlic, onion, lemon juice, and sugar. Gently press the *tarama* to extract any liquid and add to the container.
3. Whirl the blade briefly to mix. With the machine running, gradually pour in the olive oil in a thin trickle, scraping down the sides often. The spread should have the consistency of a light mayonnaise. It will thicken when chilled.
4. Season the spread with pepper sherry and more lemon juice to taste. Chill for at least 24 hours before serving as an hors d'oeuvre with crackers and toasted Pita (page 90), cucumber strips, and oil-cured black olives. Refrigerated, the spread will keep for 2 weeks.

GEFÜLLTE FISH

The name "gefüllte fish" is a puzzler to people whose knowledge of German or Yiddish exceeds their knowledge of fishy dishes. *Gefüllte* does mean stuffed, but present-day gefüllte fish is more like a stuffing than a stuffed fish. The explanation is that the chopped fish mixture was formerly (and still, but rarely) wrapped in fish skins before being cooked, creating, in effect, a stuffed fish.

This traditional Jewish dish has become so popular in America that supermarkets all stock it. The use of freshwater fish in its preparation is customary because the dish originated in the inland areas of Central Europe, where pond fish were cultivated because, obviously, saltwater fish were not available. We prefer the whitefish and pike combination, but the inclusion of carp is traditional. A horseradish accompaniment —Prepared Horseradish (page 183) or Horseradish with Beets (page 184)—is also traditional, and to our minds, altogether desirable.

(*continued*)

Makes 10 large cakes

> Approximately 1½ pounds each pike, whitefish, and impeccably fresh carp, or a combination of whitefish and pike only (or whatever fish is available) to make about 2½ pounds cleaned fish fillets and 1½ pounds or more bones, heads, and skin (if extra bones and heads are available—be sure gills are removed—get these, too, for a richer stock)
> 2 cups minced onion
> 2 eggs
> 1 teaspoon sugar
> 1 teaspoon finely ground white pepper
> 5 teaspoons salt
> 2 tablespoons matzo meal
> Big pinch of grated nutmeg (unorthodox, but delicious)
> ¼ cup cold water
> 1 carrot, coarsely cut up
> 1 rib celery
> 1 teaspoon whole black peppercorns
> 2 bay leaves
> Few sprigs parsley
> 6 cups water, more if necessary
> 2 cups bias-cut, ½-inch-thick carrot slices
> 2 small onions, cut into ¼-inch slices

1. Bone and skin the fish (or have the fishman do it), reserving all the trimmings.

2. Cut the fish into 2-inch cubes and combine half in a food processor with 1 cup of the minced onion. Process to a medium-coarse texture—do not make a paste. Scrape into a bowl and repeat with the remaining fish and minced onion.

3. In another bowl beat together the eggs, sugar, white pepper, 3 teaspoons of the salt, the matzo meal, and the nutmeg.

4. Gradually beat the egg mixture into the fish, whipping with a wooden spoon to incorporate the egg evenly. Beat in ¼ cup cold water, then cover and refrigerate for at least 1 hour.

5. Meanwhile, combine the fish bones, heads, and skins, the coarsely cut-up carrot, celery, remaining 2 teaspoons salt, peppercorns, bay leaves, parsley, and at least 6 cups water. Simmer, partly covered, for 45 minutes, then strain into a 12-inch skillet. The broth should be about ¾ to 1 inch deep; add water if it is not.

6. Gently form the fish into 10 ovals about 1 inch thick (use about

½ scant cup of mixture for each). Press a carrot slice firmly into the center of each fish cake.

7. Bring the broth to a boil and drop in the remaining carrot slices and onion slices.

8. Gently place the fish ovals in the liquid. Bring to a simmer, then lower the heat and cook below a simmer, covered, for 1 hour 15 minutes. Do not let the liquid boil or the cakes will get ragged. Uncover and cook 15 minutes longer, then remove from the heat and let the cakes cool in the broth.

9. Arrange the fish, carrots, and onions in a deep platter. Cover with plastic and chill. Strain the broth through several layers of cheesecloth into a pan or shallow dish and chill it until it is jellied. Chop the jelly and scatter it over the fish to serve it; or, if the jelly is too soft—which sometimes happens if you haven't got enough bones for the broth—simply pour the soft jelly over the fish.

Dairy Products

Notes on Dairying

If any of the following recipes seem equivocal about the time required for a certain step, such as the formation of cheese curd, there are several reasons why we can't be precise. First of all, milk is a most unpredictable substance. No two batches are identical, chemically or bacteriologically. In addition, the weather and the kinds of bacilli in the environment have always influenced the dairymaid's or dairyman's efforts. Other variables to contend with include pasteurization, packaging, shipping, and the holding of milk and cream for sometimes unknown periods in supermarkets, all of which affect your dairying results. The relative freshness of the raw ingredients will affect the maturing time as well as the flavor of yogurt, fresh cheese, or sour cream—indeed, of all fermented dairy products. Use the freshest possible buttermilk, yogurt, or sour cream when any of these are called for as "starters"; their beneficial bacilli grow weak as age creeps up, and success can't be guaranteed if you use a starter that is too old.

Some of our recipes call for rennet, once to be found in every grocery store. It's now mainly a drugstore item (though some supermarkets stock it), and it can also be obtained by mail order (see Mail-Order Sources of Supplies, page 309). We specify "dessert" rennet tablets, not the concentrated rennet used professionally in cheese making. Rennet is a milk coagulant, of course, but it does nothing to develop the flavor of cheese; so we call for rennet for coagulation, plus a lactic-acid starter (in these recipes, buttermilk), which starts flavor development through slight fermentation while the curd forms. Certain cheeses—ricotta, for instance—require neither rennet nor a lactic-acid starter; lemon juice or vinegar accomplishes the coagulation, and a ripened flavor is not wanted.

You can control the degree of tartness of fresh cheese to some extent by refrigerating the curd during its draining period. Similarly, yogurt or sour cream can be left to ferment until you have the degree of tartness you like. You can also control the density of cream cheese or laban (yogurt "cheese") by draining it for a longer or shorter time.

All fermented dairy products thicken upon chilling, but fermentation almost ends when chilling is complete. However, this doesn't mean your homemade delicacies will last forever—the organisms that cause spoilage are always present. Optimum keeping times are indicated in the recipes. As we include no additives to prevent spoilage, these keeping times are shorter than for the commercially produced counterparts of your dairy products.

RICOTTA

Unlike most other fresh cheeses—cottage and cream cheese, for example—the curd of this bland, light cheese is formed by the direct addition of acid to the milk, not by fermentation. For that reason the time required to make it is generally short.

If you haven't used this Italian favorite before, try it in place of cottage cheese, as well as in Italian recipes for such dishes as lasagne and manicotti. You'll find it is a bit creamier than most cottage cheeses, with a much finer curd.

For a pleasant light milk dessert, sweeten ricotta slightly and top it with a sprinkling of grated chocolate or cinnamon.

Makes about 1 pound

2 quarts milk
3 tablespoons distilled white vinegar or ¼ cup strained fresh lemon
 juice
 Salt, if desired

1. Pour the milk into a heavy stainless-steel or enameled saucepan and stir in the white vinegar or lemon juice.

2. Set the pot over very low heat and bring the milk very slowly to a simmer (a reading of 200 degrees on a thermometer). There will be fine beads around the edge of the milk, which will look foamy but will not appear to be boiling.

3. Remove the pot from the heat and set it, covered, in a spot where it can remain undisturbed and where the temperature will remain fairly uniform at a reading between 80 and 100 degrees. (An unheated oven, without a pilot light, is a good spot.) Let the milk stand for about 6 hours, or until a solid curd floats above the liquid (the whey). More or less time may be required, depending on the temperature of the environment and the characteristics of the milk.

4. Line a fine sieve with doubled, dampened cheesecloth (or, better yet, two layers of very fine-meshed nylon curtain netting, dampened) and set it over a bowl. Dip the curds and whey into the sieve and allow the whey to drain off until the ricotta is yogurtlike. If you want firmer cheese, tie the corners of the cloth to form a bag and hang it up to drain further. (In warm weather, the draining might well be completed in the refrigerator.)

5. When the texture of the ricotta is to your liking, add a little salt (from ¼ to ½ teaspoon) if you wish. Store the cheese, covered, in the refrigerator. It will be at its best after it has chilled for 24 hours, and it will keep well for 4 or 5 days.

TANGY SMALL-CURD COTTAGE CHEESE

This uncooked cottage cheese tends to be tangier and finer-textured than the large-curd kind (for which a recipe follows), and it requires fewer steps in the making. We find that there are several variables in making fresh cheese—the exact age of the milk and buttermilk used and the temperature of the room, for example—so it is difficult to predict exactly how long curd formation will take. Consequently, it's a good plan to start making the cheese in the afternoon so you can check the curd the next morning, after 18 hours. By then, if matters have proceeded rapidly, the curd may be ready; if not, it may require several hours more to become firm.

The recipe may be halved if a ½-pound batch of cheese will be sufficient.

Makes about 1 pound

   5 cups skim milk
   5 cups whole milk
  ½ cup buttermilk, as fresh as possible
  2 rennet tablets (dessert type)
  ¼ cup water
  ½ teaspoon salt, or to taste
  ¼ to ½ cup heavy cream (or milk, for a lower calorie count)

1. Combine the skim milk, whole milk, and buttermilk in a stainless-steel or enameled pot and warm slowly to 100 degrees, stirring once or twice. Remove from the heat.

(continued)

2. Dissolve the rennet tablets completely in the water, stirring well. Add to the milk and mix thoroughly for about 1 minute.

3. Cover the pot and let it stand at room temperature, undisturbed, for 18 to 24 hours, or until a firm curd, its surface covered with whey (nearly clear liquid), has formed. Test the solidity of the curd by inserting the flat of a knife between the side of the pot and the curd and pulling toward the center—the curd should hold together. If it is soft, let it stand longer, covered.

4. Line a large sieve or colander, set over a bowl, with doubled, dampened cheesecloth (or, better yet, two layers of very fine-meshed nylon curtain netting, dampened). Dip as much as possible of the whey into the sieve and let it drain through, then gently dip the curds into the sieve. Let the curds drain for about 2 hours, or until dripping slows. Then tie the corners of the cloth to form a bag and hang the bag above the bowl for another hour or so, or until no more whey drips out.

5. Dissolve the salt in the cream or milk and stir gently into the cottage cheese. Refrigerate, covered, and use within 3 days.

LARGE-CURD CREAMED COTTAGE CHEESE

The large, distinct curds bathed in cream make this a "California-type" cottage cheese. Up to the point of curd formation, it is made exactly like the tangy small-curd cheese in the preceding recipe. The gentle cooking of the curd that follows takes attention and care, but it's worth the effort if you like this type of cottage cheese, which has a more defined texture as well as slightly better keeping quality than the small-curd cheese. (It keeps better because of the rinsing of the curd.)

As with all fresh cheeses, the time required for curd formation will vary, so, to give yourself scope, begin this cheese in the early afternoon and check its firmness the next morning.

Makes about 1 pound

  5 cups skim milk
  5 cups whole milk
  ½ cup buttermilk, as fresh as possible
  2 rennet tablets (dessert type)
  ¼ cup water
  ½ teaspoon salt, or to taste
  ¼ to ½ cup heavy cream

1. Combine the skim milk, whole milk, and buttermilk in a stainless-steel or enameled pot and warm slowly to 100 degrees, stirring once or twice. Remove from the heat.

2. Dissolve the rennet completely in the water, stirring well. Add the rennet liquid to the milk and stir for about 1 minute.

3. Cover the pot and let it stand at room temperature, undisturbed, for 18 to 24 hours, or until a firm curd, its surface covered with whey (almost clear liquid), has formed. Test the solidity of the curd by inserting the flat of a knife between the side of the pot and the curd and pulling toward the center—the curd should hold together. If it is soft, let it stand longer, covered.

4. When the curd is satisfactorily firm, use a long knife to cut it into rough cubes: make parallel vertical cuts ¾ to 1 inch apart across the panful of curd, then make another set at right angles to the first. Cut through the curd a third time along one of the sets of parallel cuts, with the knife held at a 45-degree angle to the bottom of the pan. Let the cut curd rest, covered, for 1 hour; more whey will appear.

5. Check the temperature of the curd (75 to 80 degrees is fairly typical) and set the pot into a larger pot containing water of the same temperature. Put the whole arrangement over very gentle heat: set it on a stove burner at lowest heat with an asbestos pad between the outer pot and the burner; or place it on an electric food-warming tray. Put a thermometer in the water bath and keep your instant-reading thermometer at hand in order to check the temperature of the curd.

6. Heat the water bath so slowly that the temperature rises only about 1 degree every 3 to 5 minutes. (Remove the pot from the heat or turn off the heat if the rise is faster than 1 degree in 3 minutes.) Check the temperature often, and every 5 minutes stir the curd very gently (with your hand or a rubber spatula) from the sides toward the center of the pot so that it will warm uniformly. (Cut any oversized curds with your spatula or a knife as you come across them.) When the curd temperature reaches 100 to 105 degrees, hold the temperature at that point for up to 30 minutes, or until a curd, when pinched, is tender-firm, no longer mushy (this is easier to judge than it sounds). Do *not* let the curds heat to the point where they become rubbery. If after half an hour the curds are still too soft, you can allow the temperature to rise to 110 degrees, stirring and testing regularly, as before.

7. Line a large sieve or colander, set over a bowl, with doubled, dampened cheesecloth (or, better yet, two layers of very fine-meshed nylon curtain netting, dampened). Dip as much whey as possible into the sieve and let it drain through, then dip the curds into the sieve. Let

the curds drain briefly, lifting the corners of the cloth in turn to shift the curds about.

8. Fill a pot with very cold water. Gather the cheesecloth full of curds into a bag shape and slosh it about for a few seconds in the cold water. Return the clothful of curds to the sieve. Change the water for a fresh batch, also very cold, and slosh the curds again, this time opening the cloth and stirring the curds with your fingers to rinse them thoroughly, still inside the cloth. Tie the corners of the cloth and hang it up to drain until the dripping stops, about 1 hour.

9. Dissolve the salt in the cream and mix gently into the drained cheese. Refrigerate and use within 3 days.

CREAM CHEESE

Is this cheese *really* different? Yes. Unless you have lingered over a mouthful of homemade cream cheese, you can have no idea of its distinctive qualities: suaveness; a rich, matured cream flavor; delicacy of texture; and a pale-cream rather than chalky color. It is somewhat softer than commercial cream cheese, but it is richer, with body derived from butterfat rather than the gummy additives that many manufacturers use, together with skim milk, in their cream cheese. To make it you need few ingredients but a bit of time and patience; few kitchen tasks are involved. The flavor develops as the curd firms and whey oozes out during the fermentation process, so give this step as much time as it needs—the time will vary according to the temperature of your kitchen. Begin to make the cheese in the afternoon or early evening so it won't need a predawn checkup; then you can finish it the next morning, or allow the curd further development during the daytime, when you can look at it occasionally.

We're fond of plain cream cheese for breakfast with toast and preserves or marmalade; spread on Date-Nut Bread (page 120) or Boston Brown Bread (page 118), cut thin, for tea sandwiches; or on crackers with a touch of Mild Hot Pepper Jelly (page 146) as an accompaniment for apéritifs. Guava shells in syrup—with a few salty crackers as a foil —are a time-honored Hispanic accompaniment.

Makes about 1 1/2 cups

1 quart whole milk
1 cup (1/2 pint) heavy cream (not ultrapasteurized)
1/4 cup buttermilk, the fresher the better
1 rennet tablet (dessert type)
1 tablespoon water
1/4 teaspoon salt, or to taste

1. Combine the milk, cream, and buttermilk in a stainless-steel, enameled, or flameproof glass saucepan. Warm the mixture over low heat, stirring, until its temperature reaches 100 degrees on an instant-reading thermometer, or until a few drops on the inside of your wrist feel neither cool nor warm. Remove from the heat.

2. Dissolve the rennet tablet completely in the water. Add the rennet to the milk, stirring thoroughly for 1 minute.

3. Cover the pot and let it rest absolutely undisturbed at room temperature for from 16 to 24 hours, or until a firm curd has formed. At this stage there will be an ample amount of clear, faintly yellowish liquid (whey) over and around a solid-appearing cake of curd.

4. Line a fine-meshed sieve with two layers of dampened cheesecloth (or, better yet, fine-meshed nylon curtain netting), cut large enough to be tied into a bag later. Set the sieve over a bowl and ladle into it first as much of the whey as possible, then the curd. Let the mixture drain until only an occasional drop of whey falls into the bowl. The curd will still be quite soft.

5. Tie the corners of the cloth to make a bag and hang it over a bowl or the sink to drain for a few hours (contrive a way to hang it in the refrigerator if the weather is hot). Work in a little salt, then refrigerate the cheese in a covered bowl; it will be fairly soft. Alternatively, if you want a firmer consistency, fold the ends of the cloth over the cheese in the sieve, then cover the cheese with a saucer or small plate. Set the sieve over a bowl that will fit in the refrigerator and weight the plate with an object weighing about a pound. Refrigerate. Double the weight after a few hours and let the cheese drain overnight, or until it is as firm as you like.

6. Remove the cheese from the cloth and work in a little more salt. Either pack it into a bowl and cover it with plastic, or mold it as follows: Line a small wicker basket, a bowl, a large, flat-bottomed cup, or a small *coeur à la crème* mold with cheesecloth. Pack in the cheese and fold the

cloth over it. Set the basket or *coeur* mold upright on a small plate, or invert the bowl or cup on a plate covered with folded paper towels (this will facilitate a little further draining). Wrap the mold and plate in plastic and refrigerate.

7. To unmold, lift the cheese by the wrapping, peel back the cloth, and invert the cheese onto a serving dish. The cheese will be at its best for 3 days, though it will keep longer.

HERBED CREAM CHEESE

Among the most popular cheeses these days are the herb-and-garlic or pepper-flavored cream cheeses that originated in France. Our version of the herbed variety is made with our Cream Cheese (see preceding recipe), which is smooth and firm but spreads sleekly. The flavoring is relatively quiet for this style of cheese, with only a whisper of garlic.

Makes 1 cup

1 clove garlic, peeled and halved
1 cup Cream Cheese (page 58)
1 tablespoon very finely minced fresh parsley
½ teaspoon finely snipped chives, or to taste
½ teaspoon dried thyme, crushed to a powder
   Pinch of dried marjoram, finely crumbled
⅛ teaspoon ground white pepper

1. Rub a small bowl thoroughly with the cut garlic; discard the garlic. Beat the cheese, parsley, chives, thyme, marjoram, and pepper together in the bowl.

2. Pack the cheese into another small bowl or, if you wish to unmold it, line a bowl, a small wicker basket, or other mold with cheesecloth and pack the cheese into it. Fold the cloth over the top and set the mold on a saucer (invert onto a saucer covered with paper towels if the mold has no holes; the cheese will drain a bit more). Wrap the mold in plastic and refrigerate the cheese for at least 12 hours to allow the flavor to develop.

3. To unmold, lift the cheese by the wrapping, peel back the cloth, and invert the cheese onto a serving dish. The cheese is at its best for 2 days or so following the mellowing period, but it will keep longer.

CREAM CHEESE WITH PEPPER

The amount of pepper you add to your own homemade Cream Cheese (page 58) when preparing this version of an imported French cheese is a matter of individual taste. Remember that finely ground pepper is decidedly "hotter" than cracked or coarsely ground pepper, and proceed accordingly.

Makes 1 cup

¼ to ½ teaspoon whole black peppercorns
1 cup Cream Cheese (page 58)

1. Crack the peppercorns in a mortar, or fold them into a cloth and hit them with a mallet.
2. Mash the cheese in a bowl and add the peppercorns. For highly seasoned cheese, use the full amount of pepper and include both fine and coarse particles. For a less peppery flavor, sieve out the finest particles and mash only the coarser bits into the cheese.
3. Mold the cheese as described for Herbed Cream Cheese (page 60), or pack it into a bowl and refrigerate it for at least 12 hours before serving. It will keep for up to a week.

SWEET BUTTER

Is it worthwhile to make sweet butter? Yes—conditionally. If you can't buy good sweet butter (and few outside of large cities can), and if you can get your hands on *real* heavy cream (not the ultrapasteurized variety), then the extremely quick and simple task of butter making is worth doing. Homemade butter will not be cheap, but it will be sweet and have a clean, fresh taste. And to our inflexible way of thinking, it is the only fit companion for your homemade breads.

Makes 1/2 to 2/3 cup

2 cups (1 pint) heavy cream, well chilled
2 to 3 ice cubes, crushed

1. Run the cream in a food processor, using either the plastic or steel knife, until the soft mass of whipped cream separates into solids and

liquid—about 2 to 3 minutes. (Or do the same in the bowl of an electric mixer, which will take longer.) Pour off the liquid and chill it to drink, or save it to use in baking or soups.

2. Add 2 to 3 crushed ice cubes to the processor or mixer bowl. If you are using a processor, be sure to cover the feed tube. (If you are using a beater, make a round of foil large enough to cover the bowl. Cut a center hole for the beaters and fit the foil over the edge of the bowl, or you will be splattered.) Run the processor briefly until the butter forms a mass on top of the blade. (For the mixer method, beat until the ice melts.) Pour everything into a fine sieve to drain.

3. Put the butter into a bowl (whether you have used processor or mixer, the procedure from here on remains the same) and press it to extract any traces of milk, which will sour if not removed. Add ice water a few times to wash the butter and knead until the liquid is clear. Press out all liquid.

4. Pack the butter in a crock, cover, and refrigerate 48 hours to develop the flavor before serving.

NOTE: At least one new food processor has a special blade for whipping cream and making butter. If you own such a machine, follow the manufacturer's instructions.

CRÈME FRAÎCHE

While there are several ways of making an approximation of the thick, slightly ripened heavy French cream called *crème fraîche,* this version comes closest to our idea of what it should be: rich and silky, with an edge that is reminiscent of the real stuff (which cannot be made at home because we lack the French starting culture). Although several editions of the French cream have recently arrived in some American specialty shops, they are breathtakingly expensive and, to our taste buds, not at all what the mother-cream is. A few we sampled were buttery, almost greasy, lacked the characteristic nutty-sour flavor, and were too thick to use as anything but a sauce enricher.

While at first glance the *crème fraîche* recipe may appear to be the same as for our heavy Sour Cream (page 63), it has a less acid taste, due to the shorter ripening period. It is further distinguished from the sour cream in that it is stirred before chilling to maintain a pouring consistency, while the sour cream has the texture of thick custard.

If you can remember, save 2 tablespoons of your first batch to make more of the luscious cream. The recipe may be doubled, quadrupled, or even octupled, depending on the extent of your abandon. *Crème fraîche* can be whipped.

Makes 1 cup

1 cup (½ pint) heavy cream
2 tablespoons sour cream

1. Combine the heavy cream and sour cream in a small saucepan and mix thoroughly with a whisk. Heat over very low heat until just barely lukewarm—about 85 degrees on an instant-reading thermometer.

2. Pour the cream into a scalded jar, cover, and let stand at room temperature until thick most of the way through, but still somewhat liquid on the bottom when probed with a chopstick or a knife blade. (Do not go beyond this point or the cream will overferment.) Thickening may take anywhere from 8 to 24 hours, depending upon the room temperature, which may be between 65 and 90 degrees; if it is lower, the cream takes forever; if higher, the cream sours. A temperature of 80 degrees is just about perfect; cream will thicken in about 12 hours at this temperature, and it continues to thicken once refrigerated.

3. When the cream has tested "done," stir it thoroughly and refrigerate for at least 8 hours before serving. Refrigerated, it will keep at least 2 weeks.

SOUR CREAM (Heavy or Light)

When made with heavy cream, this is thick, low in acidity, and creamy in both flavor and color, not bone-white like commercial sour cream. Made with light cream, it is smooth and custardlike, with a silky, light consistency.

It can be added to hot sauces as an enrichment with little danger of curdling because it is richer than "store-bought" and also because, unlike the commercial product, it contains neither rennet nor skim milk.

You can use homemade sour cream as a starter for another batch. It has a relatively long keeping time—up to 2 weeks for heavy cream, up to 7 days for light cream. The exact keeping time depends, of course, upon the freshness of the cream you started with.

This recipe can be doubled, or even tripled, successfully. For a larger batch use a larger single container, or two or three half-pint jars.

Makes 1 cup

1 rounded tablespoon sour cream
1 cup (½ pint) either heavy or light fresh cream (not ultrapasteurized)

1. Put the sour cream into a bowl. Gradually add the cream, whisking constantly until the sour and sweet creams are thoroughly mixed.

2. Pour into a scalded and cooled jar holding slightly more than half a pint. Cover with waxed paper and a lid. Let the jar stand undisturbed at room temperature, which may be from 65 to 90 degrees, for 18 to 48 hours, or until it has achieved a custardy firmness. Investigate after 18 hours by tilting the jar—the cream should retain its shape. If it passes this test, insert a knife blade into it. The top should be fairly firm, the bottom should still be slightly liquidy. (The cream will continue to thicken under refrigeration.) If necessary, allow the cream to thicken at room temperature for up to 48 hours.

3. Refrigerate the cream, covered, for 12 hours before using it.

YOGURT

Considering the enormous amount of magazine and book space that has recently been allotted to this ancient form of sustenance, you might well ask, "Why more?" Because, as every devoted cook knows, there is always more to be added. Although you probably already know that (unadulterated) yogurt is marvelously healthful; that the homemade kind is considerably more economical than store-bought (commercial brands cost two to eight times as much, depending upon the brand and market); and that yogurt is ridiculously easy to make at home, you probably have *not* tried our utterly delicious, foolproof recipe, which we happily offer below. If you have calorie worries and tremble at the use of whole milk instead of skimmed, remember that both the skimmed and whole-milk yogurts sold in stores contain about 150 calories per cup.

Makes 1 quart

1 quart whole milk
3 tablespoons plain yogurt (either commercial, or left from your last batch of homemade)

1. Bring the milk to a boil over moderate heat, stirring it fairly constantly. (Do not be tempted to leave out this step. It ensures a smooth, even curd.) Cool the milk until a thermometer reads from 95 to 110 degrees. Remove any skin that has formed.

2. Whisk the yogurt in a bowl to liquefy it. Whisk in the milk, mixing well.

3. Divide the mixture among four 1-cup jars (or you may let it incubate in the bowl, but this will take longer).

4. Cap the jars (or cover the bowl) and allow the yogurt to incubate until the proper texture is achieved, usually in about 4 to 5 hours. We have found that yogurt is at its best when incubated at 100 degrees, although an environment with a temperature anywhere between 85 and 100 degrees will do nicely (the lower temperature requires a longer incubation period, of course). Many mechanical yogurt makers overheat, producing a curdled, uneven texture in the finished product. You can keep the temperature at around 100 degrees by using one of these methods:

• Place the yogurt jars or bowl in a closed oven that has a pilot light, first testing the oven with a thermometer to be sure that the temperature is around 100 degrees.

• Place the jars or bowl in a pan of 100-degree water, cover with a towel, and set over the pilot light on the top of a gas stove. Keep a thermometer in the water to check the temperature. If it begins to rise, place the pan on a cake rack or asbestos pad to lift it away from the heat source.

• Place the jars or bowl in a pan of water, wrap the pan in a towel, and set it on a heating pad with the control at low or medium, depending upon the range of your heating pad. Keep a thermometer in the water to check.

5. No matter which method you use, start checking to see if the yogurt is set after about 4 hours. It should have the consistency of a delicate custard, so do not let it overferment in the hope that it will have a more solid consistency. Refrigerate it when just set, as it will firm up considerably as it chills. It will keep for at least a week.

(continued)

VANILLA YOGURT

Make like the plain yogurt, but add ¼ cup sugar to the quart of milk before you begin heating it. When it has boiled and cooled to 95 to 110 degrees, stir in ½ teaspoon vanilla extract. Proceed with steps 2 through 5 above.

FRUIT-FLAVORED YOGURT

Follow the recipe for Vanilla Yogurt (see above) to the point where the milk has cooled and you have whisked the yogurt starter and milk together. Spoon into each 1-cup jar 1 to 2 tablespoons of fruit preserves; apricot, apple, or prune butter; Cranberry Jelly (page 169) or Jellied Cranberry Sauce (page 168); pureed fruit for babies (apricot, peach, prune, or pear). Then pour in the yogurt mixture to fill the jars. Continue with steps 4 and 5 in the master recipe.

VANILLA FROZEN YOGURT

Although many recommend still-freezing yogurt, we have found that an electric freezer is necessary to make frozen yogurt that we consider acceptable. The advantages of making your own frozen yogurt are several: it's cheaper (especially if you made the plain yogurt to begin with), there are no chemical additives, you can control the sweetness, and you can add the natural flavor of real berries or fruit (see the following recipe). If you use the frozen yogurt immediately after it's made, you will have a texture like that of "soft-frozen" yogurt. If you freeze it hard, be sure to let it soften in the refrigerator to a creamy texture before serving it. Its flavor and texture will be at their most appealing for the first two or three days after freezing.

Makes about 1 quart

1 envelope unflavored gelatin
¼ cup water
2 eggs
¼ cup sugar
⅓ cup light corn syrup
2 teaspoons vanilla extract
2 cups Yogurt (page 64)

1. Sprinkle the gelatin over the water in a small pan and let stand for 5 minutes. Stir over low heat until the gelatin dissolves.

2. Beat the eggs until light. Add the sugar gradually, beating until the mixture is light and pale. Gradually beat in the corn syrup, then add the vanilla. Beat in the yogurt.

3. Turn the mixture into a 1- or 2-quart ice-cream freezer and freeze, following the manufacturer's directions.

4. When frozen, either serve at once or scrape into a quart container and place in the deep-freeze. If the yogurt is stored, set it in the refrigerator to soften somewhat before serving.

STRAWBERRY OR RASPBERRY FROZEN YOGURT

Makes about 1 quart

1 package (10 ounces) frozen strawberries or raspberries, thawed
1 envelope unflavored gelatin
⅓ cup light corn syrup
1 tablespoon lemon juice
⅛ teaspoon almond extract
2 eggs
2 cups Yogurt (page 64)

1. Drain the syrup from the berries into a small pan. Sprinkle the gelatin over the syrup and let stand for 5 minutes, then stir over low heat until the gelatin dissolves.

2. In the container of a food processor or a blender, combine the berries, the gelatin mixture, corn syrup, lemon juice, and almond extract and process to a fine puree.

3. In the bowl of an electric mixer beat the eggs until they are thick and pale. Stir in the berry mixture, then stir in the yogurt.

4. Turn the mixture into a 1- or 2-quart ice-cream freezer and freeze, following the manufacturer's directions.

5. Either serve the soft yogurt immediately or scrape it into a quart container and store it in the deep-freeze. If the yogurt has frozen hard, let it soften somewhat in the refrigerator before serving.

LABAN (Thick Yogurt or Yogurt "Cheese")

This tart, thick, creamy spread is particularly delicious when combined with the familiar Mediterranean flavors of garlic and olives, although it also blends well with pepper, marjoram, parsley, *cilantro* (fresh coriander), chives, or basil.

Makes about 1 cup

1 quart Yogurt (page 64), chilled
¼ teaspoon salt, or to taste
  Optional flavoring: chopped fresh herbs, dried herbs, and/or a hint of garlic

1. Line a sieve with 2 layers of rinsed cheesecloth. Pour in the chilled yogurt (saving 3 tablespoons for starting another batch, if you plan to make more). Let drain for 1 hour.
2. Tie the corners of the cloth together to make a bag. Suspend the bag over the sink or a bowl and let the liquid continue to drip out until the "cheese" is the desired consistency—usually in about 8 to 12 hours.
3. Add salt to taste and optional herbs (and/or garlic) to the *laban* and mix well. Turn it into a bowl and chill it for several hours, or even longer, before serving it with Pita (page 90), "Black" Pumpernickel (page 108), or other good bread or crackers.

"KEFIR" (Tangy Cultured Milk)

If you've not tasted this delicious Middle Eastern beverage, it can be described briefly as one of the family of cultured milk products that includes yogurt, buttermilk, and sour cream, but it resembles none of them. (We quote the term "kefir" because the kind available in this country isn't identical with the original version, which is not imported.) It is thin as buttermilk but smooth, not curdy, and has a less acid flavor than yogurt or sour cream.

To get started, purchase "kefir" (usually to be found at a health-food store). The culture acts quite rapidly to create a junketlike milk product —which, if you want to leave it in this state, is a delicate custard-curd for a snack or breakfast. If you care to preserve the "kefir" as a liquid, shake it each time you serve it to break up the curds; it then becomes a thoroughly creamy, not curdy, drink. Use a starter from a previous batch to make the next one. Flavored "kefir," as well as plain, can be used as a starter.

This explanation of the procedure for making your own "kefir" from a store-bought culture will enable you to create batch after batch at considerably less than commercial cost. Among the flavors we have tested we prefer these for which we give directions, but you may also use other pureed frozen and sweetened fruits (which we found better than fresh fruit for this purpose), such as peaches, raspberries, or blueberries.

1 quart milk, either whole or skim (whole milk makes a smoother product)
¼ cup prepared "kefir" (purchased, or from your last batch of "kefir"), of any flavor

Heat the milk to lukewarm (110 degrees). Mix in the "kefir" starter and pour into a jar. Cover and leave at room temperature for 8 to 24 hours (depending upon air temperature), until thick and like a custard. Shake the "kefir," then chill thoroughly. Shake again before serving.

"KEFIR" WITH HONEY AND VANILLA

Follow the recipe above, but add 2 tablespoons honey and ½ teaspoon vanilla extract to the mixture before chilling it.

"KEFIR" WITH STRAWBERRIES

Prepare 1 quart of plain "kefir" as directed in the master recipe. Puree a 10-ounce package of frozen strawberries in syrup (we do it in the blender). Strain out seeds in a fine sieve and combine the puree with the prepared kefir. Shake and chill.

Notes on Making Ice Cream

We start here with a moderately rich but not cloying, honest-to-goodness home-frozen vanilla ice cream, custard-based and flavored with real vanilla beans and so, technically, "French." Directions then follow for making chocolate, coffee, and strawberry ice creams, the American favorites.

ABOUT ICE CREAM FREEZERS

We used a 2-quart electric freezer that employs ordinary ice cubes and table salt. You may have another type; the directions provided by each manufacturer should be read and followed for the freezing step. In general, keep in mind that the smoothest ice cream results from a moderate (not fast) rate of freezing, with fairly finely divided ice and not too high a proportion of salt. Too-fast freezing, which can be caused by using too much salt, makes for coarse crystals; so, if you don't mind a longer freezing time, we'd advise using the minimum quantity of salt your freezer instructions mention.

ABOUT YIELDS

Experimenting with different ice-cream freezers, we found to our dismay that there is a considerable range in the volume of ice cream produced by various machines. In fact, one recipe produced exactly twice as much when we switched from one machine to another. As a rule, expect your ice-cream mixture to expand by at least 50 percent during freezing.

Homemade ice cream—in fact *any* ice cream—is at its best within a few days of its making—a good reason in itself for freezing your own.

VANILLA ICE CREAM

If you'd like to serve a French vanilla ice cream that is neither overrich nor anemic, our advice is to make your own. To our minds there is no substitute for a real vanilla bean for flavoring *real* vanilla ice cream, although extract is satisfactory for supplementing other flavors such as chocolate. If for any reason you can't get a vanilla bean when the urge for ice cream strikes, add 2 teaspoons of extract when the custard has partially cooled.

Makes about 1½ quarts

```
 3 egg yolks
   Pinch of salt
 1 cup less 2 tablespoons (⅞ cup) sugar
 2 cups milk
 2 cups (1 pint) heavy cream
 1 vanilla bean
⅛ teaspoon almond extract
```

1. In the large bowl of an electric mixer beat the egg yolks with the salt and about half of the sugar, beating until the mixture is very thick.

2. Meanwhile, heat the milk and cream with the remaining sugar almost to simmering. Remove from the heat.

3. While beating the egg-yolk mixture on low speed, slowly add about half of the hot milk and cream; mix well. Stop beating and stir the contents of the bowl into the pot of hot milk and cream.

4. Split the vanilla bean lengthwise and scrape as many of its tiny seeds as possible into the pot; add the halves of the bean pod. Cook the custard over low heat, stirring constantly, until it almost simmers (it should have thickened lightly, just enough to coat a metal spoon). Set the pot at once into a larger pan or sink containing cold water to stop the cooking.

5. Cool the custard and stir in the almond extract. Chill it thoroughly, covered.

6. Fish out the halves of the vanilla bean (rinse, dry, and store them in a jar for further use). Strain the custard into the cream can of your ice-cream freezer and freeze it according to the manufacturer's directions.

7. Transfer the finished ice cream to covered freezer containers to harden further, or "ripen," in the deep-freeze.

COFFEE ICE CREAM

Makes about 1½ quarts

½ cup coffee beans
2 cups milk
2 cups (1 pint) heavy cream
1 cup less 2 tablespoons (⅞ cup) sugar
  Pinch of salt
4 egg yolks
2 teaspoons vanilla extract

1. Preheat the oven to 350 degrees.

2. Spread the coffee beans in a pan and roast them for 5 minutes in the preheated oven. Let them cool, then grind them coarsely.

3. Combine the coffee beans with the milk and cream in a heavy saucepan and bring to a simmer, stirring. Cover, remove from the heat, and let stand for 15 to 30 minutes. Add ½ cup of the sugar and the salt and stir to dissolve.

4. In the large bowl of an electric mixer, beat the egg yolks with the remaining sugar until the mixture is very thick. Strain the coffee grounds out of the milk and cream and gradually add half the liquid to the yolk-sugar mixture, beating on low speed and scraping down the sides of the bowl with a rubber spatula. Combine with the remaining milk-cream-coffee infusion and return to the saucepan.

5. Cook the custard over medium-low heat, stirring constantly, until the mixture almost simmers and has thickened to a thin custard consistency (it will coat a metal spoon smoothly). Set the pot at once into a pan or sink containing cold water. Cool, stirring often, then add the vanilla extract. Chill thoroughly, covered.

6. Strain the custard into the cream can of your freezer and freeze according to the manufacturer's directions. Transfer the finished ice cream to a covered freezer container to harden further, or "ripen," in the deep-freeze.

STRAWBERRY ICE CREAM

Starting with berries at the perfect point of ripeness, you can, with the method given in our recipe, turn out an ice cream that is both creamy and laden with fruit, without any iciness to mar its texture. We start this ice cream a day ahead of time by "ripening" the pureed or very finely chopped berries with sugar in the refrigerator for at least 12 hours. If you don't have time for this step, mash or puree the berries thoroughly before incorporating them into the custard base.

Makes about 1 1/2 quarts

    1 quart ripe strawberries, approximately (2 1/2 cups after washing, hulling, and pureeing)
1 1/4 cups sugar
    3 eggs
    Pinch of salt
    2 cups (1 pint) heavy cream
1/2 cup milk
    2 teaspoons vanilla extract

1. Combine the pureed (or finely chopped) ripe berries with 3/4 cup of the sugar and stir well. Refrigerate for 12 to 24 hours.

2. At any point while the berries are chilling, you can make the custard base. First beat the eggs and salt with the remaining 1/2 cup of sugar in the large bowl of an electric mixer until very thick.

3. While the eggs are being beaten, heat the cream and the milk in a heavy saucepan just to simmering. When the mixture is hot, turn the speed of the beater to slow and gradually beat in about half of the hot cream and milk. Then stop the beater and stir the egg mixture into the hot milk in the saucepan. Return to medium-low heat and cook, stirring constantly, until the custard will coat a metal spoon; this will take only a few minutes. Set the pan at once in a larger pan or sink partly filled with cold water to stop the cooking.

4. Cool the custard, stir in the vanilla, and chill the mixture thoroughly.

5. Stir together the custard and sugared berries and pour the mixture into the cream can of your ice-cream freezer. Freeze the ice cream according to the manufacturer's instructions, then transfer to covered freezer containers to harden further, or "ripen," in the deep-freeze.

CHOCOLATE ICE CREAM

Makes about 2 quarts

  3 eggs
1 ¼ cups sugar
  2 cups (1 pint) heavy cream
  2 cups milk
    Pinch of salt
  4 ounces (4 squares) unsweetened baking chocolate, cut up
  2 teaspoons vanilla extract

1. In the large bowl of an electric mixer, combine the eggs with ½ cup of the sugar and beat until the mixture is very thick.

2. Meanwhile, in a heavy saucepan, heat the remaining ¾ cup sugar, the cream, milk, and salt, stirring occasionally. Heat to almost simmering, then remove from the heat.

3. Beating the eggs on low speed to prevent spattering, add a little of the hot milk at a time until about half has been combined with the eggs. Stop the mixer and pour the egg mixture, stirring, into the pot containing the remaining hot milk and cream.

4. Cook over low heat, stirring constantly, until the custard thickens enough to coat a metal spoon. Set the pan promptly into a pan or sink of cold water to stop the cooking. Let the custard start to cool.

5. Melt the chocolate over hot water. Stir it, without cooling, into the partially cooled custard; add the vanilla.

6. Chill the custard thoroughly, then strain it into the cream can of your ice-cream freezer and freeze it according to the manufacturer's directions. Transfer it to covered freezer containers to complete hardening, or "ripening," in the deep-freeze.

Breads

Breadnotes

YEAST BREADS

Hamburger Buns and Frankfurter Rolls
Honey-Bran Bread
Cracked-Wheat Bread
Sprouted-Wheat Bread
Five-Grain Bread (Health Bread)
Cinnamon-Raisin Bread
Pita (Middle Eastern "Pocket Bread")
Whole-Wheat Pita
Bagels
Pumpernickel Bagels
Bialys
Soft Pretzels
Salt Sticks
Breadsticks (Plain or Seeded)
Light Pumpernickel

SOURDOUGH BREADS

Rye Sourdough Starter
Sour Rye Bread with Caraway Seeds
Jewish "Corn" Bread
"Black" Pumpernickel
White-Flour Sourdough Starter
English Muffins
Crumpets
Westphalian Pumpernickel

SNACKS, QUICK BREADS, AND BAKING MIXES

Flaky Cheese Twists
Corn Chips
Melba Toast
Boston Brown Bread
Date-Nut Bread
Pancake and Waffle Mix
Biscuit Mix (Biscuits, Coffee Cake, Shortcake)
Corn Bread and Muffin Mix
Bran Muffin Mix

Breadnotes

For some reason unknown to us, baking with yeast alarms many accomplished cooks. If you are one of these, or if you just plain haven't yet had the pleasure of baking bread, there are a few things that might be helpful to know about ingredients and procedures before you start.

INGREDIENTS

All-Purpose Flour and Bread Flour. Although all-purpose unbleached flour may be used to make perfectly decent loaves, there is no question about the superiority of bread flour for the job. This hard-wheat flour used by professional bakers is rich in magical gluten, the mixture of wheat proteins that gives the dough its elasticity and strength to expand and hold rising gases. As bread flour is difficult to get in some places, we've included a proportion of the more readily available *gluten flour* in breads where the elastic quality is particularly desirable. It can be purchased in all health-food stores. Although it is expensive, a little goes a long way, and it can be stored for months. Without it breads will be nowhere near as crisp, chewy, or "bready."

Other Flours, Grains, and Meals. A fair number of hearty breads contain grains and meals that may not be familiar. All are available in health-food stores or specialty stores (see Mail-Order Sources of Supplies, page 308).

Whole-wheat berries (or *grains*) are simply the entire, unprocessed wheat kernels.

Cracked wheat is the whole-wheat kernel—cracked, obviously. *Bulghur*—a partly cooked, then dried cracked wheat—is also referred to as "cracked wheat," and may be used as well.

After the wheat kernel has been ground, it is called *whole-wheat flour.* Some whole-wheat flours have the bran (husk) partly sifted out, some have it all sifted out. The most common whole-wheat flour has a medium-fine texture. It is the one we mean when we specify "whole-wheat."

Wheat germ, the most nutritious part of the wheat, is oily and perishable, and therefore usually removed from the grain before grinding, for the sake of longer shelf life. Perhaps the most familiar of all health-food products, it provides distinctive texture and flavor when used in moderation.

Bran is the coarse, dry outer husk of the wheat (currently fashionable in "fiber diets"). It adds texture and a certain amount of sweetness, nuttiness, and color to bread.

After wheat, the grain we most often call for is *rye,* which comes as a light, medium, and dark flour. The coarsely cracked and ground rye is called either *rye meal* or *pumpernickel flour.* Light and medium rye (the kind most often encountered in shops) may be used interchangeably in our recipes.

Cornmeal may be yellow or white. We prefer the stone-ground meals—meals that emerge from between millstones much like those our ancestors used—as they contain the flavorful germ that is lost in the longer-lasting, degerminated supermarket variety. They are generally coarse but never as flinty-hard as mass-produced meals.

The *rolled oats* we use are the long-cooking variety. These are whole oats, husks removed, flattened between rollers to their characteristic oblong shape. If you know a shop that carries *steel-cut oatmeal* (cracked oats), it is delicious for cereal and in recipes where it can replace cracked wheat, but do not use it in recipes calling for rolled oats —or you'll break your teeth.

NOTE: All flours, grains, and meals absorb liquids at an unpredictable rate, which is determined by their degree of dryness. Therefore it is important to learn the feel of good dough, as the amount of flour needed to make the same bread can vary from day to day and with each new bag of flour.

Leavenings.   For yeast-leavened breads we have used *dry yeast,* as it is available all over the country, unlike fresh, compressed cake yeast. If you buy the rather perishable jars of dry yeast, rather than packages, you must be sure to proof it (mix it with warm water and a bit of sugar; then wait until it foams) to make sure that it is alive and perky. We call for this proofing step in all our recipes, regardless of whether packaged yeast or yeast from a jar is used, just to be on the safe side. It's no fun wasting ingredients and hanging around waiting for a heap of dough that will never rise.

Baking powder and *baking soda* are the familiar leavenings used in nonyeast or "quick" breads.

Sourdough as a leavening is treated separately (see page 104 and 110).

Sugar.   Sugar is used in small amounts in nonsweet breads for several reasons: it starts the yeast action; it acts as a flavor enhancer; it helps to brown the loaf.

PROCEDURES

Mixing dough.   This may be done by hand, with a heavy-duty mixer equipped with a dough hook, or with an ordinary electric mixer (for the first part of the mixing only). When a dough is freshly mixed (by any method) it will be sticky. It is only after it has been kneaded that it develops smoothness and a lively feel.

Kneading.   How you knead depends on your strength and body structure, but whether you do it with one hand or two—or your feet, for that matter!—what you do to the dough is generally the same. Plop the dough onto a floured working surface, preferably one that allows for a full extension of your arms, then flatten it (it will be an uneven mass at first). Fold the dough not quite in half toward you, then, with the heels of your floured hands, press into the dough and away from you. If it is a heavy dough, you may have to push it several times to stretch it somewhat. Give it a quarter turn, fold the dough toward you again, and repeat the pushing, turning, and folding, flouring the board and your hands as needed. In about 5 to 10 minutes the dough will become springy and elastic, no longer a resistant, sullen lump. The gluten being developed by your dedicated kneading will be forming a fine, elastic interior mesh to enclose the tiny air bubbles that will be produced by the action of the yeast. When the dough has been sufficiently kneaded, the surface will be smooth and often marked with tiny blisters.

Rising.   When you set the dough to rise, be sure that the bowl is large enough. We like to use one that has had cup measurements indicated on the outside with a permanent ink marker. That way, if you put in 5 cups of dough, you can be sure that it has doubled in volume when it reaches the 10-cup mark. Ideally, dough should rise in a draft-free place at a constant temperature—preferably around 80 degrees. A higher temperature will speed up rising, but we prefer the flavor developed in the dough by a slower rise. At temperatures much lower than 80 degrees the dough will rise perfectly well; but it will take much longer.

Rising times in all bread recipes are only general indications. Be guided by the degree to which the loaf has risen. Some loaves are baked before the dough doubles in volume, others are left to rise until doubled. To test whether dough has doubled in volume—which most recipes require at some point—poke two fingers about an inch into the dough. The indentations should remain. At this point the dough will be ready to punch down.

Punching Down.   This means deflating the dough and turning it inside out. Punch a fist into the center of the dough in a bowl. If the dough is to rise in the bowl again, roll the smashed-in dough from the sides of the bowl to the center and turn it over. If it is to be formed into loaves, roll it from one side of the bowl to the other, making a rough cylinder. Knead the dough for a minute to soften it up for molding, then form it into a rounded shape on the work surface, cover it as directed (with a cloth or plastic), and let it "relax" for a few minutes. This makes it more cooperative when you shape it into loaves.

Shaping of the Loaves.   This is described in each recipe.

Storing.   Before you store loaves of bread, they should be cooled thoroughly on racks so they do not become moist. When the loaves are completely cooled, they may be wrapped, sealed, and frozen for months. Or store them for several days at room temperature, in a bowl with a cloth over it (if the air is reasonably humid), or wrapped in waxed paper. Or wrap in plastic and store for up to a week in the refrigerator.

All breads are improved by a brief reheating in a 325-degree oven. If they have become a bit stale, place in a brown paper bag sprinkled with water and heat through in a low oven until refreshed and crisp-crusted, about 15 minutes.

HAMBURGER BUNS AND FRANKFURTER ROLLS

Buns of your own making will actually be a contribution to a picnic or cookout, not just a puffy hassock for a hamburger or a fluffy chaise longue for a frank. These rolls have texture and the good flavor of butter and eggs.

Makes about 20 large buns or 36 medium-sized hot-dog rolls

2 cups milk
¾ stick (6 tablespoons) unsalted butter

2 teaspoons salt
3 tablespoons (packed) light brown sugar
¼ cup warm (110-degree) water
2 packages dry yeast
1 egg
6 to 7 cups all-purpose flour, or as needed
½ stick (4 tablespoons) melted unsalted butter (for brushing the rolls)

1. In a saucepan, combine the milk, ¾ stick butter, salt, and 2 tablespoons of the brown sugar. Stir over medium heat until the butter melts. Let cool to 110 degrees.

2. Meanwhile, combine the warm water, the remaining tablespoon of brown sugar, and the yeast in a bowl. Let stand until foamy, about 10 minutes.

3. In a large mixing bowl (or the large bowl of any electric mixer), beat the egg briefly, then beat in the yeast mixture and the milk-butter mixture. Gradually beat in 4 cups of the flour; beat until the thick batter is very elastic.

4. Make a ring of 2 cups of the remaining flour on a kneading surface. Pour the batter into the center and mix it into the flour roughly, using a dough scraper or a pancake turner. Then knead thoroughly, adding sprinkles of flour if needed to make a light and very elastic dough just firm enough to handle, not stiff or heavy. Form into a ball.

5. Turn the dough around in a buttered bowl and place with the greased side up. Cover with plastic and let rise until doubled, 45 minutes to 1 hour.

6. Punch down the dough, re-cover the bowl, and let the dough rise again until doubled, about 30 minutes.

7. Turn the dough out onto a very lightly floured kneading surface and knead just enough to expel air. Form into a ball, cover with a towel, and let rest for 10 minutes.

8. Halve the dough and refrigerate one piece, wrapped in plastic. (This will prevent its rising too much as you shape the first half.) Roll out the remaining half of the dough ½ inch thick and cut into rounds. For large buns, a canning-jar screw band for wide-mouthed jars (3½ inches across) is a good cutter; for medium-sized buns, use a large-sized biscuit cutter (2¾ inches).

9. Place the rounds of dough on lightly greased baking sheets about 1 inch apart (they should just touch each other after baking). Cover with a towel and set to rise until doubled while you roll out and shape the second half of the dough into either more hamburger

buns or frankfurter rolls (see directions below for shaping and baking these).

10. While the buns or rolls are rising, preheat the oven to 400 degrees. Have the melted butter ready.

11. Brush the buns with the butter and bake them for 18 to 20 minutes, placing the pans on the middle and upper shelves of the oven and switching their positions midway in baking. The buns are done when the tops and bottoms are a good golden brown. Brush again with butter and cool, covered with towels, on racks.

SESAME-TOPPED HAMBURGER BUNS

Follow the directions above through placing the buns on the pans (in step 9), then beat the white of one egg lightly with 1 tablespoon water and brush over the tops of the buns. Sprinkle the buns generously with sesame seeds. After rising, brush the buns with melted butter; brush again at the end of baking.

FRANKFURTER ROLLS

1. Follow the recipe for the hamburger buns (above) through step 7. Then roll out half of the dough (refrigerate the rest meanwhile) into a sheet a scant ½ inch thick and about 15 inches long and 8 inches wide. With a sharp knife or a pastry wheel, trim the edges and divide the dough crosswise into 3 sections each about 5 inches long. Cut each section into 6 strips about 5 inches long and 1¼ inches wide.

2. Flatten each dough strip until it is 2 inches wide and fold it firmly in half lengthwise, with the seam at the side. Round the tips of the rolls with your fingers and lay them ½ inch apart in rows on a greased baking sheet. Leave an inch around the edges of the pan and an inch between rows. (The rolls will expand until their sides touch as they bake.)

3. Repeat with the second half of the dough. Let rise and bake as directed for the hamburger buns, but only for about 12 to 15 minutes. Brush with melted butter after baking and cool, covered with towels, on racks.

HONEY-BRAN BREAD

A rather light, all-purpose loaf given distinction by the addition of flavorful, fiber-rich whole-wheat flour and unprocessed bran. The honey lends aroma and color, but it does not make this a "sweet bread." We use it for breakfast toast and for sandwiches.

1 1/2 cups milk
1/2 stick (4 tablespoons) unsalted butter
1/3 cup honey
4 teaspoons salt
1/2 cup warm (110-degree) water
2 teaspoons sugar
2 packages dry yeast
1 cup whole-wheat flour
1 cup unprocessed coarse bran
4 to 4 1/2 cups all-purpose flour, or as needed
2 to 3 tablespoons melted unsalted butter (for brushing the loaves)

1. In a saucepan, combine the milk, 1/2 stick butter, honey, and salt and stir over medium heat until the butter melts. Cool to 110 degrees.

2. Meanwhile, in a large mixing bowl, combine the warm water with the sugar and yeast. Let stand until very foamy, about 10 minutes.

3. Beat the cooled milk mixture into the yeast mixture, then beat in the whole-wheat flour and bran; beat thoroughly. Gradually add all-purpose flour until the mixture is too stiff to beat.

4. Sprinkle 1 to 1 1/2 cups of the remaining all-purpose flour in a ring on a kneading surface. Put the dough in the center and mix roughly with a dough scraper or a pancake turner. Knead very thoroughly, adding more flour if needed to prevent stickiness, to make a medium-stiff dough. Knead until the dough is elastic and has a slight sheen.

5. Form the dough into a ball and place in a large, buttered bowl. Turn it around once or twice and place it buttered side uppermost. Cover the bowl with plastic and set the dough to rise until doubled in volume, about 1 hour.

6. Punch the dough down, turn it onto a very lightly floured kneading surface, and knead just enough to expel the remaining air. Halve the dough, cover with a towel, and let rest for 10 minutes.

7. Form each half of the dough into a loaf. To make a pan loaf, we like to roll out the dough into a rectangle 1/2 inch thick and about as wide as the length of the pan. Beginning with a short side, roll up the dough jelly-roll fashion, pinching the rolled portion to the flat portion every half turn or so. Pinch the ends closed. Fit each loaf snugly into a greased 9 × 5-inch loaf pan, shaping it higher in the center than at the sides and ends. Let the dough rise again until doubled; it should rise about 1 inch above the pan rim.

8. While the loaves are rising, preheat the oven to 425 degrees.

(continued)

9. Brush the loaves with melted butter and bake them in the center of the oven for 15 minutes. Reduce the oven setting to 350 degrees and bake the loaves for about 20 minutes longer, or until slightly shrunken from sides of pans. Turn the loaves from the pans, set them on the oven shelf, and bake them for 5 minutes more, or until a firm rapping on the bottom produces a hollow sound. Brush the tops again with butter.

10. Cool the loaves, covered with a towel, on a rack.

CRACKED-WHEAT BREAD

This is not meant to be a replica of the Italian wheat bread, baked in a similar shape, but the breads do have a good deal in common. This loaf is slashed and tapered like the long, narrow European loaves, but has a chewiness added by the cracked wheat grains. Like most crusty free-form loaves, this bread perks up when slipped into a warm oven for a short spell before the meal.

Makes 4 long loaves weighing about 12 ounces each

      2 cups water
      1 tablespoon plus ½ teaspoon salt
      1 cup cracked wheat
  1 ½ cups warm (110-degree) water
  1 ½ tablespoons (packed) dark brown sugar
      2 packages dry yeast
      ½ cup unprocessed coarse bran
      3 tablespoons vegetable oil
  1 ½ cups whole-wheat flour
      5 cups all-purpose flour, or as needed
      Cornmeal (for sprinkling the pans)

  Glaze:

  1 teaspoon cornstarch, boiled until clear in ⅔ cup water and cooled, or
      1 egg white, beaten until foamy with 2 tablespoons water

1. Boil the 2 cups water in a saucepan, add the ½ teaspoon salt, then stir in the cracked wheat. Simmer, covered, for 5 minutes, stirring occasionally. Cool.

2. In a large mixing bowl, stir together ¾ cup of the warm water, the brown sugar, and the yeast. Let stand until very foamy, about 10 minutes.

3. Beat into the yeast mixture the bran, the remaining tablespoonful of salt, the remaining ¾ cup warm water, and the oil. Beat in the cracked wheat, then the whole-wheat flour. Beat very thoroughly.

4. Make a ring of 4 cups of the all-purpose flour on a kneading surface. Pour the dough into the center of the ring and mix it into the flour roughly with a dough scraper or a pancake turner. Knead thoroughly, adding more all-purpose flour if needed to prevent stickiness, until the dough is elastic.

5. Form the dough into a ball, turn it around in a large, oiled bowl, and place it with its oiled side up. Cover the bowl with plastic and let the dough rise until doubled in volume, about 1 hour.

6. Punch down the dough, re-cover the bowl, and let the dough rise again until doubled, about 45 minutes.

7. Turn the dough out onto a lightly floured kneading surface, knead it a few strokes to expel air, and divide it into quarters. Roll each piece of dough into a ball, then cover with a towel and let rest for 10 minutes.

8. Sprinkle cornmeal onto two baking sheets large enough to accommodate two long loaves each. Form each ball of dough into a flattened oval about 12 inches long. Roll each up into a tapering loaf, pinching the seam closed as you go, ending with a 14-inch loaf about 2 inches in diameter. Place two of the loaves, seams down and well apart, on each of the baking sheets. Cover with towels and let rise until doubled, about 30 minutes.

9. While the loaves are rising, preheat the oven to 400 degrees.

10. Paint the loaves lightly with the glaze of your choice, cornstarch or egg white. Using a single-edged razor blade or a very sharp knife, make 3 or 4 diagonal slashes, holding the blade almost parallel to the surface, about ¼ inch deep in the top of each loaf.

11. Bake the loaves for 20 minutes, with the pans on the middle and upper shelves of the oven. Brush them again with the glaze and switch pan positions. Reduce the heat to 350 degrees and bake for 20 minutes longer. Test a loaf for doneness: if it doesn't sound hollow when the bottom is rapped, remove the loaves from the pans onto the oven shelf and bake them for 5 to 10 minutes longer.

12. Cool the bread on racks, uncovered.

SPROUTED-WHEAT BREAD

If you have ever chewed on a kernel of wheat—a tough and relatively tasteless bit of raw material—you'll be intrigued by the transformation wrought by the sprouting of the kernels. The sprouted seeds develop a sweetness that, joined with the sesame seeds and toasted wheat germ, give this bread a fine, full flavor. It is, by the way, one of the "new" breads, not one that would have been familiar to our grandmothers.

Makes 2 loaves

For sprouting:

⅓ **cup wheat berries (grains), picked over**
1 cup water

Dough:

1½ **cups warm (110-degree) water**
 2 **tablespoons plus ½ teaspoon (both packed) light or dark brown sugar**
 1 **package dry yeast**
 2 **tablespoons safflower or other relatively tasteless vegetable oil**
1 ½ **teaspoons salt**
 2 **tablespoons cider vinegar**
 1 **tablespoon molasses**
4 ½ **cups whole-wheat flour, or as needed**
 ⅓ **cup toasted wheat germ**
 ¼ **cup sesame seeds**
 2 **tablespoons melted unsalted butter (for brushing the loaves)**

1. To sprout the wheat, soak the berries in the water overnight, or for about 12 hours. Drain, place in a quart jar covered with nylon mesh or several layers of cheesecloth held in place by a screw band. Set out of direct light (or, better yet, in a cupboard) and allow to sprout for about 2 days, or until the sprouts are ½ to ¾ inch long. Rinse the sprouts with tepid water 3 or 4 times daily and drain them well; don't let them stand in water between rinsings. When they're ready, you will have about 1¼ cups of sprouts.

2. To make the bread, combine ½ cup of the warm water with the

½ teaspoon brown sugar and the yeast. Let stand until very foamy, about 10 minutes.

3. In a large mixing bowl, stir together the remaining cup of warm water, the 2 tablespoons brown sugar, oil, salt, vinegar, and molasses. Beat in thoroughly 1½ cups of the whole-wheat flour, then the yeast mixture. Beat in the wheat germ, sesame seeds, and thoroughly drained wheat sprouts. Work in enough of the remaining whole-wheat flour, about 3 cups, to make a stiff dough. Knead thoroughly on a floured board, adding more whole-wheat flour as needed, until the dough is elastic and no longer sticky.

4. Form the dough into a ball, turn it around in a large, buttered bowl, and place it so its buttered side is up. Cover the bowl with a towel and let the dough rise until doubled, 1 hour or more.

5. Punch the dough down and divide in half. Let rest for 10 minutes, covered with a towel. Form each piece of dough into a pan loaf as follows: Roll out the dough into a rectangle about ½ inch thick and as wide as the length of the pan. Beginning with a short side, roll the dough up jelly-roll fashion, pinching the rolled portion to the flat portion every half turn or so. Pinch the ends closed. Fit each loaf snugly into a buttered 8 × 4-inch pan, shaping it higher in the center than at the sides and ends. Cover with a towel and let rise until doubled.

6. While the loaves are rising, preheat the oven to 350 degrees.

7. Bake the loaves for 45 to 55 minutes in the center of the oven. When the bread shrinks slightly away from the sides of the pans, turn out a loaf and rap it on the bottom. If the sound is hollow, the bread is done. If the sound is dull, place both loaves, out of the pans, on the oven shelf and bake them a few minutes longer.

8. Brush the tops of the loaves with butter and cool them, covered with a towel, on a rack.

FIVE-GRAIN BREAD (Health Bread)

Like an all-purpose whole-wheat sandwich bread, but enriched with robust oats, corn, and rye. The rather high proportion of gluten flour increases the protein content, which is another reason why loaves similar to this are often called "health bread."

(*continued*)

Makes 2 loaves

   ¼ cup molasses
   2 tablespoons salt
   1 cup milk, scalded
   1 cup water
   1 cup rolled oats (regular, not quick-cooking or instant)
   ¼ cup yellow cornmeal
   1 cup pumpernickel flour (rye meal)
   1 cup warm (110-degree) water
   2 packages dry yeast
   ¼ cup (packed) dark or light brown sugar
   ½ stick (4 tablespoons) unsalted butter, softened
1 ½ cups gluten flour
1 ½ cups whole-wheat flour
   3 cups all-purpose flour, or as needed

1. In the large bowl of an electric mixer, mix together the molasses, salt, scalded milk, water, rolled oats, cornmeal, and pumpernickel flour; beat for about 10 minutes.

2. Meanwhile, combine the yeast with the warm water and brown sugar. When the yeast mixture has doubled in volume, add it to the batter. Add the butter and mix well. Beat in the gluten flour and whole-wheat flour.

3. Spread about 2 cups of the all-purpose flour in a ring on a kneading surface and scrape the dough into the middle. Mix, then knead, adding more flour as needed, until the dough is elastic and no longer sticky.

4. Form the dough into a ball and place dough in a buttered bowl, turning it around once or twice and leaving it with the buttered side up. Let rise, covered with plastic, until doubled, about 1½ hours.

5. Punch the dough down and let it double again.

6. Turn the dough out onto a kneading surface, knead it a few strokes to expel air, and divide it in two. Let rest, covered with a towel, for 10 minutes.

7. Form each piece of dough into a pan loaf as follows: Roll out the dough into a rectangle about ½ inch thick and as wide as the length of the pan. Beginning with a short side, roll the dough up jelly-roll fashion, pinching the rolled portion to the flat portion every half turn or so. Pinch the ends closed. Fit each loaf snugly into a greased 9 × 5-inch pan, shaping it higher in the center than at the sides and ends. Cover with a towel and let rise until the dough has risen slightly above the rims of the pans.

8. While the loaves are rising, preheat the oven to 350 degrees.

9. Bake in the center of the oven for 50 to 60 minutes, or until the loaves are well browned and rapping on the bottom of one produces a hollow sound.

10. Cool the loaves, uncovered, on a rack.

CINNAMON-RAISIN BREAD

Smells as good as it sounds and tastes as good as it smells, especially toasted. A spiral of cinnamon and raisins patterns and spices each slice of this slightly sweet, old-fashioned tea loaf.

Makes 2 loaves

1 ½ cups raisins
   ½ cup warm (110-degree) water
   1 package dry yeast
   ½ cup sugar
   1 cup milk
   ½ stick (4 tablespoons) unsalted butter
   1 tablespoon salt
   ⅛ teaspoon grated nutmeg
1 ½ cups whole-wheat flour
   2 eggs, beaten
3 ½ to 4 cups all-purpose flour, or as needed
   Milk (for brushing the dough)
   4 teaspoons ground cinnamon mixed with 2 tablespoons sugar

1. Set the raisins to soak in enough hot tap water to cover.

2. Combine the warm water and yeast with a pinch of the sugar and let rise until very foamy, about 10 minutes.

3. Heat the milk, remaining sugar, butter, salt, and nutmeg until the mixture is lukewarm and the butter is partly melted. Pour into a large mixing bowl.

4. Beat in the whole-wheat flour, then the yeast mixture, eggs, and 3 cups of the all-purpose flour. Knead until smooth on a lightly floured surface, adding all-purpose flour as necessary to make a medium-soft but manageable dough.

5. Form the dough into a ball and turn it around in a buttered bowl; place the buttered side up. Cover the bowl with plastic and let the dough rise until doubled, about 1 hour.

(continued)

6. Punch the dough down, turn it out onto a kneading surface, and cut it in half. Roll each half out to make a rectangle measuring about 7 × 20 inches. Brush all over with milk and sprinkle with half of the cinnamon-sugar mixture. Drain the raisins and pat them dry. Sprinkle half of them evenly on each rectangle of dough. Beginning with a short end, roll up each rectangle tightly and pinch the ends closed. Fit each, seam down, into a greased 8 × 4-inch loaf pan.

7. Cover the pans with a towel and let the dough rise for about 1 hour, or until risen 1 inch above the edges of the pans.

8. While the loaves are rising, preheat the oven to 350 degrees.

9. Bake the loaves in the center of the oven for about 45 minutes, or until they are a good golden brown and slightly shrunken from the sides of the pans.

10. Turn the loaves out of the pans and cool, covered with a towel, on a rack. For the best flavor, wrap the cooled loaves in plastic and let them mellow for 24 hours before serving.

PITA (Middle Eastern "Pocket Bread")

Since we first home-made these ballooning breadlets (which are fun to make), commercial bakers have joined the ranks of the Middle Eastern bread makers who used to be solely responsible for them, with the result that stores are flooded with all manner of expensive and intricately packaged facsimiles.

These flat, round pockets of thin, chewy yeast bread are sealed all around the edges (which is why they puff up in the oven) and need only a slit-space in an edge through which to stuff or overstuff them with as exotic or domestic a filling as your mood dictates. Or use them as they are commonly served in their lands of origin—quartered or torn—as a sopper- or scooper-upper.

NOTE: The gluten flour in the two pita recipes that follow is not a casual component—it makes the difference between puffy pockets and undersized Frisbees. In other words, results are mighty unpredictable if you rely only on all-purpose flour.

Makes 14 individual loaves

2 ¼ cups warm (110-degree) water
  1 teaspoon sugar
  1 package dry yeast

  1 tablespoon olive oil
  2 teaspoons salt
  1 cup gluten flour
4 ½ cups all-purpose flour, or as needed
  Cornmeal (for sprinkling the baking sheets)

1. Combine ¼ cup of the warm water, the sugar, and the yeast in a large mixing bowl and let stand until very foamy, about 10 minutes.

2. Beat in the remaining warm water, the olive oil, and salt. Beat in the gluten flour and beat vigorously for 2 to 3 minutes. Gradually add all-purpose flour until the mixture is too stiff to beat, then turn it out onto a floured kneading surface and knead well, adding enough additional all-purpose flour to make an elastic, nonsticky, but not-too-stiff dough.

3. Form the dough into a cylinder about 14 inches long and cut into 14 slices. Lay the slices 2 or 3 inches apart on a floured towel. Cover with a dry cloth, then a well-dampened one, and let them rise until doubled, about 1 hour.

4. On a floured surface, roll each piece of dough into a round about 6 inches in diameter. Lay the rounds on baking sheets sprinkled with cornmeal, spacing them at least 2 inches apart. (You will need four or more pans for this quantity of dough.) Cover with dry cloths topped with damp ones and let the loaves rise for 30 minutes; the dough should be not quite doubled.

5. While the loaves are rising, preheat the oven to 475 degrees.

6. If yours is a gas oven, put one pan directly on the oven floor and bake the loaves for 4½ minutes (they will balloon), then transfer the pan to the top shelf, at the same time putting another pan of pita on the oven bottom. At the end of the second 4½-minute period, remove the upper pan, move the lower pan to the upper shelf, and put the third pan on the bottom, proceeding in this way until all the loaves are baked. If yours is an electric oven, follow the same leapfrog method, but bake the loaves first on a shelf placed as close as possible to the bottom of the oven before transferring them to the upper shelf.

7. As the bread is removed from the oven, stack the rounds and wrap them in a dry towel, then a damp one. Keep adding to the stack and rewrapping it, then let all the loaves cool thoroughly (unless you want to serve some of the bread at once). They will deflate but the pockets will remain. Store in plastic bags, or freeze. Before serving, rewarm the pita.

WHOLE-WHEAT PITA

Makes 14 individual loaves

1 package dry yeast
1 teaspoon sugar
2 ¼ cups warm (110-degree) water
2 teaspoons salt
1 tablespoon olive oil
1 ½ cups all-purpose flour
1 cup gluten flour
2 ½ cups whole-wheat flour
   Cornmeal (for sprinkling the baking sheets)

1. Combine the yeast, sugar, and ¼ cup of the warm water and let stand until very foamy, about 10 minutes.

2. In a large mixing bowl, combine remaining 2 cups of warm water, salt, and oil. Beat in the all-purpose flour, then the gluten flour, and beat well. Add the yeast mixture and beat vigorously (on high speed, if using a machine) for 2 or 3 minutes.

3. Add whole-wheat flour until the batter is too stiff to beat. Put most of the remaining whole-wheat flour in a ring on a kneading surface and pour the dough into the middle. Mix roughly with a dough scraper or a spatula, then knead until the dough is extremely elastic, adding flour as needed to keep the dough from sticking.

4. Form the dough into a cylinder about 14 inches long and cut into 14 slices. Place the slices 2 or 3 inches apart on a floured towel. Cover with another dry cloth, then a damp one, and let rise for about 1 hour, or until doubled.

5. Roll out each piece of dough on a lightly floured board to form 6-inch rounds. Sprinkle three or four large baking sheets very lightly with cornmeal and place the pita rounds on them at least 2 inches apart. Cover with a dry towel, then a damp towel, and let rise for 30 minutes, until not quite double.

6. While the loaves are rising, preheat the oven to 475 degrees.

7. Place one pan of pita on the oven floor of a gas oven (or on the lowest shelf of an oven heated by electricity) and bake for 4½ minutes, until the rounds have ballooned but are not browned. Move the pan to the topmost shelf and place the second pan in the lower position. Bake

for 4 to 4½ minutes, or until the pita on top are lightly browned and the lower ones have ballooned. Remove the upper batch from the oven, place the bottom batch on the top shelf, and put the next baking sheet in the lower position. Bake as for the first batch, continuing with the fourth panful if you have used four pans.

8. Stack the hot pita as they are finished and wrap them in a dry towel, then a damp one. Let them cool for 15 minutes before serving or cool completely, wrap in plastic, and refrigerate or freeze. Rewarm the pita before you serve them.

BAGELS

No two ways about it. If you haven't got a bagelry near by and you're devoted to these adult teething rings, you have to make your own; the frozen kind from supermarkets could never satisfy a true bagel devotee. These are water bagels, which, along with pretzels, are among the few breadstuffs simmered in water before they're baked. We've yet to produce a bagel as sleek and uniform as those made by the pros, but ours are properly chewy (although they have only a modicum of gloss), and they have more flavor than even the best bakery bagels we sampled.

Makes 12

2 cups warm (110-degree) water
1 teaspoon sugar
1 package dry yeast
½ cup gluten flour
4 ½ cups all-purpose flour, or as needed
1 tablespoon salt

Water bath:

4 quarts water
4 tablespoons sugar
2 tablespoons salt

1. In a small bowl, combine ½ cup of the warm water, the sugar, and the yeast. Stir and let stand till foamy, about 10 minutes.

2. In the large bowl of an electric mixer, combine the gluten flour, 2 cups of the all-purpose flour, the salt, and the remaining 1½ cups warm water. Add the yeast mixture and beat for 5 minutes on medium-

low speed. Cover the dough and let it rise until it collapses, about 2 hours. (When the dough has collapsed, the sides of the bowl will show its former, higher level.)

3. Stir 2 more cups all-purpose flour gradually into the dough. Spread the remaining flour on a working surface and turn the dough out onto it. Knead until smooth and shiny.

4. Place the dough in an ungreased bowl and let rise, covered, until doubled in bulk, 1 hour or more.

5. Punch down the dough. Turn out onto a board and cut into 12 pieces. Cover with a dry towel, then a damp one, and let rest for 10 minutes.

6. Removing one piece at a time from under the towel, begin making the bagel shapes. Roll each piece into a "snake" about 8 inches long. Moisten and overlap the ends; pinch them together firmly. The bagel should be a uniform ring with a center hole no smaller than 1½ inches. As each bagel is finished, place it on a dry towel. When all are formed and on the towel, place another dry towel, then a damp one, over them and let them rise for about 30 minutes, or until they are puffed ("half proofed") but not doubled.

7. While the bagels are rising, preheat the oven to 425 degrees.

8. Make the water bath by combining the water with sugar and salt in a large pot and bring to a simmer. When the bagels are ready—risen, but not doubled—drop about three at a time into the simmering water. Keeping the water at a bare simmer, cook the bagels for 1 minute on each side.

9. Remove the bagels with a slotted spoon, holding a towel under the spoon. Place them on a large baking sheet (at least 14 × 17 inches) covered with baking parchment (do *not* try using a greased pan); the bagels, which should all fit on the sheet, will be rather close together.

10. Bake in the center of the preheated oven for 10 minutes; the bagels should be set but not browned. Turn them over and return the pan to the oven. Bake for about 5 minutes more, or until the bagels are browned.

11. Cool the bagels on a rack. Store in a plastic bag in the refrigerator if you'll be using them within a day or two, or wrap and freeze for months.

PUMPERNICKEL BAGELS

These have little in common with water bagels except their shape. They are really grainy, nicely puffed pumpernickel rolls in a doughnut form. Because the crust of a pumpernickel roll is the best part, and rolls in this shape have more crust than others, it might be argued that these are the best of all possible pumpernickel rolls! Incidentally, what looks like a lot of sugar in the recipe isn't. The deeply browned sugar used to color and flavor the dough loses almost all sweetness in its caramelized state.

Makes 20

3 tablespoons plus 1 teaspoon sugar
¼ cup boiling water
1 cup warm (110-degree) water
2 packages dry yeast
1 tablespoon salt
2 tablespoons melted butter or lard, or vegetable oil
1 cup skim milk, scalded and cooled to room temperature
1 cup pumpernickel flour (rye meal)
1 ½ cups medium rye flour
4 cups all-purpose flour, or as needed

Egg wash:

1 egg beaten with 1 tablespoon water

1. In a very small skillet, bring the 3 tablespoons sugar to a boil, stirring it over moderate heat. It should melt to a rich, dark brown. Staying well away from the probability of spluttering, add the boiling water and stir to dissolve the caramel. Pour the solution into a dish and cool for about 10 minutes in the refrigerator.

2. Combine the warm water, yeast, and the remaining teaspoon of sugar and let stand until very foamy, about 10 minutes.

3. In a large mixing bowl, combine the salt, shortening, cooled milk, and liquid caramel. Add the yeast mixture. Stir in the pumpernickel and rye flours, then 2 cups of the all-purpose flour. Spread 1 cup of the remaining all-purpose flour on a work surface and turn the dough out onto it. Gradually incorporate the flour, kneading in as much more as necessary to make a fairly stiff dough. Knead well until the dough is no longer sticky.

(continued)

4. Form the dough into a ball and place in an oiled bowl, turning a few times to coat the dough. Cover with plastic and place in a not-too-warm spot (a high temperature during rising will tear this dough). Let the dough rise until doubled, about 1½ hours.

5. Punch the dough down, halve it, and roll it into two 10-inch cylinders. Cover them with a towel and let the dough relax for 10 minutes.

6. Cut each cylinder into 10 pieces. Cover the pieces with a dry towel, then with a damp one, and let them rest another 10 minutes.

7. Roll each piece into a "snake" about 8 inches long, tapered at the ends (meanwhile, keep the unshaped dough covered). Wet both ends of the dough slightly, overlap them about an inch, and gently but firmly pinch the seam together. Place the finished bagels on two large baking sheets covered with baking parchment, cover them with a towel, and let rise until they are not quite doubled. (Be sure that the center hole is 2 inches in diameter at this time; if not, stretch the bagel to enlarge the center.)

8. While the bagels are rising, preheat the oven to 425 degrees.

9. Brush the risen bagels lightly with the egg wash (don't let it drip onto the pan, or it will burn) and bake them for 10 minutes on two shelves close to the center of the oven. Switch the pans and bake the bagels 5 to 10 minutes more, or until they are well browned.

10. Cool the bagels on a rack. They will keep for a day or two in a plastic bag at room temperature, or may be frozen for months.

BIALYS

Another bread for those who love the chewiness of real water bagels and pretzels. This one, less dense than the aforementioned, is lightly sprinkled with poppy seeds and minced onion. Eat bialys sliced, toasted, and buttered, or stuffed with tongue, ham, or corned beef.

Makes 16

    2 cups warm (110-degree) water
    1 package dry yeast
    2 teaspoons sugar
2 ½ teaspoons salt
1 ¼ cups gluten flour
3 ½ cups all-purpose flour, or as needed

Topping:

1 tablespoon vegetable oil (or lard, if preferred)
1 ½ teaspoons poppy seeds, or to taste
⅓ cup finely minced onion (or up to ½ cup, if you like)
½ teaspoon salt

1. In a large mixing bowl, combine ½ cup of the warm water, the yeast, and the sugar and let stand until foamy, about 10 minutes.

2. Mix the remaining 1½ cups warm water, salt, gluten flour, and all-purpose flour into the yeast mixture. Knead vigorously on a floured surface until smooth (the dough will be soft).

3. Form the dough into a ball and place in a greased bowl; turn it around and place it with its greased side up. Let rise, covered with plastic, until tripled in bulk, about 1½ hours.

4. Punch the dough down, turn it over, cover, and let rise until doubled.

5. Punch the dough down and roll it into two cylinders. Cut each into 8 rounds, lay them flat, cover with a towel, and let them rest.

6. Meanwhile, prepare the topping by mixing the oil, poppy seeds, onion, and salt; set aside.

7. Pat the dough into flattened rounds a little higher in the middle than at the edge, each about 3½ inches in diameter. Place on a lightly floured board, cover with a dry towel and then a damp towel, and let rise until increased by about half in bulk ("half proofed"). This will take about 30 minutes; do not let overrise.

8. Press the bottom of a small jar or a shot glass about 1 inch in diameter into the center of each bialy to make a deep indentation. Spread the topping over the bialys. Let them rise for 15 minutes more, until three-quarters proofed; do not let them double.

9. While the bialys are rising, preheat the oven to 425 degrees.

10. Carefully transfer the bialys to two large (14 × 17-inch) ungreased baking sheets. Bake on the upper and lower shelves of the oven for 6 to 7 minutes, then switch the shelf positions and reverse the pans front to back and bake until the bialys are evenly and lightly browned, about 5 to 6 minutes more.

11. Cool on racks. Store the bialys in a plastic bag in the refrigerator if they'll be eaten within a day or two, or freeze them for several months.

SOFT PRETZELS

You no longer need to hang around street corners waiting for dubiously sanitary vendors to fill any pretzel yens you may harbor. Thanks to the magic of gluten flour, you can make these blown-up chewy (not crunchy) versions of the familiar hard pretzel. They are a wonderfully satisfying, salty, yeasty, wheaty snack all alone. Or you can serve them with a pea soup or other thick vegetable pottage for an amiable winter one-dish meal.

Makes 12

1 ½ cups warm (110-degree) water
  1 teaspoon sugar
  1 package dry yeast
  1 teaspoon salt
¾ cup gluten flour
  3 cups all-purpose flour, or as needed

  Water bath:

1 quart water
3 tablespoons baking soda
1 tablespoon sugar

  Topping:

1 tablespoon coarse sea salt

    1. In a small bowl, combine ½ cup of the warm water with the sugar and yeast. Let proof until fluffy, about 10 minutes.
    2. Combine the remaining 1 cup warm water, salt, gluten flour, and 1 cup of the all-purpose flour in the large bowl of an electric mixer; beat until well blended. Add the yeast mixture and beat on medium-low speed for 4 or 5 minutes. Stir in 1½ cups more flour.
    3. Turn the dough onto a floured working surface and knead until very smooth and shiny, adding about ½ cup flour, or the amount needed, as you knead.
    4. Form the dough into a ball and place in an ungreased bowl. Cover the bowl with plastic and let the dough rise until doubled in bulk, about 1 hour or more.

5. Punch down the dough, cut into 12 equal pieces, and cover with a sheet of plastic. Roll each piece to form a long rope about 16 to 18 inches long, with tapered ends. Form each into a pretzel shape as illustrated. Lay each shaped pretzel on a lightly floured board. Let the pretzels rise until not quite doubled, about 30 minutes.

6. While the pretzels are rising, preheat the oven to 425 degrees.

7. Make the water bath. In a 9-inch enameled or stainless-steel skillet, combine the water, baking soda, and sugar. Bring to a simmer. Slide three pretzels at a time into the bath; keep it at a bare simmer and cook the pretzels for 20 seconds on each side, flipping them gently with a skimmer. Remove them with the skimmer, draining them over the pan. Place on a towel for a moment, then flip them onto a large parchment-covered baking sheet, with their original topsides up. Sprinkle sparingly with the coarse salt. Repeat with the remaining pretzels.

8. Bake the pretzels in the center of the oven for 15 minutes, or until nicely browned.

9. Cool the pretzels to lukewarm and eat them fresh; or wrap and freeze them after they have cooled completely.

SALT STICKS

A childhood memory of frequently being favored with chewy salt sticks in a neighborhood bakery prompted us to re-create this old-fashioned Central European bread. Perhaps your children will enjoy the exacting task of unfurling a crusty baked salt stick without making any tears (and rolling up the raw dough, too, for that matter).

(continued)

Makes 32

1 cup skim milk
1 tablespoon lard or unsalted butter
½ cup water
1 tablespoon salt
2 teaspoons plus a pinch of sugar
½ cup warm (110-degree) water
1 package dry yeast
1 cup gluten flour
1 cup rye flour
2 ¾ cups all-purpose flour, or as needed

Glaze:

1 egg white, beaten with 1 tablespoon warm water

Topping:

4 teaspoons caraway seeds
4 teaspoons coarse (kosher) salt

1. In a saucepan, heat together the skim milk, lard or butter, water, salt, and 2 teaspoons sugar until the fat melts. Let cool to 110 degrees in the large bowl of an electric mixer.

2. Meanwhile, combine the warm water, pinch of sugar, and yeast in a bowl and let stand until foamy, about 10 minutes, then add to the skim-milk mixture.

3. Mix in a bowl the gluten flour, rye flour, and 2¾ cups all-purpose flour. Add 2 cups of the mixed flours to the yeast mixture and beat for 5 minutes on low speed. Add the remaining flour gradually, scraping the dough onto a floured board and kneading when the dough becomes too stiff to beat. Knead until very smooth, using additional all-purpose flour, if needed, to make a medium-stiff dough.

4. Form the dough into a ball and turn around in a buttered bowl. Put the buttered side up, cover with plastic, and let rise until doubled, about 1 hour or more.

5. Punch the dough down, turn onto a working surface, and divide into four pieces. Let the pieces rest, covered with a towel or plastic, for 5 minutes.

6. Roll out each piece into a 10-inch round. Cut into eight wedges, then roll each tightly from the wide end to the point, stretching and elongating the dough as you roll. Place on a parchment-covered or

lightly greased large (14 × 17-inch) baking sheet with the point of each roll underneath, leaving about 1½ inches between salt sticks. Form the rest of the dough—you will fill two baking sheets.

7. Let the salt sticks rise, covered, for about 45 minutes, or until almost doubled.

8. While the salt sticks are rising, preheat the oven to 400 degrees.

9. Coating half of the sticks on one sheet at a time, brush them with the egg-white glaze and sprinkle them with 1 teaspoon each of the caraway seeds and coarse salt; press into the surface of the dough. Repeat with the remaining sticks.

10. Bake the salt sticks on the upper and lower shelves of the oven for 5 minutes, then exchange shelf positions and turn the baking sheets front to back. Bake for 3 minutes, then reduce the oven temperature to 250 degrees and bake for 10 to 15 minutes longer, or until the rolls are an even golden brown with no soft white spots on the sides. Don't let them get too brown, but be sure they are baked to a crunchy gold.

11. Cool on a rack. The salt sticks may be frozen; to freshen them, reheat them in a 350-degree oven for 10 minutes.

BREADSTICKS (Plain or Seeded)

Crisp, keepable, quickly made, these might easily replace pretzels in your life—or at least keep them company on the snack shelf. You can make them plain, but if you take our busybody advice, you'll stick in the seeds. Breadsticks make pleasant picnic fare and look lovely in a glass or mug on the table at meals.

If you'd like to make baton-length breadsticks, cut the dough into 16 pieces and roll each into a 16-inch rope.

Makes 32

⅔ cup warm (110-degree) water
½ teaspoon sugar
1 package dry yeast
1 teaspoon salt
2 tablespoons olive oil
2 cups all-purpose flour, or as needed
    Optional: 4 teaspoons fennel seeds or caraway seeds, or 2 tablespoons poppy seeds

1. Combine the water, sugar, and yeast in a small bowl and let rise until foamy and doubled, about 10 minutes.

(continued)

2. In the large bowl of an electric mixer, combine the yeast mixture, salt, oil, and 1¼ cups of the flour. Beat for 4 to 5 minutes on medium speed.

3. Spread ½ cup of the remaining flour on a kneading surface and mix with the dough. Knead, adding more of the remaining flour as needed to make a medium-stiff dough. Knead until the dough is extremely smooth and satiny.

4. Form the dough into a ball, place in an oiled bowl, and turn around; place with the oiled surface upward, cover with plastic, and let rise until doubled, about 1 hour.

5. Punch down the dough; knead the seeds (if you are using them) into the dough in the bowl and let it rest for 5 to 10 minutes, covered with plastic.

6. On your kneading surface, divide the dough into 32 pieces and cover them with plastic wrap. Roll one piece at a time to form a rope about 7 to 8 inches long—they'll be very thin. Place the breadsticks about ½ to ¾ inch apart on a lightly greased 11 × 17-inch baking sheet. Leave to double, about 45 minutes.

7. While the breadsticks are rising, preheat the oven to 325 degrees.

8. Bake the breadsticks in the center of the oven for 25 minutes, or until nicely browned all over. After the breadsticks have been in the oven for 5 minutes, spray them (without removing them from the oven) with water, using a "mister" of the type used for refreshing the leaves of house plants. Repeat after 5 minutes, then complete the baking.

9. Cool the breadsticks on a rack and store them airtight. They will keep for weeks.

LIGHT PUMPERNICKEL

When you're not in the mood for the punch of pumpernickel or other very dark, grainy breads, you might want to try this substantial but milder hybrid. Slightly sweet and beery, it combines amicably with smoked meats.

Makes 1 loaf

1 ⅓ cups dark beer
   ¼ cup yellow cornmeal, plus additional for sprinkling the pan
   1 tablespoon lard
1 ½ teaspoons salt

1 tablespoon molasses
¼ cup warm (110-degree) water
1 package dry yeast
½ teaspoon sugar
1 cup whole-wheat flour
¾ cup rye flour, or as needed
⅔ cup gluten flour

Glaze:

1 teaspoon cornstarch, boiled with ⅔ cup water until clear (2 to 3 minutes) and cooled

1. Heat the beer to a simmer and stir in the cornmeal. Add the lard, then remove from the heat, stir in the salt and molasses, and cool to 110 degrees.

2. Meanwhile, combine the warm water, yeast, and sugar in a small bowl and let rise until foamy, about 10 minutes.

3. Add the yeast mixture to the beer-cornmeal mixture. Beat in the whole-wheat flour, rye flour, and gluten flour. Mix well, turning out onto a board lightly dusted with rye flour when too stiff to beat; knead until elastic, sprinkling with more rye flour if needed to prevent stickiness.

4. Form the dough into a ball and place in a greased bowl, turning to coat. Place with greased side up, cover with plastic, and let stand until doubled in bulk, 1½ hours or more.

5. Punch down the dough and let it rest for 10 minutes.

6. With lightly oiled hands, form the dough into a 7-inch ball with a flattened base. Sprinkle a little cornmeal into a 9-inch layer-cake pan. Place the dough in the center, cover with plastic or a foil tent, and let double.

7. While the dough is rising, preheat the oven to 375 degrees.

8. Brush the loaf with the cornstarch glaze and, using a single-edged razor blade or a very sharp knife, cut a tic-tac-toe design (two sets of parallel lines at right angles to each other) in the top.

9. Bake the bread in the center of the oven for 50 minutes to 1 hour, brushing again with the glaze after 20 minutes. When done, the bread will sound hollow when rapped on the bottom with the knuckles.

10. Cool on a rack and wrap airtight for storage in the refrigerator or freezer.

RYE SOURDOUGH STARTER

The 4-cup batch of starter made by this recipe is enough to bake any of our rye breads requiring a rye starter, with enough left over to serve as the nucleus for another baking. This starter is considerably thicker than the White-Flour Sourdough Starter (page 110), which we use for the English Muffins on page 111 and other breads.

When you "feed" leftover starter—which should be done every 2 weeks or so—add a little rye flour and water, using 3 parts of flour to 2 of water. To build up a small amount of starter to a quantity large enough for baking, do the job in several steps, never adding a larger measure of flour than the amount of starter on hand. Let the starter stand at room temperature overnight or for up to 24 hours, until it is bubbly and no longer smells floury. To increase further, add more flour and water in the same proportions and again let the starter ferment until it is bubbly enough to use. Store leftover starter in the refrigerator between bakings and "feedings," and for indefinite storage freeze it. Thaw, then feed the starter and let it ferment at room temperature before use.

Makes about 4 cups

  1 package dry yeast
  3 cups tepid (80-degree) water
3 ½ cups medium rye flour
  1 small onion, peeled and halved

1. Dissolve the yeast in 2 cups of the tepid water, then beat in 2 cups of the rye flour, beating until no lumps remain. Add the onion, cover loosely with a cloth, and let stand at room temperature for 24 hours.

2. Remove the onion. Beat in 1 cup tepid water, then 1½ cups rye flour. Cover with the cloth and let stand for 24 hours longer. The starter should now be pleasantly sour-smelling, almost beery, and bubbly. (Depending upon the temperature of the room, a slightly longer or shorter period of fermentation may produce this result.)

TO USE: The starter is now ready for use and can be refrigerated for up to 24 hours before use, without further feeding. If you must hold the starter longer before use, the night before it is wanted add ½ cup tepid water and ¾ cup rye flour and let it stand at room temperature over-night.

SOUR RYE BREAD WITH CARAWAY SEEDS

These tawny-crusted loaves have a crackled surface and the proper rye tang, enhanced with caraway seeds (which you can omit, if you like, but they lend much character to the bread). If you keep the bread for a few days (we think it improves in flavor for at least 24 hours after baking), restore the crispness of the crust by warming the loaf briefly in the oven before slicing it.

Makes 2 loaves

1 package dry yeast
¼ cup warm (110-degree) water
   Pinch of sugar
1 tablespoon salt
1 cup tepid (80-degree) water
2 cups active Rye Sourdough Starter (page 104), stirred down before
   measuring, at room temperature
3 tablespoons caraway seeds
1 cup medium rye flour, or as needed
1 cup gluten flour
2 ½ to 3 cups all-purpose flour
   Cornmeal (for sprinkling the baking sheet)

Glaze:

1 teaspoon cornstarch, cooked in ⅔ cup water until translucent (2 to 3
   minutes), then cooled

1. Combine the yeast, warm water, and sugar and let stand until very foamy, about 10 minutes.

2. Dissolve the salt in the tepid water and stir the mixture into the sourdough starter. Beat in the yeast mixture, then the caraway seeds. Beat in the rye flour, about ½ cup at a time, then beat in the gluten flour.

3. Spread 2 cups of the all-purpose flour in a ring on a kneading surface and pour the dough into the center of the ring. Mix roughly with a dough scraper or a pancake turner, then knead just until thoroughly

mixed, adding as much of the remaining white flour as necessary to make a medium-stiff dough, not too heavy.

4. Scrape the kneading surface, dust it with rye flour, and knead the dough very thoroughly until it is elastic and smooth-surfaced. Don't overflour the board; keep the dough as close as possible to medium-stiff, not heavy.

5. Form the dough into a ball and place in an ungreased bowl; cover with plastic and let rise until doubled in bulk, at least 1 hour.

6. Turn the dough out onto your kneading surface, dusted lightly with rye flour, then expel the air from it and form it into two smooth balls. Cover with a towel and let rest for 20 minutes, meanwhile sprinkling cornmeal on a large (11 × 17-inch) baking sheet.

7. Flatten each ball of dough into an oval about 12 inches long and 1 inch thick. Beginning at a long edge, roll the dough up and pinch the seam closed. Make a slightly pointed oval loaf about 12 inches long and higher than it is wide. Place, seam down, on the cornmeal-covered baking sheet. Repeat with the second half of the dough, leaving ample space between the loaves.

8. Cover the loaves with a towel and let them rise until they have reached "three-quarters proof" (not quite doubled). When they have reached this point, the light pressure of a finger should barely dent the side of a loaf.

9. While the loaves are rising, preheat the oven to 425 degrees, and put a large, shallow pan containing 2 inches of boiling water on the bottom (or on the lowest shelf, if yours is an electric oven).

10. Brush the loaves with the cornstarch glaze. With a single-edged razor blade or a very sharp knife, held almost parallel to the surface, cut three diagonal slashes ¼ inch deep in the top of each.

11. Bake for 15 minutes in the center of oven, then lower the heat to 350 degrees, remove pan of water, and bake the bread for 30 minutes longer. Brush the loaves again with the glaze. Set them directly on the oven shelves for 10 to 15 minutes, or until there is a hollow sound when you rap on the bottom.

12. Cool on a rack, uncovered. Wrap in plastic and store at room temperature. The bread may be frozen.

JEWISH "CORN" BREAD

The name of this bread is a mystery to us. Although theories about the word "corn" in its name abound, we've not yet encountered one that we find acceptable in either historical or etymological terms. Call it what you like, but if you've a fondness for it, you'll probably *have* to make it unless you live in the Big Apple; as far as we know, it's a New York specialty. Bakers lucky enough to find a supply of them enhance their "corn" bread with a sprinkling of so-called "black caraway" seeds, which have nothing much in common with the familiar caraway seeds that bedeck other breads. Imported from North Africa or the Middle East, "black caraway," a member of the *Nigella* genus, is often known as *chernushka* and can be obtained from some spice merchants or by mail order (see Mail-Order Sources of Supplies, page 307), and occasionally in health-food stores.

Makes 2 large loaves

1 ½ cups warm (110-degree) water
  1 package dry yeast
  ½ teaspoon sugar
  4 teaspoons salt
  3 cups Rye Sourdough Starter (page 104), measured after stirring down, at room temperature
  2 cups gluten flour
3 ½ cups all-purpose flour, or as needed
  Cornmeal (for sprinkling the baking sheets)

Glaze:

1 egg white beaten with 2 tablespoons water

Optional topping:

2 teaspoons "black caraway" (*chernushka*) or regular caraway seeds

1. Combine ½ cup of the warm water, the yeast, and sugar and let stand until doubled in bulk, about 10 minutes.
2. Dissolve the salt in the remaining warm water in a mixing bowl. Mix in the sourdough starter, then the yeast mixture, then the gluten flour and 2 cups of the all-purpose flour; make a soft dough.
3. Spread 1½ cups flour on a kneading surface and turn the dough out onto it. Knead, adding more flour if necessary to make a soft dough that will hold its shape. Do not overknead—the dough should be only slightly elastic, even a bit sticky.
4. Form the dough into a ball and put in an ungreased bowl; cover with plastic, and let rise until doubled in bulk, about 1½ hours.
5. Turn the dough out onto a lightly floured surface and knead it a

few strokes to expel air. Cover with a towel and let rest for 15 minutes.

6. Divide the dough in half. Form each half into a loaf by flattening it to an inch-thick oval about 12 inches long, then rolling it up from one long side. Pinch the seam closed. Shape the ends of the oval loaves neatly and place them on two cornmeal-dusted baking sheets, seam down. Cover with towels and let rise until "three-quarters proofed," or not fully doubled.

7. While the loaves are rising, set a large roasting pan containing 2 inches of boiling water on the oven floor (or the lowest shelf of an electric oven) and preheat the oven to 400 degrees.

8. Brush the loaves with egg-white glaze, being careful not to let the glaze drip onto the pan, as it sticks and burns. With a single-edged razor blade or a small, sharp knife, cut three diagonal slashes, holding the blade almost parallel to the surface, about ¼ inch deep on each loaf. Sprinkle the loaves with "black caraway" or caraway seeds, if you like.

9. Bake for 30 minutes on the middle and upper shelves of the oven, then brush again with glaze, exchange shelf positions, and remove the water pan. Bake for 20 to 30 minutes longer, or until there is a hollow sound when you rap the bottom of a loaf.

10. Cool the bread on racks.

"BLACK" PUMPERNICKEL

Most so-called pumpernickels do not contain pumpernickel flour (rye meal), which is essential to authenticity. Except in the most Old World bakeries, pumpernickel is just dyed rye bread. If you yearn to approach the real thing, here's how.

Makes 2 loaves

½ cup plus ½ teaspoon sugar (this will color, not sweeten)
½ cup boiling water
2 cups warm (110-degree) water
2 packages dry yeast
1 tablespoon plus 2 teaspoons salt
2 cups Rye Sourdough Starter (page 104), measured after stirring down, at room temperature
1 cup pumpernickel flour (rye meal)
1 cup medium rye flour
1 cup gluten flour
3 tablespoons unsweetened cocoa
4 cups all-purpose flour, or as needed
Cornmeal (for sprinkling the baking sheets)

Glaze:

1 egg white beaten with 2 tablespoons water

1. In a small saucepan stir the ½ cup sugar over moderate heat until it reaches a medium-dark brown color; when the entire mass is frothing and seething, pour in the boiling water (avert your face while you do this). Stir to dissolve the caramel; cool.

2. Mix ½ cup of the warm water with the ½ teaspoon sugar and the yeast. Let stand until very foamy, about 10 minutes.

3. In a mixing bowl, stir the salt into the remaining 1½ cups warm water until dissolved. Add the yeast mixture, the cooled liquid caramel, and the sourdough starter and mix. Beat in the pumpernickel flour, rye flour, gluten flour, and the cocoa. Stir to blend thoroughly. Gradually stir in about 3 cups of the all-purpose flour, enough to make a dough that leaves the sides of the bowl.

4. Spread 1 cup of all-purpose flour on a kneading surface and turn the dough onto it. Knead the dough until it is somewhat elastic but still rather soft and sticky; don't overknead. Add a little more flour if necessary to prevent sticking, but do not make a stiff dough.

5. Form the dough into a ball and put into a large, ungreased bowl; cover with plastic and let it rise until doubled in bulk, about 1½ hours.

6. Punch the dough down, turn it out onto a lightly floured surface, cover with a towel, and let it rest for 15 to 20 minutes, meanwhile sprinkling two baking sheets with cornmeal.

7. Cut the dough in half and pat each half into a rough rectangle 1 inch thick. Fold each crosswise in thirds, pat out flat again, and fold into thirds, again crosswise. Form into a neat oval or rectangular loaf, with the seam side down and the ends pinched tightly closed. Place the loaves on the cornmeal-dusted baking sheets, cover with towels, and let rise until not quite doubled in bulk.

8. While the loaves are rising, preheat the oven to 425 degrees, putting a large pan containing 2 inches of boiling water on the bottom (or on the lowest shelf, if an electric oven).

9. Brush the risen loaves lightly and quickly with the beaten egg white and water; don't let the glaze drip onto the pan, or the bread will stick. Cut three diagonal slashes in the top of each loaf, using a single-edged razor blade or a small, sharp knife held almost parallel to the surface.

10. Put the bread into the oven and reduce the temperature setting to 400 degrees. Bake for 30 minutes, then remove from the oven, brush

with glaze again, and return to the oven, switching the shelf positions. Remove the pan of water. Bake for about 20 minutes longer, or until done (test by rapping on the bottom of a loaf with your knuckles—the sound should be hollow, not dull).

11. Cool on a rack, then wrap the bread and let it mellow for a day or so before serving.

WHITE-FLOUR SOURDOUGH STARTER

This tangy batter is the key ingredient of our English Muffins (page 111) and many other sourdough breadstuffs as well. This recipe makes 3 cups, enough to make a large batch of muffins, with enough left over to serve as a nucleus for a future baking. The starter keeps well in a covered jar in the refrigerator so long as it is "fed" with a small amount of flour and an equal amount of water about every 2 weeks—this keeps the yeasts alive. Or freeze it for indefinite storage; it will require reviving by "feeding" after it thaws.

If liquid gathers on the surface of stored starter, stir it in before adding flour and water. Your starter will be good so long as it responds to feeding and has a pleasantly tangy odor. If neglected, it may develop a pink or greenish tinge and an unpleasant odor. If that should happen, start over.

To increase a small amount of leftover starter to a quantity large enough for a baking, add flour and water in equal quantities, but never exceed the proportion of a cup of flour to a cup of starter. Let the mixture ferment, lightly covered, at room temperature until very bubbly; then, if you need still more starter, add more flour and water and ferment again.

Makes 3 cups

   2 cups tepid (80-degree) water
   ½ teaspoon sugar
   1 package dry yeast
   2 cups all-purpose flour

Mix the water, sugar, and yeast until dissolved. Beat in the flour until the batter is smooth. Pour into a clean 2-quart jar and cover with a cloth. Let stand at room temperature for 2 or 3 days, or until the starter has a sharp, almost winy odor and is bubbly (it will be full of lively bubbles after a short time and will continue to bubble, more sedately, until it is sufficiently sour). Exact times can't be given, as weather and temperature affect the rate of fermentation.

TO USE: If not to be used at once, cover the starter with a lid and refrigerate it. It will be lively enough to use for about 18 hours; if refrigerated longer, "feed" it lightly and let it become bubbly at room temperature —usually a matter of letting it stand overnight—before using it.

ENGLISH MUFFINS

For muffins with the correct tangy flavor and holey texture, we like to use White-Flour Sourdough Starter (page 110). Our muffin recipe makes a large batch—we suggest you wrap and freeze any muffins you won't use within two days or so. If you have gluten flour, substitute 1 cup for 1 cup of the all-purpose flour.

Makes about 20 four-inch or 24 to 26 smaller muffins

> 2 cups White-Flour Sourdough Starter (page 110), stirred down before measuring, at room temperature
> 1 teaspoon sugar
> 1 ½ cups milk, scalded, then cooled to 100 degrees
> 5 to 6 cups all-purpose flour, or as needed
> 2 teaspoons salt
> 3 tablespoons melted unsalted butter or shortening
> Cornmeal (for sprinkling the baking sheets)

1. In a large mixing bowl or the large bowl of an electric mixer, combine the starter, sugar, and milk. Gradually mix in 3 cups of all-purpose flour and beat thoroughly until an elastic batter—the sponge —is formed.

2. Cover the bowl and set it in a warm spot. Let the sponge rise until it becomes very bubbly and then collapses to about its original volume. (If the collapse comes when you're not on the spot, no harm is done; you can tell it has occurred by the "high-water mark" indicating the original volume of the risen sponge.) This will take from 2 to 3 hours—or it could take much longer, due to weather conditions or other variables (so be warned!).

3. Beat the salt into the sponge, then beat in the melted butter or shortening. Gradually add 2 to 3 cups of all-purpose flour, just enough to make a medium-stiff dough. Knead very thoroughly on a

lightly floured board. The dough should be smooth and elastic; it's almost impossible to overknead it.

4. Form the dough into a ball and turn several times in a buttered bowl, then place buttered side up. Cover with plastic and let rise until doubled in bulk, 1 to 2½ hours, usually.

5. Turn the dough out onto a floured surface. With floured hands pat it out a scant ½ inch thick. Let it rest a few minutes, meanwhile sprinkling cornmeal on two baking sheets.

6. Using a 4-inch cutter for large muffins or a 3-inch one for medium muffins, cut the dough into rounds (you can use a well-washed can of the appropriate size, both ends removed). Transfer the rounds to the prepared baking sheets, placing them 1½ inches apart. Gather the dough scraps, pat them out again, and cut out the rest of the muffins. Press the center of each muffin with the palm of your hand (this prevents "peaking"). Cover with a cloth and let rise until light but not more than half again their original height, 15 to 30 minutes.

7. Heat an ungreased griddle (or an electric skillet, set at 400 degrees). Transfer the muffins to the hot pan, a few at a time, placing them at least an inch apart and bake for 10 minutes, or until the rising has stopped (the tops will be firm to a light touch) and the undersides are lightly browned. (Adjust your heat, if necessary.) Turn the muffins, press them lightly with a spatula, and bake the second side about the same length of time, or until lightly browned.

8. Cool the muffins on a rack and bake the remaining batches. If unbaked muffins begin to over-rise while earlier batches are baking, set them in the refrigerator until their turn comes. Store cooled muffins airtight for up to 4 days, or wrap and freeze them for future use.

TO SERVE: Split the muffins with the tines of a fork, toast them, and butter them liberally; serve hot.

CRUMPETS

A true British crumpet is a dense article rather like an English muffin, but thinner and full of holes. Don't split these (they're only about half an inch thick)—just toast them, butter the holey side lavishly, and serve with jam.

Our recipe is for a classic crumpet; unlike some, it calls for no eggs or butter. If you want to add these, reduce the liquid by 2 tablespoons and add an egg and 1 tablespoon of melted butter; but we'd advise you to try the recipe "straight" first, and then compare.

English muffins are not (despite some directions to the contrary) properly baked in rings, but crumpets are. The rings we used are 4 inches in diameter. If you don't have them or can't find them at a kitchenware shop, you can improvise rings by collecting tuna-fish cans or others of an appropriate size, removing the bottoms as well as the tops, and buttering them well before use.

Makes 10 to 12

½ cup warm (110-degree) water
¼ teaspoon sugar
½ package (scant 1½ teaspoons) dry yeast
1 cup milk, scalded, then cooled to 100 degrees
¾ teaspoon salt
2 cups all-purpose flour
⅛ teaspoon baking soda
¼ cup slightly warm (100-degree) water
Unsalted butter (for greasing the muffin rings)

1. Combine the warm water, sugar, and yeast in a mixing bowl and let proof for 10 minutes, until slightly foamy.

2. Add the milk to the yeast mixture, then beat in the salt and flour, ½ cup at a time. Beat very vigorously, using an electric mixer if you have one. The batter should be elastic and slightly heavy; it's almost impossible to overbeat it. (The harder you attack the batter, the more authentically holey your crumpets will be.)

3. Cover the bowl, set it in a warm place, and let the batter become very bubbly and then collapse (it will fall back to about its original volume, leaving a "high-water" mark on the bowl.) This usually takes 2 to 2½ hours, but may take longer.

4. Dissolve the baking soda in the ¼ cup slightly warm water and mix into the batter. Let the batter rest in a warm spot for 30 minutes, or until it is again bubbly.

5. Heat a griddle (or an electric skillet, set at 400 degrees). Butter the insides of muffin rings or clean, dry tuna cans. Set the rings on the griddle and leave them until they are just hot to the touch.

6. Ladle about ¼ cup of bubbly batter into each ring; it will rise briskly. Bake 5 to 8 minutes, until all the bubbles have broken and the top no longer looks wet. With a pancake turner turn the crumpets, rings and all; the crumpets will drop free of the rings. Lift off the rings and bake the second side of the crumpets for 5 to 6 minutes, until the

crumpets feel light and have dry sides and lightly browned bottoms. Remove to a rack to cool.

7. Butter the rings again and repeat the baking, making as many batches as necessary. If the kitchen is warm and the batter is rising too vivaciously, you can set it in the refrigerator between batches. Baked crumpets, well cooled, can be stored in plastic bags at room temperature for a few days. Refrigerate or freeze for longer storage. Toast before serving.

WESTPHALIAN PUMPERNICKEL

A very dark, dense, and damp bread, virtually unleavened, this loaf is baked slowly, covered, until the coarse grains become barely amenable to the tooth. The long fermentation of the dough develops a unique, slightly sourish, nutty flavor that appeals especially to those who relish intensity and assertiveness in breadstuffs.

If you like, double the recipe and make two loaves, as the bread keeps well and takes up a good deal of oven time.

Makes 1 loaf

    2 tablespoons sugar
1 ¼ cups boiling water
    ½ cup cracked wheat
1 ½ teaspoons salt
    1 tablespoon vegetable oil
    1 tablespoon molasses
    ½ cup White-Flour Sourdough Starter (page 110), stirred down before measuring, at room temperature
2 ½ cups pumpernickel flour (rye meal)
    All-purpose flour (for kneading)

1. In a small, heavy saucepan, melt the sugar over medium heat. Let it become a very deep brown (it will smoke). Standing well back, add the boiling water, then stir until the caramel has dissolved. Remove from the heat.

2. Put the cracked wheat, salt, oil, and molasses in a mixing bowl. Pour the hot caramel liquid in, stir, cover, and let stand until lukewarm (110 degrees).

3. Stir in the sourdough starter, then mix in the pumpernickel flour, ½ cup at a time, to make a moderately stiff but workable dough. Cover

the bowl and set it in a quite warm place (about 90 to 100 degrees) for 8 hours. The dough will become somewhat leavened but not light.

4. Turn the dough out onto a lightly floured kneading surface and knead it just enough to shape it into a flat-topped loaf that will fit an oiled 8 × 4-inch loaf pan. Place it in the pan and fit a piece of aluminum foil over the pan, pressing it snugly around the rim. Let the dough rest in a warm place for 30 minutes.

5. Set the pan in an unheated oven, then turn the heat to 275 degrees and bake the bread, covered, for 3 hours.

6. Remove the bread from pan and cool it on a rack, covered with a towel.

FLAKY CHEESE TWISTS

Made with a shortcut puff pastry, these twists are richer in cheese and sure to be fresher tasting than packaged cheese sticks of any type. If you make these twists in warm weather or in a warm kitchen, the dough may soften as you work. If this happens, call a halt while you refrigerate the dough for a few minutes to allow it to become firm again.

If you have stored baked twists for a few days before serving, freshen them in a warm oven for a few minutes before offering them with drinks, or perhaps with the salad course.

Makes about 5 dozen

2 ½ cups instant-type flour
  1 teaspoon salt
  2 sticks (1 cup) unsalted butter, chilled and cut into bits
½ cup ice water, or as needed
  1 cup finely grated sharp Cheddar cheese
  1 teaspoon paprika (medium-hot, if available)
¾ teaspoon coarse (kosher or sea) salt
  2 tablespoons very fine, dry bread crumbs
  1 egg
  1 tablespoon water

1. Whisk together the flour and 1 teaspoon salt thoroughly. Add the butter bits and, using your fingers or a pastry blender, blend into a flaky mixture. Sprinkle in the ice water gradually and mix lightly with a fork. Add just enough water to make the dough bits adhere to each other;

don't overmix. Form the dough into a brick, wrap in plastic, and chill for at least 1 hour or as long as 12 hours.

2. When ready to bake the twists, halve the pastry, return one-half to the refrigerator, and roll out the remaining half on a lightly floured surface to make a rectangle measuring 8 × 12 inches. Turn the pastry so that a long side faces you and brush off all surplus flour. Fold the short ends to meet in the center and again brush off flour, then fold the pastry like a book where the ends meet at the center. Roll the folded pastry out again, this time to an oblong measuring 7 × 10 inches. Working quickly, repeat the folding, brushing, and rolling twice (a total of three foldings and rollings), ending up with a 7 × 10-inch oblong. Stop at any point to refrigerate the dough if it gets too soft.

3. Cover a large baking sheet with waxed paper and sprinkle it lightly with flour. Lay the pastry on the paper and roll it out to 9 × 12 inches. Chill. Roll and fold the second half of the pastry. Chill both halves of the pastry, uncovered, for 30 minutes; or, if you like, cover closely with plastic and chill for up to 12 hours.

4. Combine the cheese, paprika, coarse salt, and bread crumbs in a bowl. Beat the egg with the 1 tablespoon water in another bowl.

5. Preheat the oven to 400 degrees.

6. Slide one sheet of dough, on its waxed paper, onto the work surface. Brush it lightly with the egg mixture and sprinkle it with one-fourth (about ¼ cup) of the cheese mixture, pressing it into the surface. Cover with another sheet of waxed paper and turn the dough over. Peel off the waxed paper from the top, then coat its surface with egg and another quarter of the cheese mixture, pressing it in as before.

7. Quarter the sheet of dough (a pastry wheel does this well), then cut each quarter into strips ½ inch wide and 4 inches long. Twist each strip to pencil-thinness (they will lengthen as you twist) and place them, ½ inch apart, on an ungreased baking sheet. Press the ends of the twists onto the pan to prevent unrolling.

8. Bake for about 10 minutes, until the cheese sticks are golden brown, then remove to racks to cool. When cool, trim off any unsightly flattened ends.

9. Repeat the forming and baking procedure with the second half of the dough. When all are done, store, airtight, for up to 2 weeks in the refrigerator or for up to a week at room temperature. The baked twists may also be frozen. However stored, they improve with brief warming before serving.

CORN CHIPS

Crisp, golden, as rich in corn flavor as tortilla chips but more tender. The essential ingredient—*masa* flour or *masa harina*—is packaged by at least one major cereal manufacturer with nationwide distribution and is to be found in Hispanic markets and in some supermarkets in large cities. *Masa* flour, made from specially processed corn, has a taste all its own. Cornmeal cannot be substituted for it. These chips can be made in double or triple batches, but they are so quick to make that you can have them fresh on short notice.

    1 cup warm (100-degree) water
    1 egg yolk
    1 teaspoon salt
    ¾ cup masa harina, or as needed
      Corn oil for frying

1. In a mixing bowl, whisk the water, egg yolk, and salt together until thoroughly mixed. Gradually add enough *masa harina* to make a soft dough, just stiff enough not to stick to your fingers.

2. In a heavy skillet, or an electric one, preheat frying oil at least 2 inches deep to 375 degrees.

3. Fit a cookie press or pastry bag with the plate designed to make a flat, ribbed shape and fill it with the *masa* dough.

4. Press out into the hot oil a few short lengths of dough, enough to cover only about half the surface of the frying oil. Fry the ribbons, turning them once, just until they are golden brown. Lift the corn chips from the oil with a slotted spoon or skimmer and drain them on a cookie sheet covered with paper towels. Repeat until all the *masa* dough has been used.

TO SERVE OR STORE: Serve the chips while they are still warm, or cool them completely and store them airtight. To serve chips after storage, freshen them briefly in a warm oven. They will keep for up to a week.

MELBA TOAST

Making Melba toast is laughably simple *if* you have very thin white bread to begin with. Use either your own homemade loaves, sliced about half the normal thickness, or, if available in your town, a firm, homemade-type bread sliced extra-thin.

Halve the slices into rectangles, lay them directly on the oven shelves, and warm them—"bake" sounds too hot—until they are thoroughly dry and crisp, slightly golden (your oven temperature should be very low—well under 200 degrees). Turn the slices once or twice to minimize curling.

Another method, which takes a bit longer, is to spread the slices on an electric "keep-warm" serving tray set at its highest heat. Turn them somewhat more often, as they are being dried by bottom heat only. They will take longer to "melba," but the results are good.

Pack the fragile Melba toast in containers with airtight lids when it is cool. It will keep indefinitely.

Use the same method for whole-wheat bread, or for rounds of "party" rye bread. You could also bake your own rye bread, using any of our recipes in this section, in loaves of small diameter for making rye Melba toast.

BOSTON BROWN BREAD

A truly American bread and a traditional accompaniment for baked beans Boston-style. This bread is equally good warm or cool, spread with Cream Cheese (page 58) or Sweet Butter (page 61), or made into tea sandwiches. It isn't overly sweet, which explains why it goes well with such diverse accompaniments.

Our recipe describes how to bake the bread in the oven. If you prefer damper (perhaps more traditional) loaves, or if the oven is otherwise engaged, set the molds on a rack in a steamer or deep pot with enough boiling water to come halfway up their sides. Cover the pot and steam for 2 hours, or until the bread tests "done."

Makes 2 cylindrical loaves

¾ **cup raisins or currants**
1 **tablespoon all-purpose flour**
⅛ **teaspoon baking powder**
¾ **cup molasses**
1 **egg**
2 **tablespoons melted unsalted butter**
1 ¾ **cups buttermilk**
1 **cup rye flour**
1 **cup whole-wheat flour**
1 **cup yellow cornmeal, preferably stone-ground**
1 **teaspoon baking soda**
1 **teaspoon salt**
¼ **teaspoon ground black pepper (optional)**

1. Preheat the oven to 375 degrees. Grease two 1-pound coffee cans or other cylindrical containers with a 4- to 5-cup capacity.

2. Toss together, in a small bowl, the raisins, all-purpose flour, and baking powder.

3. In a large bowl, beat together the molasses, egg, melted butter, and buttermilk until well blended.

4. Combine the rye and whole-wheat flours, cornmeal, baking soda, salt, and the optional pepper, then sift the mixture through a coarse-meshed sieve into the buttermilk mixture, stirring just until combined. Fold in the floured raisins.

5. Turn into the prepared coffee cans; the mixture should come one-half to three-fourths of the way up the sides. Cover with greased waxed paper, then cover tightly with foil tied in place with string. Set the molds in a deep casserole or pot, set the pot in the preheated oven, and add boiling water to come halfway up the sides of the molds. Bake for 2 hours, or until the top of a loaf springs back when pressed lightly.

6. Remove the molds to a rack and let stand for 5 minutes. Run a knife around the inside of each mold and unmold the bread onto a serving dish, to be cut into slices while hot; or cool the bread on a rack, wrap the loaves in foil, and refrigerate or freeze.

TO REHEAT: Replace the bread in a steaming container, cover with foil, and steam briefly to reheat; or simply heat the bread, wrapped in foil, in the oven until heated through.

DATE-NUT BREAD

The honeylike sweetness of dates, unencumbered by a confusion of spices, distinguishes this light, classic tea loaf. Nuts and dates really *do* have a natural affinity. It is no accident that they have been paired since biblical times.

Makes 1 loaf

      1 cup boiling water
      1 cup chopped dates
    ½ stick (4 tablespoons) unsalted butter, at room temperature
    ½ cup (packed) dark brown sugar, sieved if lumpy
    ¼ cup sugar
      1 egg
1 ¾ cups all-purpose flour
    ½ teaspoon salt
    ½ teaspoon baking powder
    ½ teaspoon baking soda
    ¾ cup coarsely chopped pecans or walnuts

1. Preheat the oven to 350 degrees. Grease an 8 × 4-inch loaf pan.

2. Pour the boiling water over the dates; let stand until needed.

3. With an electric mixer or by hand, beat the butter until creamy in a large bowl. Gradually beat in the sugars and cream well; beat in the egg. Beat in the dates and their liquid (at lowest speed, if you're using a machine).

4. Sift together the flour, salt, baking powder, and baking soda and add gradually, on lowest speed, to the creamed mixture; stir in the nuts. Turn the mixture into the greased loaf pan.

5. Bake in the center of the oven for 45 minutes, or until a cake tester inserted in the center of the loaf emerges clean and dry.

6. Cool the loaf in its pan on a rack for 15 minutes before turning it out onto the rack to cool completely. Wrap airtight; the loaf will keep well for at least a week, refrigerated. Freeze for longer storage.

PANCAKE AND WAFFLE MIX

If you're a serious cook, it may seem far-fetched to make ready-measured batches of a mix such as this, but for some of us morning sleepyheads (and/or night people), having a good mix like this one on hand means that pancakes and waffles will appear more often at breakfast; few of us are geared up to start measuring and sifting in the dawn's early light, and a good mix is the answer.

This mix, used with either sweet milk or buttermilk, makes characterful pancakes, with the flavor of good grains and with a high-rising, almost crunchy texture. The waffles are equally good. If you own a bowl big enough to blend a double batch, by all means double the recipe and make enough mix for half a dozen good breakfasts.

A suggestion for real sleepyheads: Use the mix to make extra waffles, underbaking them slightly as suggested in the waffle recipe. Cool them on a rack, then store them in closed plastic bags in the freezer. Quickly reheated in a toaster (no need to thaw them), they will be crispy and very good, if not quite as flavorful as fresh-baked waffles.

Makes 3 batches, each sufficient for 12 to 14
four-inch pancakes or 5 large waffles

1 cup rye flour
1 cup whole-wheat flour
2 cups all-purpose flour
1/2 cup yellow cornmeal, preferably stone-ground
1/3 cup sugar
2 tablespoons baking powder
2 1/2 teaspoons salt
1/2 teaspoon baking soda

1. Sift the flours, cornmeal, sugar, baking powder, salt, and soda into a bowl, using a wide meshed sieve. With a large whisk, mix them very thoroughly for at least 30 seconds.

2. Measure the mix into three plastic bags or other containers, putting 1¾ cups into each. (If any mix is left over, divide it among the bags.) Close the containers and store them at room temperature.

(*continued*)

PANCAKES

12 to 14 four-inch pancakes

2 eggs (or 3, for richer pancakes)
1 ¼ cups milk
  2 tablespoons melted unsalted butter
  1 batch (1¾ cups) Pancake and Waffle Mix (see above)

1. In a mixing bowl, beat the eggs with a whisk until they are well mixed, then whisk in the milk and the melted butter.

2. Add the mix and stir the batter with a fork or the whisk just until the dry ingredients are moistened—it will be a little lumpy. (The pancakes will be better if you don't stir the batter until it is smooth.)

3. Bake the pancakes on a hot griddle, greased or not, depending on the manufacturer's instructions (400-degree setting for electric griddles or skillets), ladling out a scant ¼ cup of batter for each cake. Turn the pancakes when one or two of the bubbles on top have burst and the edges begin to lose their gloss, then bake the second side until no more steam rises, or until the light touch of a finger leaves no imprint. Serve the pancakes at once on warmed plates.

BUTTERMILK PANCAKES

12 to 14 four-inch pancakes

  1 batch (1¾ cups) Pancake and Waffle Mix (see above)
¼ teaspoon baking soda
  2 eggs
1 ⅔ cups buttermilk, or more if needed (the thickness of buttermilk
      varies)
  2 tablespoons melted butter

1. Sift the mix and the soda together.

2. In a mixing bowl, beat the eggs with a whisk until well mixed, then whisk in 1⅔ cups of the buttermilk and the melted butter.

3. Add the sifted dry ingredients and mix and bake the batter as described above. (If the batter is too thick, add a little more buttermilk.)

WAFFLES

Makes 5 waffles (9 × 4¹/2 inches each)

2 eggs
1 ¼ cups milk
2 tablespoons melted unsalted butter
1 batch (1¾ cups) Pancake and Waffle Mix (see above)

1. Preheat your waffle iron.

2. Separate the eggs, putting the whites into a small bowl and the yolks into a mixing bowl.

3. With a rotary beater or a whisk, beat the whites until they form firm peaks. With the same beater beat the yolks until they are well mixed, then beat in the milk and the melted butter.

4. Stir the mix into the liquid ingredients, blending it in just until the dry ingredients are moistened (don't try to achieve a smooth batter). Fold in the beaten egg whites.

5. Bake the waffles in the preheated waffle iron, following the manufacturer's recommendations for heat settings and for greasing. When no more steam emerges from the edges of the baking waffle, open the iron and check the waffle for doneness; if it is not as brown as you'd like, close the iron and bake the waffle a moment or two longer. Serve on warmed plates.

TO STORE: If the waffles are to be frozen for future reheating in a toaster, bake them only to a light gold. Cool them on a cake rack, then wrap them airtight for freezer storage.

BISCUIT MIX

Another one of the few mixes that we think worthwhile to have around. We can just about always use hot biscuits to liven up or fill out a mundane meal. And having the mix on hand ensures a quick coffee cake, even on the dreariest Sunday when no one would dream of going out to get something special. As for shortcake, it's a delight whenever summer fruits (or poached winter ones, for that matter) are handy. We find shortcake outrageously filling for dessert, so we prefer to have it for a weekend breakfast—deliciously alone.

(*continued*)

Makes 3 batches (scant 2 cups each)

4 ½ cups all-purpose flour
  5 teaspoons baking powder
  1 teaspoon salt
  5 tablespoons solid vegetable shortening
  3 tablespoons unsalted butter, cut into tiny pieces

1. In a bowl, whisk together the flour, baking powder, and salt. Add the shortening and butter. Blend with your fingertips, a pastry blender, or an electric mixer until the fat particles are no longer visible.

2. Divide the mixture evenly among 3 airtight containers. Close and refrigerate for up to a month.

BISCUITS

Makes about 12 two-inch biscuits

  1 batch (scant 2 cups) Biscuit Mix (see above)
  ⅔ cup milk

1. Preheat the oven to 475 degrees.

2. Pour the mix into a bowl and make a hole in the center. Pour in the milk and blend quickly, stirring from the center outward, just until there are no dry bits of flour remaining.

3. Turn the dough out onto a lightly floured surface, then pat it or roll it out to form a rectangle about ½ inch thick. With a 2-inch cookie cutter, cut out circles and place them on an ungreased baking sheet. Roll out the scraps and cut more biscuits until all the dough is used up.

4. Place the baking sheet in the oven; turn the oven temperature down to 425 degrees. Bake the biscuits for 12 to 15 minutes, until they are very lightly browned. Serve immediately.

COFFEE CAKE

Makes 1 eight-inch-square cake

Topping:

  ½ cup all-purpose flour
  ¼ cup (packed) light or dark brown sugar
  ½ teaspoon ground cinnamon
2 ½ tablespoons unsalted butter, cut into small bits

Batter:

   1 batch (scant 2 cups) Biscuit Mix (see above)
   ½ cup sugar
   ¾ cup milk
   1 egg
   ½ teaspoon vanilla extract

   1. Preheat the oven to 350 degrees. Grease an 8-inch-square pan.
   2. In a bowl, combine the flour, brown sugar, cinnamon, and butter for the topping. With a pastry blender or your fingers, work the mixture together until the butter is barely visible. Reserve the topping.
   3. In a bowl, whisk together the mix and the sugar. Beat together the milk, egg, and vanilla and add to the mix, stirring just to blend.
   4. Turn the batter into the prepared pan and smooth it with a spatula. Squeeze the topping into small chunks in your hand, then break into nuggets and sprinkle them over the batter.
   5. Bake the cake for 30 to 35 minutes, or until a cake tester or skewer inserted in the center comes out clean. Let cool slightly in the pan and serve warm.

SHORTCAKE

Makes 10 two-and one-half-inch shortcakes

   1 batch (scant 2 cups) Biscuit Mix (see above)
   2 tablespoons sugar
   ⅓ cup heavy cream
   ⅓ cup milk
   1 tablespoon melted unsalted butter

   1. Preheat the oven to 475 degrees.
   2. Pour the mix into a bowl and whisk with the sugar. Make a hole in the center. Pour in the cream, milk, and melted butter and blend rapidly, stirring from the center outward just until there are no dry bits of flour remaining.
   3. Turn the dough out onto a lightly floured surface, then pat or roll out to form a rough rectangle slightly thicker than ½ inch. Cut with a biscuit cutter 2½ inches in diameter; place on an ungreased baking sheet. Roll out the scraps and cut more shortcakes.
   4. Place the baking sheet in the oven; turn the oven temperature

down to 425 degrees. Bake the shortcakes for 12 to 15 minutes, until they are very lightly browned.

TO USE: Split the shortcakes, butter them if you wish, fill with fruit, and serve with cream, plain or whipped.

CORN BREAD AND MUFFIN MIX

Ready to use, a flavorful mix for either corn bread or muffins. To make the mix, use either regular yellow or white packaged cornmeal, or, if you can get it, stone-ground meal, which tends to be coarser, richer in the taste of corn, and less hard-textured than factory-ground meal. If you have ever used the light, sweet packaged corn-bread mixes, this will seem dense and crunchy by comparison.

Makes 5 cups of mix, enough for 2 batches of corn bread
or 24 corn muffins

2 ⅔ cups cornmeal
    2 cups all-purpose flour
    2 to 4 tablespoons sugar, to taste
    2 teaspoons salt
    2 tablespoons baking powder

Combine all the ingredients in a large bowl and mix very thoroughly with a whisk. Measure 2½ cups mix into each of two plastic bags and close the bags securely. Store at room temperature.

CORN BREAD or CORN MUFFINS

1 eight-inch-square pan of bread or 12 medium corn muffins

2½ cups Corn Bread and Muffin Mix (see above)
    2 eggs
    1 cup milk
    ½ stick (4 tablespoons) unsalted butter, melted

1. Preheat the oven to 400 degrees. Grease an 8-inch-square pan or 12 muffin cups.
    2. Empty the mix into a mixing bowl.
    3. Beat the eggs until well mixed. Beat in milk, then the melted butter. Stir into the dry ingredients only until they are moistened; don't overmix.

4. Spoon the batter into the prepared pan or muffin cups. Bake muffins for 20 minutes, bread for 25 to 30 minutes. Either is done when firm and golden brown. Serve hot.

BRAN MUFFIN MIX

Bran muffins made with this mix are not sweet and cakelike, but branny and wheaty. If you are accustomed to a sweet muffin, you may want to use the full amount of sugar indicated. Muffins made with the smaller measure of sugar will have only a hint of sweetness, making for a better contrast when you heap a morsel with Bitter Orange Marmalade (page 164).

Enough for 2 batches of 12 two-and-one-half-inch muffins each

   1 cup unprocessed coarse bran
   2 cups whole-wheat flour
   1 cup all-purpose flour
  ¼ to ½ cup sugar, to taste
   2 tablespoons baking powder
   2 teaspoons salt

1. Stir all the ingredients together thoroughly, using a whisk. If you suspect there may be any lumps, sieve through a coarse strainer and whisk again to mix thoroughly.
2. Measure 2 cups of the mix into each of two plastic bags. Depending upon how much you have aerated the mix in stirring, you will have a little left in the bowl. Divide it between the batches. Store, closed airtight, at room temperature.

BRAN OR RAISIN-BRAN MUFFINS

12 two-and-one-half-inch muffins or 8 three-inch muffins

   2 eggs
   1 cup milk
  ½ stick (4 tablespoons) unsalted butter, melted
   1 batch (a little over 2 cups) Bran Muffin Mix (see above)
  ¼ cup raisins (optional)

1. Preheat the oven to 425 degrees. Grease muffin cups.
2. Beat the eggs with the milk, then whisk in the melted butter. Stir

in the mix just until it is moistened; don't overmix. (If you are using the raisins, dump the mix onto the liquid, top with the raisins, and mix just until moistened.)

3. Divide among the muffin cups and bake for 20 minutes, or until the muffins are firm and slightly shrunken from the sides of the cups. Serve at once. Leftovers may be stored in plastic bags, refrigerated, for later rewarming in a moderate (300- to 350-degree) oven.

Pickles and Relishes

On Pickles and Relishes
Kosher-Style Dill Pickles ("Half-Sours")
Pickled Green Tomatoes, Kosher Style
Bread and Butter Pickles
Cornichons (Tiny French Sour Cucumber Pickles)
Crisp Pickled Green Beans
Pickled Okra
Pickled Jerusalem Artichokes
Marinated Artichoke Hearts
Olives with Bay and Rosemary
Marinated Mushrooms
Caponata
India Relish
Sweet Red Pepper Relish
Mild Hot Pepper Jelly
Peach or Nectarine Chutney
Mango Chutney

On Pickles and Relishes

Some of the favorite pickles and relishes we've chosen for this section require no special "canning" equipment or procedures. The "crock" pickles, either naturally fermented or made sour with vinegar, can be prepared in any large ceramic or glass jar as well as a crock, and can later be refrigerated in any jars you have handy. Jars or plastic containers with tight covers can be used for the preparations to be kept in the refrigerator or freezer—Marinated Artichoke Hearts (page 140) and Caponata (page 143), for example.

However, those pickles and relishes to be processed by a "canning" method—we specify a boiling-water bath—require the same equipment and procedures described in the Pointers on Preserving on pages 153–56. In addition, the processing procedure is outlined in all recipes requiring it, and exact processing times are given.

KOSHER-STYLE DILL PICKLES ("Half-Sours")

These Eastern European favorites have become widely known in the United States, thanks largely to delicatessens. Unfortunately, many of the kosher-style pickles presently encountered at these places are rank with garlic oil and other shortcut flavorings used in place of the fresh dill, garlic, and pickling spices needed for the pungency that enhances the natural cucumber flavor.

Making your own half-sours or full-sours is an easy task, feasible wherever and whenever fresh cucumbers, preferably of a pickling variety, are available. Choose stubby cucumbers 4 to 6 inches long—a size often known by the market designation of "Kirbys." They must of course be unwaxed, firm, unblemished, with no sign of softening or wrinkling. In the Northeast, at least, greengrocers seem to stock them virtually the year round.

With this method, you can control the flavoring and the degree of sourness (produced by natural fermentation, not by vinegar). Take the pickles from the spiced brine while they are still mainly white inside (in from 3 to 10 days, depending upon temperature and environmental bacilli) and you have half-sours. Leave them until they are jade-green throughout and you have full-sours.

A USEFUL TIP: When fresh dill with flower heads can be obtained, buy a good supply. Cut off any roots, rinse and shake dry the bunches, and fold them into plastic bags. Tie the bags shut and freeze the dill until it is needed for pickling, then take from the bag whatever amount you need. If fresh or frozen dill is not to be had, dill seeds can be used— about a teaspoonful will replace a handful of dill stalks.

Makes 8 to 10 pickles

   8 to 10 full-sized, unblemished pickling cucumbers, or as many as will "swim" freely in the brine
   Good handful of stalks of fresh dill, with flower heads (and these preferably in bud), plus ¼ teaspoon dill seeds if the dill lacks flower heads
   4 cloves unpeeled garlic, flattened
   1 gallon water
   ½ cup coarse (kosher) salt
   4 teaspoons Pickling Spice (page 201)

1. Make sure your cucumbers are unblemished, then wash them well, being sure to scrub off any sand. Put them into a very clean crock large enough to cover the pickles with at least 2 inches of brine. Add the dill and garlic.

2. Bring the water, salt, and pickling spice to a boil and boil, covered, for 5 to 10 minutes. Cool *completely,* then pour over the pickles, being sure they are well covered with brine.

3. Put a heavy plate on top of the cucumbers to hold them under the surface and cover the crock with a cloth. Let stand at room temperature, checking daily and skimming if any scum appears.

4. After 2 or 3 days taste the brine and, if you like, add more spices. Let the pickles ferment for 3 days at least, then check for degree of "doneness" by cutting off a slice. (Return the cucumber to the brine if it isn't ready.) When they are pickled to your taste, transfer them to glass jars, pour some of the brine (including a share of the spices) over them, cover them, and refrigerate. (They will keep well for several weeks but will slowly become more pickled, despite the refrigerator cold.) If you prefer full-sour pickles, leave them in the crock until they

are a translucent green throughout, then transfer them to jars, add spices and brine, and refrigerate as for half-sours.

PICKLED GREEN TOMATOES, KOSHER STYLE

Like half-sour cucumber pickles, these pickled tomatoes are a traditional Jewish delicacy that has become a favorite outside its original culinary community. This recipe produces a tomato pickle with a fresh taste that is sometimes missing in the commercial versions, which are often flavored with extracts rather than real dill and garlic.

Try making your own pickled green tomatoes at any time during the summer or early fall. Choose only *completely* green, hard tomatoes with no sign of ripening. Don't use any that show whitening areas, a slight yellowing, or any tinge of pink.

The fermentation produces the naturally acid flavor of these pickles —no vinegar is used. After pickling, the tomatoes will keep in the refrigerator for several months.

Small to medium, completely green tomatoes

Other ingredients, <u>per quart</u> of water used:

   2 tablespoons coarse (kosher) salt
   1 teaspoon Pickling Spice (page 201)
   ½ teaspoon mustard seeds, slightly bruised
   ¼ teaspoon whole black peppercorns, slightly bruised
      Handful of stalks of fresh dill, preferably with flower heads (and
      these preferably in bud), plus ¼ teaspoon dill seeds if the
      dill lacks flower heads
   1 medium unpeeled clove garlic, slightly flattened

   1. Sort and rinse the tomatoes, measure them by quarts, and put into a large, clean crock or bowl. Pour in cold water to cover the tomatoes by 2 to 3 inches. Measure the water into a pot and note how many quarts you have. Prick each tomato in several places with a fork and return them to the crock.

   2. To the water in the pot add salt, pickling spice, mustard seeds, and peppercorns in the required amounts and bring the solution to a boil. Simmer for 5 minutes, then cool *completely*.

(continued)

3. Add the dill (and dill seeds, if used) and garlic to the tomatoes in the crock, distributing them evenly. Pour in the brine and spices. Put a clean, heavy plate on the tomatoes to hold them under the surface.

4. Cover the container loosely with a cloth and let the tomatoes stand in a fairly cool spot (70 degrees is ideal) for 1 to 3 weeks, until they have become as tangy and flavorful as you like them. The time required will depend partly on their size, partly on the temperature of the spot where they are fermenting. Check the tomatoes daily; if a white scum (harmless) forms on the brine, skim it off.

5. When the tomatoes are pickled to your taste, transfer them to clean, dry jars, strain some brine over them, adding sprigs of dill from the crock if you like, put on lids, and refrigerate.

BREAD AND BUTTER PICKLES

This is a time-honored "country" pickle, enough of a favorite to have passed from the repertoires of grannies and great-aunts into the production lines of commercial packers.

Use firm, slender cucumbers; be sure they have not been waxed. The ice will help to keep the cucumbers crisp in spite of the necessary salting period. Some people like oniony bread and butter pickles. If you're one of them, use the larger quantity of onions called for in the recipe.

Makes 5 or 6 pints

   3 quarts unpeeled, not too thinly sliced cucumbers (about ⅜ inch thick)
½ cup coarse (kosher) salt
   Crushed or cracked ice (about 2 trays of cubes)
   1 quart cider vinegar
   3 cups sugar
   1 teaspoon turmeric
¼ teaspoon ground cloves
   4 teaspoons mustard seeds
   2 teaspoons celery seed
¼ teaspoon ground ginger
   Optional: ½ teaspoon whole black peppercorns
   2 cups to 1 quart sliced onions (the same thickness as the cucumbers)

1. Mix the cucumbers with the salt in a ceramic, glass, or stainless-steel bowl. Mix in the crushed ice and let stand for 3 to 4 hours.

2. In a stainless-steel or enameled kettle, combine the vinegar, sugar, and the turmeric, cloves, mustard seeds, celery seed, ground ginger, and optional black peppercorns and bring to a boil. Lower the heat and simmer for 10 minutes, then turn off the heat and cover.

3. Drain the cucumbers thoroughly, removing any unmelted ice. Bring the pickling solution again to a boil, add the cucumbers and sliced onion, cover, and bring quickly to a simmer. Watching closely, and pushing the vegetables under the surface to insure even heating, bring the pickles to a full boil and boil for exactly 2 minutes.

4. Following the Pointers on Preserving on pages 153–56, ladle the pickles into clean, hot canning jars, distributing the spices equally. Fill the jars with the pickling liquid to within ½ inch of the rims. Wipe the rims, put on two-piece lids, and fasten the screw bands.

5. Put the jars on a rack in a deep kettle half full of boiling water and add boiling water to cover the lids by 2 inches. Bring to a hard boil, then cover the pot and boil (process) for 5 minutes (for pint jars) or 10 minutes (for quarts).

6. Remove the jars from the boiling-water bath and let cool. Let the pickles mellow for about a month before serving.

CORNICHONS (Tiny French Sour Cucumber Pickles)

If you can find (or grow) tiny cucumbers (or gherkins, even harder to find in the market or in seedsmen's catalogues), a bounteous supply of these choice pickles can be yours at the cost of very little effort. *Cornichons* command astronomical prices in fine-food shops, so the low cost of your *cornichons* is an added incentive to making them.

If you have a garden, plan to grow a pickling variety of cucumber (catalogues identify these), and pick them when they are about an inch long. If you have no garden space but live near truck-farming country, you may be able (as we were) to persuade a farmer who plants "pickles" to let you go into the field to harvest tiny cucumbers, 1 to 3 inches long, which are tedious to pick and so are seldom seen in the market.

We tried various flavorings with our batches of *cornichons.* To our taste, the cucumbers preserved in fine white wine vinegar with no additions but salt, peppercorns, and fresh tarragon sprigs were the best. (Don't be tempted to use a harsh or cheap distilled vinegar instead of white wine vinegar—the whole effort is likely to be rendered pointless.)

(continued)

You might like to add a few mustard seeds to each jar; and many *cornichon* connoisseurs like to pickle the cucumbers with a few pearl onions.

Tiny cucumbers (or gherkins, if available), 1 to 3 inches long

Other ingredients, <u>per quart</u> of cucumbers:

3 tablespoons coarse (kosher) salt or pickling salt
4 to 6 bushy sprigs fresh tarragon
½ teaspoon whole black peppercorns
White wine vinegar to cover pickles generously

1. If at all possible, prepare the cucumbers the day they are picked. Wash or scrub them well to free them of all earth or sand—you may need a terrycloth washcloth or even a soft brush. Dry each cucumber completely as you finish cleaning it and drop it into a ceramic, glass, or stainless-steel bowl. Mix in the amount of salt required and let stand, stirring once or twice, for 24 hours. Brine will form.

2. Drain the cucumbers and dry them thoroughly. Drop them into large, very clean canning jars (half-gallons are convenient) or crocks, filling each container only about two-thirds full. Add the tarragon and peppercorns, then pour in white wine vinegar to cover the cucumbers by at least 1 to 2 inches—they should "swim" freely.

3. Cover the jars or crocks with plastic (and lids, if you have them), set them in a cool spot, and let the cucumbers pickle for about 4 weeks; they will then be ready to use. They will keep for up to a year, perhaps longer. They may be transferred, with enough of the vinegar to cover them well, into small jars.

NOTE: If you start with a small quantity of cucumbers and your pickling crock or jar is not comfortably filled, more cucumbers may be salted, drained, dried, and added, with peppercorns and tarragon in proportion, during the first few days of pickling. The newcomers will soon catch up with the original batch.

CRISP PICKLED GREEN BEANS

These crunchy beans are free of harsh acidity and inappropriate sweetness, not too hot or pungent. Their fresh greenness is set off by a touch of dill, the warmth of a little red pepper. Serve as a nibble with vodka drinks or with cheese, or as a relish at picnics.

For putting up average-sized beans, we like straight-sided, wide-mouthed 12-ounce canning jars, each of which will accommodate about 20 beans without kinks or crowding. If you're lucky enough to have tiny beans to pickle, the straight-sided half-pint jars will be the right size, in which case reduce the seasonings proportionately. The processing time will be the same—5 minutes—for either size of jar.

Ingredients per 12-ounce jar:

⅛ teaspoon dried red pepper flakes (or a pinch of cayenne pepper, or a
    very small dried hot red pepper)
1 small clove garlic, peeled but left whole
    Small handful of fresh dill heads, or ½ to 1 teaspoon dill seeds
    Very fresh young green snap beans, as straight as possible (about 20
        per 12-ounce canning jar)
½ cup white wine vinegar
½ cup water
1 tablespoon coarse (kosher) salt

1. Into each clean 12-ounce jar put the indicated amount of red pepper flakes (or cayenne or small dried hot red pepper), garlic, and dill heads or dill seeds.

2. Wash, drain, and remove the stem ends of the beans (the tender tip ends needn't come off). Fit the beans into the jars, cutting any that are too long; allow ½ inch of space at the top.

3. In a saucepan, bring the appropriate amounts of vinegar, water, and salt to a boil, then, following the Pointers on Preserving on pages 153–56, fill the jars with the boiling liquid to within ¼ inch of the rims. Wipe the rims, put on two-piece lids, and fasten the screw bands.

4. Put the jars on a rack in a deep kettle half full of boiling water and add more boiling water to cover the lids by 2 inches. Bring to a hard boil, cover the pot, and boil (process) for 5 minutes.

5. Remove the jars from the boiling-water bath and let cool. Let the pickles mellow for a few weeks before serving.

PICKLED OKRA

A tender-crisp pickle, peppery and tart, a surprise to those who have only tasted okra as a cooked (and pleasantly bland and gelatinous) vegetable. This Southern favorite is often offered by specialty shops and sellers of mail-order foods.

Unfortunately, many store-bought okra pickles are vastly oversweetened and blindingly hot with red pepper. In okra time—summer and fall—do try making your own and control these factors. Your pickles will be ready to eat after about 6 weeks of mellowing in the jar.

Makes 6 pints

2 pounds young okra pods
3 small dried hot red peppers or ¾ teaspoon dried red pepper flakes
3 medium cloves garlic, peeled and split
3 teaspoons mustard seeds
1 ½ teaspoons dill seeds
2 cups cider vinegar
2 cups rice vinegar or white wine vinegar
2 cups water
5 tablespoons coarse (kosher) salt

1. Wash the okra well and cut off any darkened stem tips. Be careful not to cut into the okra caps; leave at least a stub of stem. Drain well.

2. Into each of six clean pint canning jars put half of a dried hot pepper, seeds removed (or ⅛ teaspoon red pepper flakes); half a clove of garlic; ½ teaspoon of the mustard seeds; and ¼ teaspoon dill seeds.

3. Pack the okra into the jars, standing the pods upright and alternating stem ends and tips; pack just firmly enough to keep the pods upright.

4. In a saucepan, bring the vinegars, water, and salt to a full boil, then, following the Pointers on Preserving on pages 153–56, fill the jars with the boiling liquid to within ½ inch of the rims. Wipe the rims, put on two-piece lids, and fasten the screw bands.

5. Put the jars on a rack in a deep kettle half full of boiling water and add more boiling water to cover the lids by 2 inches. Bring to a hard boil, cover the pot, and boil (process) for 5 minutes.

6. Remove the jars from the boiling-water bath and let cool. Let the pickles mellow for about a month before serving.

PICKLED JERUSALEM ARTICHOKES

One of us confesses to having been forced to dispose genteelly of more than one sample of Jerusalem artichoke pickles offered on various occasions—they were either syrupy-sweet or bitingly hot, with none of the taste of the tuber surviving the pickling process.

Our pickled Jerusalem artichokes, however, have a clean, perky vegetable taste and a crisp texture, and, although peppery, they are spiced with discretion.

In case you're not familiar with these pickles, which are especially favored in the South, you can buy them as "artichoke pickles" at a lofty price in a fancy-foods shop or by mail order; or you can try this recipe while the makings are in season—fall through spring. Serve them as you would any hot-sweet pickle or condiment.

Makes 4 pints

3 pounds Jerusalem artichokes or "sunchokes" (to make about 2 quarts after paring and slicing)
Coarse (kosher) salt as needed
Water as needed
1 medium onion, sliced
4 very small dried hot red peppers or ½ teaspoon dried hot red pepper flakes, more if desired
2 teaspoons mustard seeds, slightly bruised
1 teaspoon celery seed
4 whole allspice berries
2 cups cider vinegar
1 cup water
1 cup distilled white vinegar
⅔ cup (packed) light brown sugar
1 tablespoon salt
1 medium bay leaf, broken into 4 pieces

1. Scrape or pare the thin skin from the Jerusalem artichokes and slice them ¼ inch thick. (If they are small, they may be left whole, or halved.)

2. To measure the amount of water needed for the brine, put the Jerusalem artichokes in a plastic bag and put in a ceramic, glass, or

stainless-steel bowl (do not close the bag; just hold it above the water). Pour in enough water to cover the bagged vegetables generously, then remove the bag from the water and the Jerusalem artichokes from the bag.

3. Dissolve coarse salt, using 1/4 cup per quart of water, in the water in the bowl, then add the artichokes, and let them stand in the brine, covered, for 12 to 18 hours.

4. Rinse and drain the artichokes and pat the pieces dry. Distribute them and the onion rings equally among four clean, dry pint canning jars.

5. In a stainless-steel or enameled pan, combine the dried hot red peppers, mustard seeds, celery seed, allspice, cider vinegar, water, white vinegar, sugar, salt, and bay leaf to make a pickling solution. Bring it to a boil and boil for 5 minutes.

6. Following the Pointers on Preserving on pages 153–56, pour the hot solution into the jars, being sure that each has its share of the herbs and spices; the liquid should come to within 1/4 inch of the rims. Wipe the rims of the jars, cover them with two-piece canning lids, and fasten the screw bands.

7. Put the jars onto a rack in a deep pot half full of boiling water and add boiling water to cover the jars by at least 2 inches. Bring to a hard boil, cover pot, and boil (process) for 15 minutes.

8. Remove the jars and let cool. Store for at least 2 weeks before serving.

MARINATED ARTICHOKE HEARTS

Never let it be said that we scorn the harvest from the frozen-food bins at the market. As a matter of fact, there is no way you might hope to make this appetizer (unless you live in the limited artichoke-growing country in California) were it not for the fact that small, tender artichoke hearts are frozen and shipped nationwide; we don't recommend using the tinned artichoke bottoms or hearts, which taste strongly of the citric acid used in the canning process.

These marinated artichokes are tastier and cheaper than the canned or bottled versions, domestic or imported, encountered in delicacy departments. Make your own little antipasti by arranging the artichokes on serving plates with oil-cured black olives, Italian salami, a bit of provolone, and our Breadsticks (page 101), preferably the fennel-flavored ones.

Makes 1 pint

1 package (10 ounces) frozen artichoke hearts, thawed
5 cups boiling water
¼ cup white wine vinegar
¼ cup water
1 clove garlic, peeled but left whole
¼ teaspoon sugar
¼ teaspoon dried thyme
1 ½ teaspoons coarse (kosher) salt
½ teaspoon dried basil
½ teaspoon dried oregano
⅛ teaspoon dried red pepper flakes
¼ cup olive oil, or as needed
¼ cup vegetable oil, or as needed

1. Drop the artichoke hearts into the boiling water. Boil them gently for 5 minutes, then drain them and dry them well on paper towels. Pack them into a pint jar.

2. In an enameled or stainless-steel saucepan, bring to a boil the vinegar, water, garlic, sugar, thyme, salt, basil, oregano, and pepper flakes. Pour the hot mixture over the artichokes, then add the olive and vegetable oils, pouring in enough to come almost to the rim of the jar. Seal tightly. Refrigerate the artichokes for 1 week before serving, turning the jar upside down occasionally to mix the seasonings. The artichokes will keep for about 2 weeks longer.

OLIVES WITH BAY AND ROSEMARY

There are uncounted ways of preparing olives, and every specialty food shop offers them in variously cured or flavored guises. To make your own herb-seasoned olives, purchase some brined green olives, preferably cracked. If you can't find cracked olives, buy those with pits and hit each one gently on one side with a rolling pin or a meat pounder, just hard enough to crack the flesh without expelling the pit.

Herbed olives last indefinitely and are a pleasure to have on hand as an impromptu hors d'oeuvre. Be sure to save the luscious aromatic oil to use in salads or marinades.

(continued)

Makes about 1 pint

2 cups (about 10 ounces) small green olives with pits, preferably
   cracked
2 bay leaves
1 tablespoon dried rosemary
½ lemon, cut lengthwise, then crosswise into thin slices
1 teaspoon whole black peppercorns, bruised
   Olive oil to cover
2 or 3 cloves garlic, peeled but left whole

1. If necessary, crack the olives as described above. Rinse the olives and layer them in a clean jar with the bay leaves, rosemary, lemon slices, and peppercorns. Pour in enough good olive oil to barely cover the olives (they will sink a bit). Add the garlic and cover the jar.

2. Let the olives stand at room temperature for at least 2 weeks, stirring or shaking well daily, before serving them. They will keep for months, preferably refrigerated. Allow to reach room temperature before serving.

MARINATED MUSHROOMS

This familiar component of the antipasto platter is available in a quality range that runs the gamut from the soybean oil-packed version usually available in neighborhood supermarkets to the elegantly presented mushrooms packed in delicate olive oil that are found in the best Italian specialty shops. Mushrooms seem to respond well to olive oils both bold and fragile, so choose your oil according to preference.

Makes about 1 quart

6 cups water
2 tablespoons coarse (kosher) salt
1 ½ pounds small, white mushrooms, trimmed and rinsed
¾ cup mild white wine vinegar
1 tablespoon coriander seeds
2 bay leaves
1 teaspoon sugar
½ small cinnamon stick
½ teaspoon whole black peppercorns
½ teaspoon dried thyme
1 clove garlic, peeled and halved
¾ cup olive oil, approximately

1. Combine the water and 1 tablespoon of the salt in a saucepan and bring to a boil. Add the mushrooms and boil for 2 minutes, then drain, reserving ¾ cup of the liquid.

2. In an enameled, flameproof glass, or stainless-steel saucepan, combine the reserved mushroom liquid, vinegar, coriander seeds, bay leaves, sugar, cinnamon, peppercorns, thyme, and the remaining 1 tablespoon salt. Boil for 5 minutes.

3. Pack the mushrooms into a clean quart jar and pour the pickling liquid over them. Add the garlic clove and olive oil, using whatever amount is necessary to fill the jar, then cap the jar. Refrigerate for at least a week before serving, shaking the jar at least once a day. The marinated mushrooms will keep, refrigerated, for several weeks.

CAPONATA

If you are familiar with this Italian eggplant appetizer only in its canned or bottled form, you will probably be delighted to know that you can make your own during the season—summer and early fall—and freeze it successfully. We tried many recipes before we settled on this flavorful version in which the vegetables remain fairly firm, not softened to a near puree, as is sometimes preferred.

Makes about 6 cups

1 ½ pounds unpeeled eggplant, cut into ¾-inch cubes
  1 tablespoon coarse (kosher) salt
  ½ cup olive oil
  1 cup coarsely diced onion (½-inch dice)
  3 or 4 medium sweet red peppers, cut into ¾-inch squares (to make 2½ cups)
  1 cup coarsely diced celery (½-inch dice)
  Ripe Italian-type tomatoes (about 8 medium), pureed in a food processor or blender (to make 2 cups puree)
  ¼ cup red wine vinegar
  2 tablespoons sugar
  ½ teaspoon minced garlic
  ¼ cup pitted, sliced oil-cured black olives
  2 to 3 tablespoons capers (the smallest available)
  Salt and ground black pepper to taste

1. Sprinkle the eggplant with the coarse salt and toss the cubes. Let them drain in a colander for 30 to 60 minutes, then pat dry with paper towels.

(*continued*)

2. Preheat the oven to 375 degrees.

3. Heat the olive oil in a 12-inch skillet and sauté the onion, peppers, and celery over moderately high heat for 5 minutes, stirring. Add the eggplant and toss for another 5 minutes. Add the tomato puree, wine vinegar, sugar, and garlic and stir for 2 minutes longer.

4. In the skillet (if its handle is ovenproof) or a baking dish, bake the *caponata*, uncovered, for 20 minutes. Add the olives and capers and stir well. Bake for 15 minutes longer, or until most of liquid has evaporated.

5. Cool the *caponata,* then taste and season with salt and pepper. Refrigerate, covered, for 24 hours before serving. The *caponata* will keep for at least a week in the refrigerator, or for at least 6 months frozen in plastic containers.

INDIA RELISH

A certain amount of browsing through cookery reference libraries has yielded no clue as to how India relish got its name, but it seems likely that the array of spices invariably included may have something to do with the matter.

Our relish includes the most traditional ingredients: cabbage, cucumbers, sweet green peppers, and onions. This is a good relish for hamburger time. Because it's not very sweet, it can be used where chopped sour pickles might be called for, as in coleslaw and a number of mayonnaise-based sauces.

Makes about 5 pints

8 six-inch unwaxed, unpeeled cucumbers, chopped medium coarse (to make 5½ cups)
1 pound sweet green peppers, cored and seeded and chopped medium coarse (to make 1⅔ cups)
3 medium onions, chopped medium fine (to make 1⅔ cups)
6 tablespoons coarse (kosher) salt
¾ pound cabbage, chopped medium fine (to make 3 cups)
1 cup (packed) light brown sugar
3 cups cider vinegar
½ cup light corn syrup
2 tablespoons mustard seeds
1 teaspoon celery seed
½ teaspoon turmeric
½ teaspoon ground black pepper

½ teaspoon ground ginger
¼ teaspoon ground mace
1 tablespoon dry mustard
½ teaspoon Curry Powder (page 196)
1 small clove garlic, minced to a paste
2 tablespoons olive or vegetable oil

1. Combine the chopped cucumber, green pepper, and onion with the salt in a ceramic, glass, or stainless-steel bowl and let stand from 6 to 12 hours, as convenient.

2. Drain the salted vegetables well and put into a large bowl. Mix in the chopped cabbage.

3. In a stainless-steel or enameled kettle, combine the brown sugar, vinegar, corn syrup, mustard seeds, celery seed, turmeric, pepper, ginger, and mace. Boil for a minute or two, then pour over the vegetables. Stir and let stand for about 3 hours.

4. Strain the pickling liquid back into the kettle, keeping out ½ cup. Combine the ½ cup liquid in a bowl with the dry mustard, curry powder, garlic, and olive or vegetable oil, stirring until smooth. Add to the liquid in the preserving pot and bring to a boil.

5. Return the vegetables to the pot; bring just to a full boil, stirring the vegetables from the sides toward the center so they heat uniformly.

6. Following the Pointers on Preserving on pages 153–56, ladle the relish into hot, clean pint or half-pint canning jars, leaving ½ inch headspace. Cover with two-piece lids and fasten the screw bands.

7. Put the jars on a rack in a deep kettle half full of boiling water and add boiling water to cover the lids by 2 inches. Bring to a hard boil, cover the pot, and boil (process) for 5 minutes.

8. Remove the jars from the boiling-water bath and let cool. Let the relish mellow for at least a month before serving.

SWEET RED PEPPER RELISH

A brilliant cardinal-red relish with a sweet and sour tang that briskly points up the flavor of cold meats or fowl. Alternatively, use as a jam on crackers spread with Cream Cheese (page 58). If you'd like your relish to be "hot" as well as sweet and sour, add a few drops of Pepper Sherry (page 183) or Chili Vinegar (page 189) at the end of cooking. Or try a pleasant variation that is a special favorite of ours: replace the mustard seeds with ¼ teaspoon fennel seeds.

Makes 4 half-pint jars

3 to 4 very large sweet red peppers, chopped (to make 4 cups)
2 tablespoons coarse (kosher) salt
1 ½ cups white wine vinegar
2 ½ cups sugar
1 teaspoon mustard seeds, slightly crushed

1. Mix the chopped red peppers and salt and let stand overnight in a ceramic, stainless-steel, or enameled container, refrigerated.

2. Drain off and discard the liquid and put the peppers into a stainless-steel or enameled pot with the vinegar, sugar, and mustard seeds. Bring to a boil, then lower the heat to medium and cook, stirring occasionally, until the peppers are translucent and the relish is the consistency of marmalade, but syrupy. (If the relish begins to thicken too much before the peppers are translucent, cover the pot and lower the heat for a few minutes while the peppers complete the necessary cooking without too much evaporation.) Don't overcook, or a too-stiff relish will result.

3. Following the Pointers on Preserving on pages 153–56, ladle the relish into hot, clean half-pint canning jars, leaving ½ inch of headspace. Wipe the rims, put on two-piece lids, and fasten the screw bands.

4. Put the jars on a rack in a deep kettle half full of boiling water and add boiling water to cover the lids by 2 inches. Bring to a hard boil, cover the pot, and boil (process) for 10 minutes.

5. Remove the jars from the boiling-water bath and let cool. The relish will be ready to use as soon as you like.

MILD HOT PEPPER JELLY

Only medium-hot, this jelly is for those who love sweet-tart-spicy accompaniments for cold meats, or as a companion for salty crackers and Cream Cheese (page 58).

The color of the jelly is amber by courtesy of food coloring, which is optional. If a drab-looking jelly is preferable to using coloring, by all means omit the tint. The pectin is essential—peppers, unlike citrus fruit and apples, contain none.

A CAUTION ABOUT HANDLING HOT PEPPERS: Either work carefully at the sink, rinsing your hands frequently and avoiding touching your face (especially around the eyes), or wear rubber gloves; the hot peppers can irritate the skin very quickly.

Makes 5 eight-ounce glasses, plus a "taster"

**3 medium sweet green peppers, seeded, deribbed, and chopped or
   ground (to make 1⅔ cups, with juice)
   Enough small, fresh hot peppers, seeded, deribbed, and coarsely
   chopped, to make about ½ cup (about 12, depending on their size)
2 cups cider vinegar
½ teaspoon salt
5 ½ cups sugar
   1 bottle (6 ounces) liquid pectin
   2 drops red plus 3 drops yellow food coloring (optional)**

1. Combine the sweet and hot peppers with the cider vinegar in a stainless-steel or enameled saucepan and simmer for 15 minutes. Pour the mixture into a jelly bag or sieve lined with two layers of cheesecloth and let it drain through into a bowl without squeezing. Discard the pulp.

2. Measure 1½ cups of the drained infusion into a 4-quart stainless-steel or enameled saucepan. (Any leftover portion of the liquid can be put into a small bottle and used as a "hot" seasoning.) Add the salt and bring to a simmer. Add the sugar and stir over high heat until the mixture comes to a full boil that can't be stirred down; boil hard for 1 minute. Stir in the pectin and remove from the heat. Stir in the food coloring, if used.

3. Following the Pointers on Preserving on pages 153–56, pour the jelly into hot, sterilized jelly glasses, leaving ½ inch headspace, or small, straight-sided canning jars, leaving ⅛ inch headspace. Seal at once with melted paraffin or sterilized two-piece lids.

4. Cool and store.

PEACH OR NECTARINE CHUTNEY

The fruit in this chutney, as in most spicy fruit condiments, lends mainly substance and chunkiness rather than its own flavor. Because the texture is important, we specify very firm fruit. Peach or nectarine chutney is a pleasant, tart-sweet companion for cold roast pork, lamb, or fowl, as well as hot curries.

Makes about 7 half-pint jars

2 ½ pounds very firm peaches or nectarines (to make 7 cups when cut
    into ½-inch dice)
  2 cups golden raisins
1 ½ cups medium-finely chopped onion
  1 cup cider vinegar, more as desired
  1 cup water, or as needed
  ½ cup (packed) dark brown sugar
  1 cup sugar, more as desired
  2 teaspoons very finely chopped garlic
  3 tablespoons minced fresh gingerroot
  2 teaspoons mustard seeds
  2 teaspoons ground coriander
  2 sticks cinnamon (each about 2 inches long), broken in half
1 ½ teaspoons ground cardamom
  2 teaspoons salt
  ½ teaspoon turmeric
  ¼ teaspoon cayenne pepper

1. If you are using peaches, plunge a few at a time into boiling water for a few seconds. Strip off the skins. (If the fruit is quite underripe—which is okay—you may have to pare off the skins. If you are using nectarines, leave the skins on.) Cut the peaches or nectarines into ½-inch dice; you should have 7 cups of fruit.

2. Combine the fruit with all the other ingredients in a preserving kettle and bring to a boil. Lower the heat to medium and cook the chutney, stirring it frequently, until the fruit is translucent and the chutney is thick enough to mound up slightly in a spoon. If necessary to prevent scorching, add a little more water during cooking.

3. Taste the chutney and add a little more sugar or vinegar, if you wish. (Remember that the flavor of the spices will intensify as the chutney mellows in the jar.) Remove the cinnamon sticks.

4. Following the Pointers on Preserving on pages 153–56, ladle the

chutney, boiling hot, into clean, hot half-pint or pint canning jars, filling them to within $1/2$ inch of the top. Cover the jars with two-piece lids and fasten the screw bands.

5. Put the jars on a rack in a deep kettle half full of boiling water and add boiling water to cover the lids by 2 inches. Bring to a hard boil, cover the pot, and boil (process) for 10 minutes.

6. Remove the jars from the water bath and let cool. Let the chutney mellow for at least 2 weeks (4 weeks are better) before you serve it.

MANGO CHUTNEY

Although chutneys, the relishes that traditionally accompany Indian food, are usually made of freshly chopped fruits, vegetables, and spices, the one that has been most favored by British and American chutney lovers is preserved.

Unfortunately, mangoes are never bargain fare in this country (unless you live in lucky parts of Florida), but there is a great variation in prices—so keep an eye out for the best time. When you make mango chutney, you will need unripe mangoes (and probably when you want to make it, the only really ripe mangoes of the year will appear in the market). You can use part peaches (which should also be hard-unripe) to cut the cost of the mango a bit.

Makes 4 half-pints

**3 large mangoes, preferably 2 hard-unripe and 1 hard-ripe, peeled and
   sliced (to make 4 cups)
2 cups cider vinegar
1 cup sugar (or more, if you like a very sweet chutney)
1 cup coarsely chopped onion
$1/2$ teaspoon finely minced garlic
1 teaspoon very finely minced fresh hot red pepper (or more, if you like
   a hot chutney)
$1/4$ cup peeled, finely minced fresh gingerroot
1 teaspoon ground cinnamon
$1/4$ teaspoon ground allspice
2 teaspoons salt
$1/3$ cup golden raisins**

1. Combine all the ingredients in a bowl, cover it with plastic, and let stand at room temperature for 12 to 24 hours, stirring a few times.

(continued)

2. Pour the mixture into a stainless-steel or enameled pot and simmer, stirring occasionally, for about 15 minutes or until the chutney has thickened slightly. Continue to simmer, stirring more often to prevent sticking as the thickening continues. In about 15 minutes, the chutney should be thickened enough. (Do not mash the fruit as you stir; the slices of fruit should remain intact, not become jamlike.)

3. When the chutney has reached the desired consistency (it will thicken a very little bit after processing), and following the Pointers on Preserving on pages 153–56, ladle it into four clean half-pint canning jars, filling them to within ½ inch of the tops. Cover the jars with two-piece lids and fasten the screw bands.

4. Place the jars on a rack in a deep kettle half full of boiling water and add boiling water to cover the lids by at least 2 inches. Bring the water to a hard boil, cover the pot, and boil the water vigorously (process) for 5 minutes.

5. Remove the jars from the water and let cool. Store the jars in a dark place for at least 2 weeks, preferably more, before serving.

Preserves, Sweet Sauces, and Jellies

Pointers on Preserving

If you are a somewhat experienced (or very experienced) preserve maker, you may want to skip this discussion. If you do, be reminded that there has recently been a good deal of rethinking about processing times for foods that are sealed in a water bath (we don't go into pressure canning here), so be sure that you follow the times given in the recipes, even though you may be tempted to follow your past practices.

Pots and Pans. For cooking preserves you'll need a roomy pot of stainless steel or heavy enameled metal. An aluminum pot can be used, but don't let foods containing acid—which means almost all preserves—stand in it unnecessarily long.

For use as a water-bath canner for processing, any deep pot is fine. Set a canning rack in it, if the regular type of rack (holding up to seven quart jars) will fit. These racks prevent jars from touching and possibly cracking. If such a rack won't fit your pot, use a cake rack or a folded towel in the bottom to keep jars from coming in contact with the hot metal, which could also break the jars.

Jars and Jelly Glasses. For preserves to be processed, use *only* jars manufactured for canning, not recycled mayonnaise jars and the like. But any kind of jar or glass that can be boiled to sterilize it can be used for preserves to be sealed with wax (about which more a little farther along). Be sure canning jars are not cracked and that their edges aren't nicked. (A small nick in the edge of a glass to be sealed with wax can be disregarded.)

Lids for Sealing. Canning jars are of several types, meant to be sealed with lids of several designs, but we have used only standard "Mason" jars, with threaded tops and two-piece lids. These lids consist of a flat cover rimmed with sealing compound and held in place by a separate, reusable screw band. These are sometimes called "dome" lids, although the "dome" is almost imperceptible. The lid portion can be used only once. Our processing directions are written for these lids, which are tightened only once, when they are put on the jars; retightening them after cooling can break the seal. If you use other types of jars and lids, follow the manufacturer's instructions.

Other Equipment.   You'll need things already in your kitchen—measuring cups, spoons, and a ladle, for instance. In addition, a wide-mouthed funnel for filling jars helps to keep the rims clean, and jar-lifting tongs, or a pair of long, strong ordinary tongs, are helpful when managing hot jars.

PROCEDURES

Processing.   This, for those to whom the term may be new, is done in either a boiling-water bath (212 degrees at sea level) or a hot-water bath (190 degrees). The food is put into the jars, lids are put on, the jars are immersed in water (1 to 2 inches over the lids) in a deep kettle and boiled (or simmered) for a specified time. Whenever processing is required, the directions and timing are given in the recipe.

The Jellying Point.   This is the temperature to which such preserves as jellies, jams, and marmalades are cooked in order to be sure they will "jell." For most preserves (there are exceptions, such as the No-Boil Grape Jelly on page 171), this is most easily determined by using a candy-jelly thermometer. The jellying point is 8 degrees above the boiling point of water at your altitude: the boiling point at sea level is 212 degrees, so the jellying point at that elevation is 220 degrees. If you don't have a reliable thermometer, you can use the "sheet test" for jelly and for jams and marmalades that have a generous amount of syrup to "jell." To make this test, you dip up some of the preserve in a cold metal mixing spoon and pour it back into the pot. So long as a stream, or individual droplets, falls, continue the cooking. Test often—as soon as two or three droplets join together on the edge of the spoon and shear off in a sheet, the jellying point has been reached. Stop the cooking at once—overcooked preserves tend to be rubbery and of poor color.

Sterilizing Jars.   This is necessary only for jellies or jams that are not to be processed. Wash and rinse the jars and boil them for 10 minutes in water to cover. Hold them in the hot water until they are needed.

Sterilizing and Applying Lids.   Sterilizing lids is necessary only when they are to be used to cover sterile canning jars that will be sealed without processing. Rinse the lids and bands (first wash the bands, if they have been used previously), then pour boiling water over them. Lids for foods to be processed need only be rinsed and kept covered with piping-hot water until they're needed; they will be sterilized during processing.

When applying lids, be sure the jar rim is spotless; wipe it with a paper towel dipped into hot water, if necessary. Lay the flat lid in place, then put on the screw band; don't combine the pieces before applying them.

Sealing with Paraffin Wax. This is fine for all jellies and for other sweet preserves with a fairly smooth texture—jams made from soft berries, for example. Jars (straight-sided small ones) or jelly glasses should be sterilized as described above. Remove them from the hot water with tongs, drain each one, and set them upright on a wooden surface or, if your countertop is chilly (this could cause cracking), on folded towels. Fill glasses or jars while they're hot.

While the jelly or jam cooks, melt new paraffin (never reuse wax) in a small, lipped vessel set into a pan of simmering water. Never try to melt wax over direct heat—it can catch on fire.

Ladle the jelly or jam into the jars, using a wide-mouthed funnel if you have one, leaving about 1/2 inch of headspace. Wipe any spills from the inside tops of the glasses with a paper towel dipped into hot water. Pour on a thin layer—scarcely more than a film—of melted wax. Tip the glass to make sure the wax covers the jelly and touches the glass all around. Let cool completely. Flaws may appear in the wax during cooling, but don't be concerned. Add a second thin layer of melted wax, making sure any thin spots or bubbles are sealed and again tilting the jar to seal the wax to the glass all around. When this layer has set, cover the jars with metal or plastic lids, or with foil or plastic held in place with a rubber band.

Cooling Preserves. Always make sure that hot jars, empty or full, are set on a surface—wood, for instance—that isn't chilly. Set jars well apart and let them cool completely before testing the seal (if two-piece lids have been used; see below), or completing the waxing, or storing.

Testing the Seal. A correctly sealed two-piece lid often goes "pop" quite loudly as the jar cools, and later a keen eye can detect that the vacuum created in the sealed jar has caused the lid to be slightly depressed in the center. To test, press each lid center; if the "dome" was still up and now goes down and stays down, the jar is sealed. For a double check, tap each lid with the bowl of a teaspoon: a clear, ringing sound means the seal is complete, while a dull sound indicates an incomplete or doubtful seal. A jar with such a lid should be refrigerated and considered unsealed—use the contents as promptly as you would if they had not been "canned."

Storing Preserves. Like pickles and relishes, preserves should be stored in a dry, cool, dark place, especially if you plan on long storage. If you have only a room-temperature kitchen cupboard, don't count on keeping the preserves for more than a year (ideally, less) if you want to use them while their color is at its best. They won't spoil if kept longer, but appearance may suffer, especially if light as well as warmth reaches the jars.

PEACHES IN RUM OR BRANDY SYRUP

Not overwhelmed with liquor but subtly spirituous, a few of these sweet peaches served with delicate biscuits are an elegant dessert any time of year.

 We offer this relatively small recipe, as preparation of the fruit in one layer makes for pretty, unblemished, evenly cooked fruit. If you have more than one skillet, make more than one batch, as the peaches improve with age.

Makes 1 quart (6 servings)

1 ½ **pounds very small, firm-ripe peaches (about 12 to 14)**
 ¾ **cup (packed) light brown sugar**
 ¾ **cup granulated sugar**
  1 **cup water**
 ⅓ **to** ½ **cup dark rum or brandy**

 1. Drop the peaches into a large pot of boiling water. Boil them for 1 minute, then remove from the water and slip off the skins.
 2. In a skillet large enough to hold the peaches in one layer, bring to a boil the sugars and the water, stirring. Add the peaches, cover, and simmer gently for about 4 minutes. Turn the fruit over, re-cover the skillet, and poach the peaches for about 4 minutes longer, or until they are barely tender.
 3. Pour the rum or brandy into a clean 1-quart canning jar. Spoon

in the peaches gently, packing them very tightly together without squashing them. Boil the remaining syrup to thicken it slightly, but don't let it caramelize. Pour the syrup slowly over the fruit, leaving ½ inch of headspace. Slip a thin knife carefully around the inside walls of the jar to release any air bubbles.

4. Following the Pointers on Preserving on pages 153–56, wipe the rim, cap the jar, place the jar on a rack in a deep kettle half full of boiling water. Add boiling water to cover the jar by 2 inches. Bring to a hard boil, cover the pot, and boil vigorously (process) for 10 minutes.

5. Remove the jar from the boiling-water bath and set on a rack or towel to cool. Store in a dark place for at least a month, preferably longer, before serving.

BRANDIED CHERRIES

Neither terribly sweet nor overly alcoholic, these cherries are fruity enough to stand alone as a dessert, without the need for ice cream or cake to mute the impact. But don't stint on the brandy, or you won't get the benefit of the subtle cherry-liquor flavor. (And don't ignore the possibility of cake and ice cream, just because the cherries don't demand it.)

Makes 2 pints

2 pounds red cherries, preferably (if available) a softer variety than the fairly tough-skinned Bing cherries, stemmed and pitted
2 cups water
1 cup sugar
½ to ⅔ cup Cognac or brandy, approximately

1. Combine the cherries and water in a heavy saucepan or skillet large enough to hold the cherries in no more than two layers. Bring to a simmer, cover, and barely simmer for about 10 minutes, or until the cherries can easily be pierced with a cake tester or a toothpick. Uncover the pan several times during the cooking and stir the cherries very gently.

2. With a slotted spoon, remove the cherries to a bowl. Boil the juices until they are reduced to 1 cup or slightly less.

3. Add the sugar and bring to a boil, stirring. Cover the pan and

simmer for 1 minute. Pour the syrup over the cherries, cover the bowl with a towel, and let the cherries stand for 12 to 24 hours.

4. Strain off the syrup into a small saucepan and bring it to a boil. Reduce the syrup to about ⅔ cup. Divide the cherries into two hot, sterilized pint canning jars and slowly add the hot syrup. Fill each jar with Cognac or brandy almost to the rim, wipe the rims, top with hot, sterilized two-piece lids, and fasten with the screw bands.

5. Invert the jars several times while hot to mix the liquor and syrup, then let them stand in a cool place for at least 1 month before serving.

CHESTNUT PIECES IN SYRUP

Spooned over ice cream, this makes the classic *coupe aux marrons.* It is a dessert sauce full of character—chestnuts in richly flavored syrup, not a syrup containing incidental chestnuts.

We have given directions for using the excellent dried chestnuts that can be found the year round, particularly in Oriental and Italian food shops; we find them wonderful to keep on hand, as fresh chestnuts are perishable and never seem to be in the market when they are wanted. Look for dried chestnuts that are clean and light-colored, with a minimum of clinging brown skin.

If you should have fresh chestnuts, use this recipe for 2 cups of shelled and skinned nuts (see To Shell and Skin Fresh Chestnuts, below). Cook them in water to cover just until they are tender—the cooking time will be much shorter than for dried nuts. Then proceed as directed for the dried nuts.

Makes about 2½ cups

   1 cup imported dried chestnuts (50 to 55 nuts), or 2 cups shelled and skinned fresh chestnuts (see below)
   3 cups water (for the syrup)
   1 cup sugar
   ½ cup light corn syrup
   ½ vanilla bean
     Cognac, brandy, or dark rum to taste (about 3 tablespoons)

1. Put the dried chestnuts and enough water to cover them by 2 or 3 inches into a saucepan and bring them to a boil over medium heat. Boil for 1 or 2 minutes, then turn off the heat, cover the pot, and let the

nuts soak for 1 to 2 hours. (Alternatively, soak the chestnuts overnight, refrigerated, in enough water to cover.)

2. Simmer the chestnuts, with the pan partly covered, over medium-low heat until they are tender (this will take from 1 to 3 hours, depending on the original dryness of the nuts). Add more boiling water if needed to keep the nuts covered as they cook. Let the chestnuts cool in the liquid.

3. Drain the nuts and, with a small, sharp knife, cut away any clinging bits of skin or blemishes. Break each nut into 3 or 4 pieces; you will have about 2 cups of nuts.

4. In a saucepan, combine the 3 cups water with the sugar, corn syrup, and the half vanilla bean, split lengthwise. Bring the syrup to a boil and boil for about 3 minutes.

5. Add the nuts to the syrup and simmer, partly covered, until the nuts are permeated with syrup and very tender, even crumbly, and the syrup has reduced by about one-half. (This cooking may be done in several stretches, if more convenient; just let the nuts sit in the syrup between periods over the heat.)

6. Remove the pieces of vanilla bean (rinse, dry, and save them for another use). Pour the chestnuts and syrup into a clean, dry jar, let them cool, then add the Cognac, brandy, or rum. Cap tightly, then store the topping in the refrigerator. It will keep for many months.

TO SHELL AND SKIN FRESH CHESTNUTS: Either follow the directions in your favorite cookbook, or try this method, a fast and easy way to do a pesky job when you don't need whole nuts:

Rinse the nuts. On a cutting board lay each one flat side down and whack it in two with a cleaver. Drop the split chestnuts into a pot of boiling water and boil for 3 minutes, then test: If the meat can be pried out easily (usually the skin stays in the shell), remove the pot from the heat and drain off some of the water (leave some water in the pan to keep the nuts hot while you shell them—cold, they don't cooperate). Holding the nuts with a cloth to protect your hands, pry out the meat with a nutpick or a small fork.

DARK CHOCOLATE SAUCE (and Variations)

Smooth, with good body, this bittersweet chocolate sauce can be made with Dutch-process cocoa (our preference) or with pure, unsweetened cocoa powder. It will enliven a wide range of desserts: spoon it over ice cream (in or out of the Meringue Shells on page 246), pudding, or cream puffs, or dress up sliced plain cake with a dollop of it. It also makes old-fashioned chocolate milk (you'll need less of this rich sauce than if you were using commercial chocolate syrup, as a little goes a long way). The method of our recipe was suggested by the way our late friend Michael Field sometimes made a thin chocolate dessert sauce.

Makes about 2 cups

    1 cup water
    1 cup sugar
    ½ cup light corn syrup
1 ¼ cups Dutch-process or regular unsweetened cocoa
    1 teaspoon vanilla extract

1. Bring to a boil and boil together, covered, for 1 to 2 minutes, the water, sugar, and corn syrup. Remove from the heat.
2. Sift in the cocoa, beating until smooth, then add the vanilla.
3. Strain into a jar for storage, or use warm. Refrigerated, the sauce keeps for many weeks.

MOCHA SAUCE

Replace half of the water with ½ cup very strong coffee.

CHOCOLATE-MINT SAUCE

Replace the vanilla with a few drops of peppermint extract, then taste; add more, if needed.

CHOCOLATE-ORANGE SAUCE

Omit the vanilla. Whisk in orange-flavored liqueur to taste (1 to 3 tablespoons).

HOT FUDGE SAUCE

This is the way we think hot fudge should be. It is thick and bittersweet and hardens *just* enough when you spoon it over ice cream.

Makes about 2½ cups

    ¾ stick (6 tablespoons) unsalted butter
     6 ounces (6 squares) unsweetened baking chocolate
     1 cup boiling water
     2 cups sugar
    ½ cup light corn syrup
    ¼ teaspoon salt
1 ½ teaspoons vanilla extract

1. Combine the butter and chocolate in a heavy saucepan and stir over low heat until melted. Stir in the water, sugar, corn syrup, and salt.

2. Turn the heat to medium and bring the mixture to a boil, stirring. Boil the sauce gently, without stirring, for about 8 to 9 minutes, or until it is thickened and smooth. Stir in the vanilla extract and serve hot. (Or you may store it in the refrigerator for months.)

TO REHEAT: Set the jar in a saucepan of cold water. Bring water slowly to a simmer, stirring the sauce until it is hot enough.

WALNUT DESSERT SAUCE

Lacking a walnut orchard of your own, the vacuum-packed canned walnuts are likely to be the freshest and tastiest. If you can buy good fresh walnuts in the fall, freeze them in their shells (or without shells) until you need them.

Our recipe produces a very thickly nutted sauce. If for some reason you prefer fewer nuts and more syrup, reduce the nuts accordingly and add more corn syrup—don't increase the maple, or it will be too strongly flavored.

(continued)

Makes 2 cups

¾ cup light corn syrup, more if needed
½ cup maple syrup
¼ cup water
¼ cup sugar
1 ¼ cups coarsely chopped walnuts

1. Combine the corn syrup, maple syrup, water, and sugar in a heavy saucepan. Bring to a boil, stirring.

2. Add the nuts and simmer the sauce, partly covered, for 30 minutes.

3. Pour into a clean pint jar, cool, cap, and refrigerate for as long as several months.

TO SERVE: If the sauce becomes too thick to pour, let it reach room temperature before serving, or stir in a small amount of light corn syrup to obtain the desired consistency.

BUTTERSCOTCH SAUCE

Basically simple, this rich amalgam seems to transcend its butter-sugar composition. A bit like caramel but with a flavor all its own, the thick, smooth sauce is full of taste, not just sweetness. When spooned over creamy vanilla ice cream, it becomes slightly chewy and candylike.

Makes 1½ to 1¾ cups

1 ¼ cups (packed) light brown sugar
¾ cup light corn syrup
3 tablespoons unsalted butter
¼ teaspoon salt
2 tablespoons water
1 teaspoon vanilla extract
½ cup heavy cream

1. In a heavy saucepan, bring the brown sugar, syrup, butter, salt, and water to a boil, stirring. Then boil the mixture without stirring until a candy thermometer reads 235 degrees, about 5 minutes.

2. Remove from the heat, then stir in the vanilla. Let the mixture cool to warm, stirring occasionally.

3. Add the cream a bit at a time, stirring to create a smooth, shiny sauce. The sauce will keep, covered and refrigerated, for up to a month.

BLUEBERRY PANCAKE SYRUP

For this favorite American pancake or waffle syrup, we've gotten the most out of the blueberry flavor by cooking the fruit the shortest time possible over low heat. Full body is added by the sugar syrup, cooked to a high temperature (the soft-crack stage, or 260 degrees). Be sure to let the blueberry syrup cool before you taste it and add the lemon juice, as tartness varies considerably in blueberries and is difficult to judge in a hot syrup.

If you want to can the syrup for indefinite keeping (see To Can the Syrup below), we'd double or triple the recipe, or increase it to the capacity of your canning kettle.

Makes about 2 pints

4 cups blueberries, stemmed, rinsed, and drained
3 cups water
2 strips lemon peel
3 cups sugar
  Lemon juice to taste

1. Pour the blueberries into a saucepan and crush them with a potato masher or a wooden spoon until most of the skins are broken.

2. Add 1 cup of the water and the strips of lemon peel and bring to a simmer. Turn the heat down to low and cook the berries for 5 minutes at just under a simmer.

3. Pour the hot berries into a strainer lined with two layers of cheesecloth (or fine nylon netting) and let the blueberry juice drip through. Twist the cloth to extract all the juice; there should be about 2 cups. Discard the berry pulp.

4. Combine the remaining 2 cups water with the sugar in a small saucepan. Bring the mixture to a boil, stirring, until the sugar is dissolved and the mixture is clear. Wash down the sides of the pan with a wet pastry brush, then boil the syrup, without stirring, until it reaches 260 degrees on a candy thermometer.

5. Add the blueberry syrup to the sugar syrup and bring the mixture

to a boil. Boil for 1 minute. Let the syrup cool, then add lemon juice to taste.

6. Pour the syrup into two pint jars and refrigerate it if you plan to use it within a month or two.

TO CAN THE SYRUP (for indefinite storage at room temperature): Following the Pointers on Preserving on pages 153–56, pour the hot syrup into canning jars, leaving ½ inch of headspace. Wipe the rims, put on two-piece lids, and fasten the screw bands. Set the jars on a rack in a deep kettle half filled with near-boiling water. Add near-boiling water (no hotter than 190 degrees) to cover the lids by 2 inches. Heat the water, with a thermometer in place, and process the jars in a hot-water bath (190 degrees) for 30 minutes; watch carefully and don't let water boil. Cool the jars on a rack.

BITTER ORANGE MARMALADE

Although admittedly difficult to track down (they are usually available in the market only for a fleeting moment in midwinter), bitter oranges (also called *bigarade* or Seville oranges) are well worth seeking if you are a lover of the best of the classic marmalades.

Early trade between Spain and Scotland brought the Seville orange to the British Isles, where the Scottish genius for preserving took over. We have read that the oranges were packed in water and sometimes floated in their barrels from shore to ship on the Spanish coast, as there was such a demand for the fruit that it was exported even from places without ports.

These ugly, blemished, thick-skinned, seedy, and almost juiceless oranges, good for nothing but marmalade and certain cooked dishes (duckling *bigarade,* for example) have made the reputation of the deservedly celebrated Scottish marmalades. Our recipe uses the entire fruit and the abundant pectin obtained by boiling the seeds, so there is a very large yield per orange—one 3-inch specimen will make about a pint of marmalade. So what seems to be an outrageous price for the oranges at the fruit store is moderate indeed when the cost of the finished product is calculated. Ask your fruit shop about ordering these oranges—the season is January and February, and the supply is small.

Makes 8 pints

6 large (3-inch diameter) bitter oranges
3 quarts water
   Juice of 2 lemons, strained
12 cups sugar, or as needed

1. Scrub the oranges well, removing any of the rusty surface patches that will come off readily. Rinse.

2. Bring the oranges to a boil in the water, in a stainless-steel or enameled pot, then cover, and cook them until they are completely tender; poke one with a chopstick to be sure. Let them cool in the water until comfortable to handle. Reserve the cooking water.

3. Break each orange open and scrape the many seeds into a stainless-steel or enameled saucepan, together with any pulp and the tough internal membranes (there won't be much of either). Set aside the skins and any pulp that is free of membrane.

4. Simmer the seeds and membranes with the original cooking water until you judge that all possible jellylike material has been extracted, about an hour. Put the seeds and membranes into a food mill (medium disc) and extract all possible liquid and pulp. Reserve.

5. Meanwhile, cut the peel in strips as thin or as thick as you prefer; this is easily done with a sharp knife on a board—stack two or three pieces of peel for the cutting. (Or use the thin-slicing blade of a food processor.)

6. Combine the sliced peel, reserved pulp, liquid and pulp from the seeds, and the remaining cooking water; you should have about 3 quarts, perhaps a bit more. Add the lemon juice.

7. Measure half of the fruit mixture (about 6 cups) into a large preserving pan and add an equal amount of sugar. Bring to a boil, stirring, and boil rapidly, stirring often, until the marmalade reaches the jellying point (see page 154). Remove from the heat, stir for 3 to 5 minutes to cool slightly, then ladle into hot, sterilized jars, leaving ¼ inch of headspace, and seal, following the Pointers on Preserving on pages 153–56.

8. Make the second batch of marmalade in the same fashion. (If you wish to postpone making this batch, you can refrigerate the cooked fruit mixture for a few days.)

PLUM-RUM CONSERVE

Although this particular delicacy may not be familiar to shoppers in specialty food stores, the conserve category certainly must be. Imported fruit-preserve combinations, always expensive, are generally well represented in the best food shops. The Plum-Rum Conserve below and the Brandied Apricot Jam that follows are two of our favorites in this genre. Serve them on water biscuits, toasted brioche, or fine toasted white bread with Cream Cheese (page 58); or use either conserve or jam as a cookie or cake filling.

Makes 4 half-pint jars

2 pounds red plums, stoned and sliced (to make 4 to 5 cups)
1 cup water
3 cups sugar
1 cup coarsely chopped walnuts
⅓ cup dark rum, or to taste

1. Combine the plums and water in an enameled, stainless-steel, or flameproof glass saucepan and simmer for 3 minutes. Add the sugar and return to a simmer, stirring. Remove from the heat and let stand overnight, or from 12 to 24 hours, covered with a towel.

2. Boil the plums gently, stirring now and then, until the mixture begins to get thick and sticky. From then on, you must stir constantly. Boil until the conserve reaches 225 degrees on a candy-jelly thermometer. This usually takes about half an hour, but time will vary with juiciness of the fruit.

3. Remove the saucepan from the heat and stir in the nuts, then add the rum.

4. Following the Pointers on Preserving on pages 153–56, ladle the conserve into four hot, sterilized half-pint jars, leaving ¼ inch of headspace, and seal with sterilized two-piece lids. Store for at least 2 weeks before serving.

BRANDIED APRICOT JAM

As fresh apricots are usually expensive, hard to come by, and often tasteless (unless you have your own tree or live near an orchard, in which case *all* of the above are false), we've used the dried fruit, which does have some taste, for this preserve. The recipe was developed with California apricots. If you use the sweeter imported varieties, add less sugar.

Like the preceding recipe for Plum-Rum Conserve, this makes a particularly lovely gift to have on hand.

Makes about 3 half-pint jars

2 cups dried apricot halves (about 10 ounces), each cut in two
2 ½ cups water
   Juice and grated peel of 1 orange
1 ¼ cups sugar
  ½ teaspoon almond extract
  3 tablespoons brandy or Cognac

1. Combine the apricots and water in a bowl, cover, and let stand overnight, or until soft and well plumped—about 8 to 12 hours.

2. Combine the apricots and their soaking water in a saucepan with the orange peel and juice and simmer for 5 minutes.

3. Add the sugar and bring to a boil, stirring. Boil gently, stirring often, until the mixture is thick and shiny and begins to clear the sides of the pan when stirred. While the mixture thickens, be sure to stir it continually but gently, so that the fruit does not burn or get squashed. Do not allow the mixture to cook down to a puree; it should retain good-sized bits of apricot. The process should take roughly 25 to 30 minutes, but this varies.

4. Remove the preserve from the heat and stir in the almond extract and brandy.

5. Following the Pointers on Preserving on pages 153–56, ladle the mixture into three hot, sterilized half-pint jars, leaving ¼ inch of headspace, and seal with sterilized two-piece lids.

6. Cool and let mellow several weeks or more before serving.

Cranberries: Two Recipes

One fruit is used but different personalities emerge in these two versions of an American classic. The Cranberry Jelly (page 169), made with extracted juice, is tender, translucent, quite sweet; the Jellied Cranberry Sauce (see below), on the other hand, is tart, dense, assertive, with a distinct fruit-pulp texture. Both can be unmolded for serving, and both are too good to reserve for Thanksgiving and other feasts; try spreading either one on toast, for instance, or serving it with the Sunday bacon and eggs. And—a not insignificant point—making these jellies costs only a small fraction of the grocery-store price for canned jellied sauce.

Cranberries are among the most satisfactory fresh fruits to freeze and use whenever you like, not only in turkey season. Just pop the unopened bags or boxes into your freezer for virtually indefinite storage.

NOTE: See pages 212–13 for a double recipe for making your own cranberry juice and a coarse, nonjellied cranberry sauce.

JELLIED CRANBERRY SAUCE

Makes 2 half-pint jars

1 pound cranberries (about 4½ cups), stemmed and picked over
1 cup water
2 cups sugar

1. Grind the cranberries or chop them medium-coarse in a food processor, using the steel blade.
2. Combine the cranberries, water, and sugar in a saucepan. Bring to a boil, then reduce the heat, cover, and simmer, stirring occasionally, until the fruit is entirely translucent, 10 to 15 minutes.
3. Force the pulp through the finest disc of a food mill, then press it through a fine sieve to remove the seeds.

4. Reheat the sieved sauce to boiling and then, following the Pointers on Preserving on pages 153–56, pour into hot, sterilized, straight-sided half-pint canning jars, leaving ⅛ inch of headspace. Seal with sterilized two-piece lids and invert each jar for a moment, then turn right side up and cool on a rack. So sealed, the sauce will keep indefinitely.

TO USE IMMEDIATELY: If the sauce is to be used within a few weeks, it may be poured, hot, into a mold (nonmetallic) or other container, cooled, and refrigerated without sealing.

CRANBERRY JELLY

Makes 4 half-pint jars

1 pound cranberries (about 4½ cups), stemmed and picked over
2 cups water
2 ¾ cups sugar

1. Wash and drain the cranberries. Put into a saucepan with the water and bring to a boil over high heat, stirring once or twice. Reduce the heat and simmer for 5 minutes, or until completely pulpy.
2. Force the berries through the finest disc of a food mill, then through a very fine sieve. You should have 3¼ to 3⅓ cups of thick juice.
3. Return the juice to the rinsed-out saucepan and reheat to the boiling point. Add the sugar and boil rapidly, stirring, until the jellying point (see page 154) is reached.
4. Following the Pointers on Preserving on pages 153–56, pour the jelly into hot, sterilized, straight-sided half-pint canning jars, leaving ⅛ inch of headspace. Seal with sterilized two-piece lids and invert each jar for a moment, then cool on a rack. Store indefinitely.

TO USE IMMEDIATELY: If the jelly is to be used within a few weeks, it will keep well, refrigerated, in covered but unsealed jars or glasses.

Grape Jelly Two Ways

The traditional method we describe in the first recipe below yields very good jelly, but the "no-boil" recipe that follows makes jelly with a remarkable fresh-fruit flavor and aroma. For jelly made by either method, extract the juice at a low temperature: boiling the fruit during juice extraction flattens out the assertive, rich Concord flavor. Include a few slightly underripe grapes for a touch of tartness.

TRADITIONAL GRAPE JELLY

Makes 6 six-ounce glasses

3 pounds Concord grapes, ripe but not overripe
3 cups sugar

1. Wash the grapes, still in their bunches, in a colander and drain them, then remove from their stems and measure. You should have 2 quarts, which will yield about 4 cups of juice.

2. Mash the grapes thoroughly, or whirl them in a food processor fitted with the plastic blade until well pulped.

3. Pour the pulp into a large enameled or stainless-steel saucepan and heat, stirring often (if the grapes do not seem juicy, a very little water may be added), watching that the temperature doesn't go above 190 degrees (use a thermometer). Cook until the pulp and skins are very soft, about 10 to 15 minutes.

4. Drain in a jelly bag or sieve lined with several layers of cheesecloth, pressing and twisting the cloth to extract all possible juice after free dripping stops.

5. Refrigerate the juice overnight (this is to prevent tartaric acid crystals—which are harmless but unesthetic—from forming in the jelly).

6. Pour off the juice, leaving the sediment, and strain it through a fine sieve.

7. Measure the juice into a stainless-steel or enameled pan large enough to allow a full, rolling boil. (If you don't have 4 cups of juice, just figure the amount of sugar needed on the basis of ¾ cup sugar for every cup of juice.) Heat to the boiling point, then stir in the sugar. Boil, stirring, to the jellying point (see page 154). Remove from the heat.

8. Following the Pointers on Preserving on pages 153–56, pour the jelly into hot, sterilized jelly glasses, leaving ½ inch of headspace, or small, straight-sided canning jars (⅛ inch of headspace). Seal at once with melted paraffin or with sterilized two-piece lids.

NO-BOIL GRAPE JELLY

Makes 8 six-ounce glasses, plus a "taster"

**4 cups Concord grape juice, extracted, refrigerated, and strained as
described for Traditional Grape Jelly (page 170, steps 1–6)**
5 cups sugar

1. Heat the juice in a large enameled or stainless-steel pan just until
it begins to bubble all over (test it with a thermometer—the temperature should be barely 200 degrees, not "boiling," which would be 212
degrees).

2. Remove from the heat and stir in the sugar. Return to the heat
and stir just until the sugar has dissolved; do not allow the jelly to return
to a boil, or even a simmer.

3. Following the Pointers on Preserving on pages 153–56, ladle or
pour the jelly into hot, sterilized jelly glasses, leaving ½ inch of headspace, or small, straight-sided canning jars (⅛ inch of headspace). Seal
at once with melted paraffin (glasses) or sterilized two-piece lids (jars),
leaving a small jar, or "taster," unsealed.

4. Cool and store.

NOTE: With this jelly, there is an element of uncertainty. Although it has
not happened to us, we have heard—via the grapevine, natch—that on
occasion it may not "jell"—hence the usefulness of the "taster." Check
the "taster" after about 2 days. If the jelly is too soft, resign yourself to
using it as a dessert topping, and better luck next crop.

MINT JELLY

If you know only the poison-green, synthetic-tasting mint jellies often
plopped alongside roast lamb, don't imagine that we're urging you to
confect anything of that kind. Begin with good, fresh mint and you will
end with good, fresh mint flavor. Be stingy when adding color, which
is necessary—unfortunately, mint jelly *au naturel* is not a pretty shade.
A drop or two of color will be enough to achieve a pale-green tint.

If you can grow or otherwise obtain fresh peppermint (botanically

Mentha piperita), you have the best of all possible mints for jelly-making. The second choice is spearmint *(M. spicata),* but any of the common garden mints, often available at greengrocers', will make good jelly, too.

Makes 4 half-pint glasses, plus a "taster"

1 ½ to 2 cups (packed) fresh mint (mostly leaves), washed and drained
2 ¼ cups water
  ¼ cup strained fresh lemon juice
  Pinch of salt
3 ½ cups sugar
  ½ bottle (6-ounce size) liquid pectin
  1 or 2 drops green liquid food coloring

1. Crush the mint in a large saucepan, using the bottom of a glass or a bottle, or an old-fashioned wooden potato masher. Add the water, bring slowly to a boil, and boil for 30 seconds. Remove from the heat, cover, and let the mint steep for 15 minutes.

2. Pour the mint infusion through a fine-meshed strainer , pressing lightly on the leaves before discarding them. Measure 1½ cups of the infusion into a large saucepan. Add the lemon juice, salt, and sugar.

3. Bring to a hard boil, stirring constantly; when the boil cannot be stirred down, add the pectin. Return to a full, rolling boil and start timing when the boil can't be stirred down; boil for 1 minute, then remove from the heat.

4. Skim off any foam, add the food coloring, and then, following the Pointers on Preserving on page 153–56, pour the jelly into hot, sterilized jelly glasses, leaving ½ inch of headspace or straight-sided half-pint canning jars (⅛ inch of headspace). Seal at once with melted paraffin (glasses) or with sterilized two-piece lids (jars).

5. Cool and store.

SWEET BASIL JELLY

Herb jellies may seem a bit esoteric; however, we are quite passionate about this one. Basil-flavored jelly is not a robust condiment—it evokes the fragrance of honey, anise, and chervil. There is also a hint of pepperiness, as well as a good, fresh, green herbal undertone. This pale jelly seems to have been created for spreading on crisp toast or sweet, dry biscuits, perhaps over a layer of Ricotta (page 54) or Cream Cheese (page 58). It would be a mistake to pit its delicacy against strong-flavored foods, although basil, as an herb, can hold its own with some pretty aggressive flavors.

Makes 4 eight-ounce glasses, or 5 six-ounce glasses plus a "taster"

1 ½ cups (lightly packed) unblemished basil leaves, rinsed, drained, and coarsely torn, including some unopened flower heads, if available
  2 cups water
  2 tablespoons mild white wine or rice vinegar
  Pinch of salt
3 ½ cups sugar
  ½ bottle (6-ounce size) liquid pectin

1. If the basil is quite damp, pat it dry on paper towels. Chop it quickly or process it briefly in a food processor, using the steel knife.

2. Put the basil in a large saucepan; crush it well, using the bottom of a glass or bottle, or a wooden potato masher. Add the water; bring slowly to a boil and boil for 30 seconds. Remove from the heat, cover, and let stand for 15 minutes.

3. Strain 1½ cups of the basil liquid through a fine sieve into a saucepan. Add the vinegar, salt, and sugar and bring to a hard boil, stirring. When the boil can't be stirred down, add the pectin. Return to a hard boil that can't be stirred down and boil for exactly 1 minute, then remove from the heat.

4. Skim off the foam and then, following the Pointers on Preserving on pages 153–56, pour the jelly into hot, sterilized jelly glasses, leaving ½ inch of headspace, or straight-sided half-pint canning jars (⅛ inch of headspace). Seal at once with melted paraffin (glasses) or with sterilized two-piece lids (jars).

Condiments, Savory Sauces, Spices, and Seasonings

Considering Condiments
Tomato Ketchup
Marinara Sauce
Chili Sauce
Chinese-Style Plum Sauce ("Duck Sauce")
Prepared Horseradish
Horseradish with Beets
Pepper Sherry
Red Wine Vinegar
Tarragon Vinegar
Garlic Vinegar
Shallot Vinegar
Chive Vinegar
Basil Vinegar
Mint Vinegar
Dill Vinegar
Chili Vinegar
A Note on Mustard Making
Green Peppercorn Mustard
Tarragon Mustard
Coarse-Ground Mustard with Red Wine and Garlic
Horseradish Mustard
Sweet German-Style Mustard
Curry Powder
Chili Powder
Quatre Épices
Spice Parisienne
Filé Powder (Gumbo Filé)
Chinese Five-Spice Powder
Pickling Spice
Dried Mushrooms
Garlic Salt
Tarragon Preserved in Vinegar
Frozen Herbs (Parsley, Chives, Tarragon, Dill, Basil,
    Summer Savory, Sweet Marjoram)

Considering Condiments

The condiments, flavorings, and seasonings that we have chosen are ones that we feel are worth making at home—because they will either be cheaper or better (or both) than the ones you can buy. The selection runs a circuitous trail from Tomato Ketchup (page 177) to Frozen Herbs (page 204), making stops for some savory sauces—such as Chinese-Style Plum Sauce (page 181) and Chili Sauce (page 180), many flavored wine vinegars, a group of mustards, and a small choice of spice mixtures.

As before, we have selected only foods that are improved upon when homemade. Worcestershire sauce, Dijon mustard, and soy sauce, for example, are not feasible (or sensible) to produce at home—hence their exclusion, along with superfluous herb-spice mixtures invented for the uninventive (the ones along the lines of bacon-pepper-lemon-garlic-mushroom flavoring). Nor have we thought it necessary to include several categories that should never have been mass-produced in the first place, including mayonnaise and salad dressings of all persuasions. Good recipes for such preparations are to be found in any authoritative general cookbook.

TOMATO KETCHUP

If you can wait a while (preferably 3 or 4 weeks) to open a jar and taste this smooth, spicy ketchup, its flavors will have blended subtly. We like to think of ketchup in its original sense—a seasoning to be incorporated in other preparations as well as a solo table sauce.

Ketchup came to America, as might be expected, from the sauce-loving British, who learned of its virtues in the Far East. In earlier days —and still in Britain today—ketchups were made from green walnuts, mushrooms, grapes, gooseberries, and elderberries, and even from shellfish, thus returning full circle to the fermented fish sauce that was probably the original form.

(*continued*)

**8 quarts meaty, ripe Italian-type plum tomatoes (or equivalent amount
    of other tomatoes, preferably of a fleshy variety)
1 ½ cups chopped onion
    ½ cup chopped sweet red pepper (about 1 medium-large pepper)
    ½ cup chopped celery, with leaves
    2 cloves garlic, minced
    2 tablespoons salt
    2 cups cider vinegar
    1 tablespoon mustard seeds
    1 tablespoon whole allspice berries
    1 stick cinnamon (about 2 inches), broken up
    1 tablespoon whole black peppercorns
    1 bay leaf
    1 teaspoon whole cloves
    1 teaspoon ground coriander or 2 tablespoons whole coriander seeds
    ¼ teaspoon celery seed
    ¼ teaspoon dried red pepper flakes or ⅛ teaspoon bottled hot
        pepper sauce, or to taste
    ¼ cup granulated sugar
    ½ cup (packed) dark brown sugar, more if desired**

1. Wash, drain, and quarter the plum tomatoes. Boil them, stirring
occasionally, until soft, about 30 minutes. Measure 4 quarts into a large
stainless-steel or enameled pot. (Any surplus tomatoes can be saved for
another use.)

2. Add the onion, sweet red pepper, celery, garlic, salt, and vinegar.
Bring to a boil.

3. Meanwhile, in a piece of doubled cheesecloth, loosely tie the
mustard seeds, allspice, cinnamon, peppercorns, bay leaf, cloves, coriander, celery seed, and the pepper flakes, if used. Add to the tomato
mixture; add the sugars.

4. Cook over medium-high heat, stirring often, until the ketchup
thickens moderately.

5. Pour the ketchup into a large sieve and strain it, pressing hard on
the vegetables and the spice bag to extract all flavor. Discard the pulp
and spice bag and strain the ketchup again through a finer sieve for the
smoothest possible texture. Add the hot pepper sauce if pepper flakes
were not used, then taste and add more salt and sugar, if you wish.

6. Reheat the ketchup; if not thick enough, boil longer, stirring
constantly, until it mounds up slightly in a spoon (it will thicken more
on cooling).

7. Following the Pointers on Preserving on pages 153–56, ladle the ketchup into clean, hot half-pint or pint jars, leaving ½-inch headspace. Wipe the rims, put on two-piece lids, and fasten the screw bands.

8. Put the jars on a rack in a deep kettle half full of boiling water and add more boiling water to cover the lids by 2 inches. Bring to a hard boil, cover the pot, and boil (process) for 10 minutes for half-pints, 15 minutes for pints.

9. Remove the jars from the boiling water and let cool. Allow the ketchup to mellow in the jars for at least 2 weeks, better a month, before using.

MARINARA SAUCE

A light, fresh-tasting sauce with quintessential tomato flavor. Worth stocking up on when tomatoes are dead-ripe and abundant.

Makes 3 pints

6 pounds ripe Italian-type tomatoes
1 cup very finely minced onion
½ cup very finely minced celery
1 cup very finely minced carrots
½ cup olive oil
1 teaspoon sugar
  Ground white pepper to taste
  Optional seasoning (any one of the following): 2 teaspoons ground
    coriander; ½ to 1 teaspoon dried marjoram; 1 teaspoon dried basil;
    ¼ to ½ teaspoon dried oregano
1 to 2 teaspoons salt, to taste

1. Drop the tomatoes into boiling water, a few at a time. Let the water return to a boil, then remove the tomatoes and drain. Peel and chop.

2. In a large saucepan, cook the onion, celery, and carrots in the olive oil, covered, over medium-low heat for about 15 minutes, stirring a few times. Uncover and stir, over the heat, for 5 to 10 minutes longer, or until the vegetables are very soft and lightly gold.

3. Add the tomatoes, sugar, and pepper and simmer gently, covered, for 15 minutes.

4. Puree the sauce through the medium disc of a food mill. Add the optional seasoning and cook at a bare simmer until a desirable consis-

tency is reached, about 20 minutes, stirring often. Add salt to taste.

5. If you prefer a smooth sauce, work the sauce through the fine disc of a food mill.

6. Cool the sauce and refrigerate it. It will keep, refrigerated, for about a week, or for several months if frozen.

CHILI SAUCE

Chunky, thick, and spicy, this chili sauce is slightly "hot," rather sweet, vivid with the flavors of tomatoes, peppers, and onions. You'll find it has more body than most commercial chili sauces, which are usually relatively smooth.

Let the flavor of this sauce develop in the jars for a few weeks before you serve it.

Makes 6 half-pints

3 quarts ripe Italian-type tomatoes (about 5 quarts whole
    tomatoes), peeled and any hard parts removed
1 ½ cups very finely chopped onion (about 2 medium onions), drained of
    surplus juice
1 ½ cups very finely chopped sweet red pepper (about 2 medium peppers),
    drained of part of surplus juice
½ cup water, if needed
2 cups distilled white vinegar
3 tablespoons (packed) dark brown sugar
3 tablespoons granulated sugar
5 tablespoons light corn syrup
2 tablespoons plus 1 teaspoon salt
1 dried hot red pepper (about 2 inches long), or more if a very "hot"
    sauce is preferred
1 clove garlic, peeled but left whole
1 ½ teaspoons mustard seeds
1 teaspoon whole cloves
2 teaspoons broken-up cinnamon sticks
1 ¼ teaspoons whole allspice berries
1 ½ teaspoons celery seed
¾ teaspoon whole black peppercorns

1. In a large stainless-steel or enameled pot, cook the tomatoes, onion, and sweet red pepper together until the onion is translucent,

adding the 1/2 cup water if the tomatoes lack juiciness; stir occasionally.

2. Add the vinegar, sugars, corn syrup, and salt to the vegetables and continue to cook over medium-high heat, stirring occasionally, while you prepare the spice bag.

3. In a 6-inch square of doubled cheesecloth, loosely tie the hot red pepper, garlic, mustard seeds, cloves, cinnamon, allspice, celery seed, and peppercorns. Add the bag to the vegetables in the pot and continue to cook, stirring occasionally and pressing the spice bag against the side of the pot to help extract flavor. Cook until the sauce is considerably reduced, about 1 1/2 hours; it should be chunky, not smooth.

4. Taste for spiciness, remembering that the flavor of the spices will continue to develop in the sauce during storage. If the flavor is acceptable, remove the spice bag, pressing it against the side of the pot (or in a sieve held over the pot) to extract all juices. More salt, sugar, corn syrup, or vinegar may be added at this point, according to taste.

5. Continue to cook the sauce, stirring it almost constantly and bewaring of splashy "plops," until the sauce is thick enough to release no thin liquid when a spoonful is put upon a plate.

6. Following the Pointers on Preserving on pages 153–56, ladle into clean, hot half-pint or pint jars, leaving 1/2 inch of headspace. Wipe the rims, put on two-piece lids, and fasten the screw bands.

7. Put the jars on a rack in a deep kettle half full of boiling water and add more boiling water to cover the lids by 2 inches. Bring to a hard boil, cover the pot, and boil (process) for 10 minutes for half-pints, 15 minutes for pints.

8. Remove the jars from the boiling water bath and let cool. Allow the sauce to mellow in the jars at least 2 weeks, better a month, before using.

CHINESE-STYLE PLUM SAUCE ("Duck Sauce")

More liquid and less fiery than Indian chutneys, to which it is closely related, this Chinese dip-sauce is most often served with roast pork and spring rolls. If you have not had the opportunity to eat in a fine Chinese restaurant, you may have encountered only the sickly-sweet, garlic-laden pink substance labeled "duck sauce" but bearing no resemblance whatsoever to the pungent, fruity real thing. Incidentally, you don't need to wait to cook a Chinese meal to savor this sauce; it may be served as you might a homemade chili sauce or a sweet-and-hot chutney.

(*continued*)

> 3 or 4 medium-large sweet red peppers
> 2 ½ pounds peaches or apricots, stoned and quartered (weight before preparation)
> 2 ½ pounds plums (preferably red), stoned and quartered (weight before preparation)
> 5 ½ cups cider vinegar
> 2 ½ cups water
> 1 ½ cups granulated sugar
> 2 cups (packed) light brown sugar
> ½ cup light corn syrup
> ½ cup peeled, chopped fresh gingerroot
> 2 tablespoons coarse (kosher) salt
> ¼ cup mustard seeds, lightly toasted in a small skillet
> 1 medium onion, quartered
> 2 small hot fresh green peppers (about 2 inches long), or more if your taste runs to "hot," seeded and diced; or 3 dried hot red peppers (each about 1½ inches long), seeds removed, crumbled
> 4 to 6 large cloves garlic, minced
> 1 stick cinnamon

1. Place the sweet red peppers directly over a gas flame or under the broiler and keep turning them until the skin is burned almost black. Let stand for 5 minutes, then wrap in a plastic bag and let stand for 15 minutes. Quarter lengthwise; scrape off the skin and remove the seeds. Set the peppers aside.

2. Combine the peaches or apricots, plums, 3 cups of the vinegar, and the water in a large stainless-steel or enameled kettle and simmer until soft, about 25 minutes. Remove from the heat and set aside.

3. In another stainless or enameled kettle, this one very large, combine the remaining vinegar, sugars, and corn syrup and bring to a boil, stirring. Add the fruit mixture, ginger, salt, mustard seeds, onion, hot peppers, garlic, cinnamon sticks, and the skinned sweet peppers. Simmer, covered, for 5 minutes, then uncover and simmer for 1 hour, stirring now and then. Remove the cinnamon stick.

4. Press the mixture through the coarse disc of a food mill (or use the medium disc if you like a smoother sauce). Return to the kettle and boil gently, stirring, until the sauce has thickened, about 15 minutes (it will thicken more while cooling).

5. Following the Pointers on Preserving on pages 153–56, ladle the

sauce into clean, hot half-pint or pint jars, leaving ½-inch headspace. Wipe the rims, put on two-piece lids, and fasten the screw bands.

6. Put the jars on a rack in a deep kettle half full of boiling water and add enough boiling water to cover the lids by 2 inches. Bring to a hard boil, cover the pot, and boil (process) for 10 minutes for half-pints, 15 minutes for pints.

7. Remove the jars from the boiling water and let cool. Allow the sauce to mellow in the jars for at least 2 weeks, better a month, before serving.

PREPARED HORSERADISH

Before the advent of the electric blender and the food processor, grating horseradish was a weepy job. Even so, good cooks thought it worthwhile to prepare this condiment from scratch. Made fresh, it has a firmer texture and is immeasurably more flavorful and pungent than the bottled product.

Preparing horseradish is the work of only a few minutes, so don't make too much at a time, lest it lose its character. The unused part of a fresh horseradish root will keep for some time in a plastic bag in the refrigerator.

Toward spring, horseradish sometimes begins to sprout, and its skin may be greenish. Sprouts or greenness signal that the root must be pared deeply to remove the entire "growth" layer—you'll see the layer under the skin when you cut a cross-section. If you don't peel deeper than the growth layer, your finished horseradish may have a bitter flavor. If the skin shows no tinge of green, shallow paring or scraping is all that is required.

Fresh horseradish root, preferably without any green tinge
¼ cup vinegar (your choice of distilled white, rice, or white wine), more
      as desired
Salt as needed
Sugar as needed

1. Pare the horseradish root (or a section of it) and cut it into ½-inch cubes.

2. A handful at a time, process the horseradish cubes with ¼ cup of

vinegar in the container of an electric blender or a food processor; process it just until "grated," not reduced to a pulp.

3. When the first batch has been "grated," pour it into a strainer over a bowl. Return the liquid to the container and process the second and any additional batches of cubes, using the same vinegar each time.

4. Combine all the gratings with enough of the vinegar to moisten it well, adding more if you've made a big batch. Stir in a little salt and a small quantity of sugar—a pinch each to about ½ cup of horseradish and juice. (The sugar is a flavor-smoother, not a sweetener). Add more vinegar to taste. Store the horseradish in a glass jar, closely covered, in the refrigerator. It will keep for weeks, but it's best when fresh.

HORSERADISH WITH BEETS

Fresh horseradish combined with cooked beets, vinegar, and seasonings is a favorite Eastern European condiment. The beets mellow and sweeten the assertive flavor of the horseradish and impart their inimitable coloring.

Makes about 1½ cups

¾ cup (about 3 ounces) grated horseradish, prepared with ¼ cup Red
    Wine Vinegar (page 185) or cider vinegar as the processing liquid
    (see the preceding recipe for the grating method)
2 medium beets, cooked, skinned, and finely grated (to make about 1
    cup)
1 teaspoon salt, more if desired
¼ teaspoon sugar
    Additional red wine vinegar or cider vinegar, if desired

1. Mix the grated horseradish, grated beets, salt, and sugar thoroughly. Taste, and add more vinegar, if it is needed.

2. Spoon into a jar, cover, and refrigerate for several hours before using.

3. Before serving the horseradish, taste it and add more salt, sugar, or vinegar, if you wish. Refrigerated in a covered container, the beet horseradish will keep for several weeks.

PEPPER SHERRY

Try using pepper sherry in place of bottled hot pepper sauces of the familiar kind; you may find, like Bermudians and Caribbean islanders, that you prefer it.

After you have allowed the sherry and peppers to steep for about 2 weeks, taste the liquid with care—the mellow sherry aroma carries no hint of the fieriness the peppers have given to the wine. The best way to judge whether it's ready to use is to sprinkle a drop or two onto a bland food, then taste. Only those with palates accustomed to the hottest cuisines should taste Pepper Sherry "straight." As you use the sauce, more sherry can be added to keep up the liquid level. The flavor and fire of the original peppers will last through two recyclings at least.

Makes 1 pint

2 cups very dry sherry
4 dried hot red peppers (each about 1½ inches long), with their seeds,
or an equivalent amount of smaller or larger dried hot red peppers
(some of the tiny peppers are the hottest)

Put the sherry and peppers to steep in a clean, dry bottle that has a tight stopper or lid. The pepper sauce will be ready to use in from 2 weeks to a month. Decant it when its flavor suits you, or leave the peppers in the liquid, as you choose.

RED WINE VINEGAR

You can indeed make your own perpetual supply of red wine vinegar. You'll need to start with at least a bottle or two of unpasteurized wine vinegar of good quality. Open the bottle and use some of it. (This admits air to get the action started.) If the vinegar contains the fermentation organisms you need, it will soon show a film or scum on the surface. Contrary to general belief, you don't have to wait until it produces jellylike "mother," which is actually the product of overfermentation: it is the surface film that does the work. If there is already "mother" in your vinegar starter, you can strain it out, or leave it if the quantity is small.

EQUIPMENT: You'll need a small oak barrel of the kind used for wine making. A 2-gallon size is ideal, but you may not be able to find anything smaller than 5 gallons. Devise a well-braced support to hold the barrel horizontally at least a foot from the floor—we used an old chair whose cane seat had collapsed, leaving a frame into which the barrel's bulge fit comfortably. It should be put in an out-of-traffic spot where ordinary house temperature prevails.

You'll also need a wooden spigot and a drill for making holes about 1 inch in diameter. The barrel will already have a bung hole at its midriff, closed by, logically enough, a stopper called a bung. Get a nonmetallic funnel with a stem long enough to reach from the bung hole at least to the center of the barrel, so that later additions of wine won't disturb the surface.

PREPARING THE BARREL: Lay the barrel on its side, with the bung centered on top. Draw a straight vertical line through the center of the barrel head. Drill a hole for the spigot on the line about an inch above the lower rim. (This position will permit the vinegar to be drawn out without disturbing its surface.) Drive in the spigot with a cushioned hammer or a wooden mallet so you don't damage it. Directly above the spigot, near the top rim, drill a 1-inch hole for ventilation. Remove the bung and fill the barrel with water up to the air hole. Let the barrel soak until any leaks have been closed by the swelling of the wood, then drain it well and set it securely on its frame.

MAKING THE VINEGAR: Pour in the "starter" vinegar through the long funnel set in the bung hole. (For a 5-gallon barrel we needed about 4 quarts.) Add enough dry red wine, or a combination of dry red and dry white, to immerse the tip of the funnel. Tack or tape netting or window screening over the air hole to keep out inquisitive fruit flies (they materialize from nowhere). Leave the funnel in place, either covered with plastic or with the bung set inside it.

Now time does the work. After 3 or 4 weeks, draw off some vinegar and judge whether it's ready to use; if not, pour it back. When the vinegar has a taste that is more vinegary than winy, draw off vinegar as you need it; or, preferably, take enough vinegar to equal the amount of starter vinegar you began with. Fill bottles almost to the top and cover them closely; this virtually stops fermentation, although the vinegar seems to mellow a bit after bottling. If your vinegar is too strong, dilute it with water when bottling it or when you use it. If you want to forestall any possible further fermentation, scald the vinegar, or boil it for just a moment, before bottling it.

KEEPING THE PROCESS GOING: Add at least enough wine to replace the vinegar you have drawn. It is feasible to use leftover wine, but don't pour dribs and drabs into the barrel as they're left from dinner. Accumulate wine leftovers, well corked, until you have at least a bottle or two to add, preferably just after you have drawn off vinegar. *Never* add any fortified wine—sherry, port, Madeira, Marsala, and the like—to your vinegar barrel.

MAKING VINEGAR WITHOUT A BARREL: Barrels can be hard to find in these days when cooperage is an almost lost art. You can use a crock—2 gallons is a good size—with a loosely fitting cover. If it lacks a cover, tie closely woven cloth over it to keep out fruit flies.

To draw off vinegar without roiling the contents of the crock, use a siphon, either improvised from plastic tubing or purchased from a dealer in wine-making equipment or aquarium supplies. When adding fresh wine, always use a funnel with its tip held well beneath the surface.

This arrangement isn't as authentic as the barrel, but it works.

TARRAGON VINEGAR

Make this with your choice of vinegars—we like the imported Japanese rice vinegar, which is quite mild, as well as white wine vinegar, which is the classic choice.

White wine vinegar
Tarragon sprigs

1. Select unwilted tarragon sprigs and remove any browned leaves. Wash the sprigs quickly and roll them in a terry towel to dry thoroughly, or whirl them in a salad dryer, then roll them loosely in a towel to rid them of all possible moisture.

2. Scald jars or bottles that have good caps and let them dry thoroughly. Poke a small handful of tarragon sprigs into a pint bottle, or a larger handful into a larger container. Fill with vinegar that has been brought just to the boiling point. Let the vinegar cool, uncovered, then cap the jars and store them.

TO USE: The vinegar will be ready to use after two weeks or so; it continues to gain flavor for some time. You can stretch the supply by adding fresh vinegar whenever you use some of the flavored vinegar.

So long as the flavor remains good, you can continue extracting the tarragon flavor in this fashion.

GARLIC VINEGAR

5 or 6 cloves garlic, peeled and halved
Red Wine Vinegar (page 185), white wine vinegar, or Oriental rice
    vinegar

1. Scald and let dry completely a pint jar that has a good cap or lid, put into it the peeled and halved garlic cloves, and fill it with vinegar that has been heated just to the boiling point. Let the vinegar cool, uncovered, then cap the jar or bottle.

2. Let the vinegar stand about 2 weeks, shaking it occasionally, then sniff: if strong enough, strain the vinegar into a second scalded, dry container, cover it, and store it at room temperature.

NOTE: For very strongly flavored vinegar, the strained vinegar may be reheated and poured over a fresh batch of garlic and the procedure repeated from that point.

SHALLOT VINEGAR

Make this as described for Garlic Vinegar (see above), using 6 to 8 peeled and halved medium-to-large shallots and white wine vinegar or Oriental rice vinegar.

CHIVE VINEGAR

Large fistful of chives
White wine vinegar or Oriental rice vinegar

1. Rinse the chives, discard any yellowed spears, and pat the chives thoroughly dry in a towel. Cut them up coarsely into 1- or 2-inch lengths and fill a scalded, dry jar loosely.

2. Scald enough white wine vinegar or Oriental rice vinegar to cover the chives well and pour it into the jar. Let the vinegar cool, then cover the jar and let it stand for about 2 weeks, shaking it occasionally.

3. Strain the bottled vinegar into a scalded, dry jar or bottle, cover it, and store it at room temperature.

BASIL VINEGAR

Make this in the same way as Chive Vinegar (see above), but simply bruise the basil leaves—don't cut them. It will probably be strongly enough flavored to be strained after a few days, or at most a week.

MINT VINEGAR

The best mint for this infusion is spearmint (although the commoner mints may be used), and either cider or a white wine or Oriental rice vinegar may be chosen. Make like Basil Vinegar (see above). Good in dressings for fruit salad.

DILL VINEGAR

Use fresh dill foliage, preferably with flower buds about to open, and make like Basil Vinegar (see above). If you have no fresh dill, use 3 tablespoons of dried dill seeds to a pint of cider vinegar, white wine vinegar, or Oriental rice vinegar. Especially good in composed salads made with potatoes, beans, or carrots, or with seafood.

CHILI VINEGAR

This is hot-hot, a condiment for those who like a peppery vinegar to sprinkle onto cooked greens or to use like a bottled pepper sauce. The strength of the chili vinegar is controlled by the proportion of peppers to vinegar and the length of the steeping time. Be sure any friend to whom you give it as a gift has a boundless affection for palate-searing foods and sauces.

Fresh, hot green, yellow or red peppers, or a mixture
Optional: Peeled garlic cloves
Distilled white vinegar

1. For each sterilized half-pint jar, wash, dry, stem, and slit open 3 to 6 fresh hot peppers. (*Caution:* Be careful in handling hot peppers:

either prepare them at the sink, rinsing your hands frequently and avoiding touching your face, or wear rubber gloves; the juice is extremely irritating to the skin.)

2. Drop the peppers into the jars and add to each jar, if you like, a small, peeled clove of garlic. Fill each jar almost to the brim with distilled white vinegar, cap it with a clean, dry lid, and let the peppers steep for about a month.

3. Check the flavor from time to time by putting a drop onto a bite of food—don't taste the chili vinegar directly, unless your tolerance for hot peppers is well established. When the flavor pleases you, begin using the vinegar, or strain it into a second sterile jar or bottle. It will keep indefinitely.

A Note on Mustard Making

If exotic mustards are hard to find in your neighborhood, or if you enjoy concocting your own *everything* to fit your own taste (as we do), you'll be glad to make the discovery that a number of mustards can be made without ferreting out secret formulas hidden by monks. And without recourse to the use of eggs, butter, and other unprofessional ingredients.

We have not tried to duplicate the wild range of flavorings that proliferate in chic shoppes (everything from strawberry to hot fudge, it seems), but instead have created several special types that *are* cheaper and/or better when made at home. We have found, for example, that the gentlefolk of Dijon make, not surprisingly, the best Dijon mustard, often at a reasonable price; and mild brown mustard is cheaper and better *when* store-bought. But some styles of mustard—particularly the coarse-grained ones—are most satisfying to make at home.

As mustard flavorings are very much a matter of personal preference, consider the five we've selected as representative kinds and experiment with flavorings: with the recipe for Tarragon Mustard (page 192) as a guide, substitute whatever dried herbs you fancy; or, following the method for Sweet German-Style Mustard (page 194), develop a balance of spices that intrigues your taste buds.

NOTE: Mustard seeds and powder of different brands absorb liquids at varying rates—the powders, especially, vary in liquid absorption and ferocity range, and some are searing indeed. The recipes are designed to achieve a proper consistency or to be on the thick side, a factor that can easily be remedied with a bit of wine or vinegar.

GREEN PEPPERCORN MUSTARD

Green peppercorns, with their brisk, aromatic bite, meld surprisingly well with the equally verve-y mustard seeds. This is a fashionable mustard—and consequently priced out of sight. So make your own plus extras for your fellow appreciators.

Makes about 1 cup

3 tablespoons mustard seeds
⅓ cup dry mustard, preferably imported
½ cup hot tap water
½ cup white wine vinegar
½ cup dry white wine or dry white vermouth
  Big pinch of ground cinnamon
½ teaspoon dried tarragon, crumbled
½ teaspoon dill seed
2 teaspoons coarse (kosher) salt
  Big pinch of ground cloves
1 teaspoon honey
1 tablespoon green peppercorns (drained water-packed or freeze-dried),
    more if desired

1. Combine the mustard seeds, dry mustard, water, and vinegar in a bowl and let stand for at least 3 hours.

2. In a small saucepan, bring to a boil the wine or vermouth, cinnamon, tarragon, dill seed, salt, and cloves. Strain into the mustard mixture and stir. Add the honey and green peppercorns.

3. Scrape into a food processor or blender and whirl to a puree.

4. Transfer to the top of a double boiler over simmering water. Cook for about 10 minutes, stirring often. (The mixture should be a bit softer than finished mustard, as it will thicken as it cools.) Crush a few more peppercorns slightly and add, if you like texture and a little more bite.

5. Scrape into a jar, cool, and refrigerate. Keeps indefinitely.

TARRAGON MUSTARD

This is a rich-textured, slightly coarse mustard—not a delicate cream. We like its body and strength with grilled meat and fish and to flavor sauces. If you prefer the smooth tarragon-scented mustard, buy it. We don't know how it's made.

Makes 3/4 to 1 cup

1/4 cup mustard seeds
1/4 cup dry white wine or dry white vermouth
1/3 cup white wine vinegar
 2 teaspoons dried tarragon
1/3 cup water
1/8 teaspoon ground black pepper
1/8 teaspoon ground allspice
 2 teaspoons honey
1 1/2 teaspoons coarse (kosher) salt

1. Combine the mustard seeds, white wine or vermouth, vinegar, and 1 teaspoon of the tarragon in a dish and let stand for 3 hours or longer.

2. Pour the mixture into the container of a food processor or blender. Add the water, pepper, allspice, honey, and salt and whirl to a fairly fine puree.

3. Scrape the mustard into the upper part of a double boiler; stir over simmering water for about 10 minutes, or until the mustard is thickened but somewhat more liquid than prepared mustard.

4. Cool. Add the remaining 1 teaspoon tarragon, scrape the mustard into a jar, and cap it. Refrigerated, it will keep indefinitely.

COARSE-GROUND MUSTARD WITH
RED WINE AND GARLIC

Robust, assertive, with a deep color from the red wine. The texture is similar to that of the French country mustards that have a little crunch left from the seeds. Use a few finely minced shallots in place of the garlic for a delicate shallot mustard. Use either one in mustard vinaigrettes.

Makes ¾ to 1 cup

¼ cup mustard seeds
¼ cup red wine
⅓ cup Red Wine Vinegar (page 185)
¼ cup water
¼ teaspoon ground allspice
½ teaspoon honey
¼ teaspoon ground black pepper
½ teaspoon pureed garlic (pressed through a garlic press), or more, if
    you are mincing the garlic with a knife
1 ½ teaspoons coarse (kosher) salt
1 bay leaf, finely crumbled

1. Combine the mustard seeds, red wine, and red wine vinegar in a dish and let stand for 3 hours or more.

2. Put the mixture in the container of a food processor or a blender and add the water, allspice, honey, pepper, garlic, salt, and bay leaf. Whirl to a fairly coarse texture.

3. Scrape into the upper part of a double boiler. Stir over simmering water for 5 to 10 minutes, or until the mustard has thickened somewhat but is not as thick as prepared mustard.

4. Scrape the mustard into a jar and let cool, then cap and refrigerate. The mustard will keep indefinitely.

HORSERADISH MUSTARD

An emphatically "hot" mustard, this is not for the timid-tongued, but for those who like a nip to the condiment accompanying their corned beef. If you can get fresh horseradish, by all means use it; it's easy to "grate" in a blender, with a little water or vinegar added to the peeled, cubed root to help with the grinding; see our recipe page 183. Fresh horseradish is more pungent than the bottled kind, so proceed with caution, reducing the quantities a bit—you can always add more at the end, or at any point while the mustard lasts.

(continued)

Makes about 1/2 cup

1/2 cup dry mustard, preferably imported
1/2 cup hot tap water
1/2 cup white wine vinegar or Oriental rice vinegar
2 teaspoons coarse (kosher) salt
1 tablespoon Prepared Horseradish (page 183) or drained bottled
    horseradish
1 clove garlic, peeled and sliced
1 teaspoon sugar
6 whole black peppercorns, crushed in a mortar, or a pinch of ground
    black pepper
2 whole allspice berries, crushed in a mortar, or a small pinch of
    ground allspice
A little dry white wine, or additional white wine vinegar, if needed

1. Stir together the dry mustard and water and let stand, uncovered, for 20 minutes, stirring once or twice.

2. In the container of a blender or a food processor, combine the vinegar, salt, horseradish, garlic, sugar, peppercorns, and allspice. Process until the garlic and horseradish have been pureed in the liquid, then strain through a fine-meshed strainer, pressing all juice from any pulp in the strainer.

3. Combine the strained liquid with the mustard-water mixture in the top of a double boiler set over simmering water. Cook, stirring constantly, for about 5 minutes, or until the mustard has thickened. (It will thicken more while cooling.)

4. Cool and taste. Add more prepared horseradish, if desired, and if the mustard seems too thick, thin it with a few drops of white wine or additional vinegar.

SWEET GERMAN-STYLE MUSTARD

The formula for this condiment—from this moment no longer secret—yields a slightly grainy, yellow-brown mustard heady with warm spices, any sharpness smoothed by the generous proportion of sweetening characteristic of this type of mustard. It is no surprise that it goes marvelously well with the whole range of German *wursts,* as well as with all smoked and cured meats, especially ham, tongue, and corned beef. For spreading the bread for sandwiches or canapés made with any of these, try creaming the butter with the mustard plus a snipping of chives or a little grated onion.

Makes 1½ cups

¼ cup whole mustard seeds
5 tablespoons dry mustard, preferably imported
½ cup hot tap water
1 cup cider vinegar
¼ cup cold water
2 large slices onion
2 tablespoons (packed) dark brown sugar
1 ½ teaspoons salt
2 small cloves garlic, peeled and halved
¼ teaspoon ground cinnamon
¼ teaspoon ground allspice
¼ teaspoon dill seeds
¼ teaspoon dried tarragon, crumbled
2 pinches ground cloves
3 tablespoons light corn syrup

1. Soak together the mustard seeds, dry mustard, hot water, and ½ cup of the cider vinegar for at least 3 hours.

2. An hour before you want to complete the mustard, combine in a saucepan the remaining ½ cup of vinegar, the cold water, onion, brown sugar, salt, garlic, cinnamon, allspice, dill seeds, tarragon, and cloves. Bring to a boil, boil for 1 minute, then cover and let stand for 1 hour.

3. Scrape the soaked mustard mixture into the container of a blender or a food processor. Strain into it the spice infusion, pressing on the solids in the strainer to extract all possible flavor. Process the mustard, covered, until the consistency is that of a coarse puree with discernible graininess.

4. Pour the mustard into the top of a double boiler set over simmering water and cook for 10 minutes, stirring often, until the mixture has thickened noticeably (it will thicken a bit more when cool).

5. Remove from the heat, add the corn syrup, and pour into a storage jar. Let the mustard cool uncovered, then put a lid on the jar and store the mustard either at room temperature or in the refrigerator.

CURRY POWDER

Although purists are correct in saying that there is no such thing as a standardized curry powder in Indian cuisine, there are several good mixtures of spices sold outside India as "curry powder." This is one version of such a seasoning. It is obviously fresher and, by intention, more delicate than any store-bought version. Make a small amount and adjust it to your taste. If you prefer a hot curry powder, add as many tiny dried hot peppers as you like to the pan with the whole spices to be toasted (first removing all their seeds), then grind them with the other spices.

Don't make a very large amount of curry powder at once, as the spice flavors tend to fade or become acrid if kept too long.

Makes 1/2 cup

Optional, although recommended: 2½ teaspoons fenugreek
20 medium cardamom pods, or enough to produce 1 teaspoon seeds
    (smack the pods with a meat pounder or flat side of a cleaver to
    crack them and release the seeds)
3 tablespoons coriander seeds
1 tablespoon cumin seeds
1 tablespoon mustard seeds
6 whole cloves
1 thin cinnamon stick (2 to 3 inches long), broken into pieces
¼ teaspoon ground mace
¼ teaspoon grated nutmeg
   Big pinch cayenne pepper
2 tablespoons ground turmeric
   Optional: Toasted dried hot red peppers (see note above) or more
   cayenne to taste

1. Preheat the oven to 225 degrees.

2. Combine the fenugreek, cardamom, coriander, cumin, and mustard seeds, cloves, and broken cinnamon in a small pan and bake for 15 minutes, shaking the pan a few times. Let cool.

3. Combine the toasted spices with the mace, nutmeg, cayenne, turmeric, and optional toasted peppers in a spice mill and grind to a powder. Store airtight.

CHILI POWDER

If you have an electric spice mill—a kitchen possession we seem to recommend often—it's the work of a few minutes to make your own blend of chili powder, a spice mixture that is wildly popular in this country. As uncounted varieties of chili peppers are grown, the kinds available vary unpredictably from one place to another. Our advice is to use whatever kind you can get. We have used *ancho* and *pasilla* chilies because we favor a rather mild chili powder. If you prefer a more fiery blend, seek hotter varieties.

Makes 1/3 to 1/2 cup

2 large dried pasilla chili peppers, preferably leathery, not brittle
1 large dried ancho chili pepper, preferably leathery, not brittle
2 teaspoons cumin seeds
1/4 teaspoon whole cloves
1/2 teaspoon coriander seeds
1/4 teaspoon whole allspice berries
2 tablespoons dried oregano
1 tablespoon Garlic Salt (page 202)

1. Remove the stems and seeds from the chili peppers. (You should have about 1 ounce of flesh.) Tear the chilies into small pieces.

2. Combine the chilies in a skillet with the cumin, cloves, coriander, and allspice and stir continuously over low heat until there is a faint crackling noise and the fragrance of the peppers is perceptible—this will take a minute or two. Cool completely in a dish.

3. Combine in batches in a spice mill with the oregano and garlic salt and grind to a fine powder. Mix, then store airtight.

QUATRE ÉPICES

Although the name of this spice mixture means "four spices" in French, it may contain five spices—as our version does—or even more. Many chefs keep a supply of their favorite blend on hand for enlivening meat or meat-flavored dishes ranging from soups and stews to sausages and intricate galantines and pâtés; such a mixture is usually what is meant when the simple word "spices" appears in certain recipes translated from the French. (But there are other French seasoning mixtures—such as Spice Parisienne, our version of which appears below—that include herbs as well as spices and, like *quatre épices,* are made in many versions.)

Ours is a well-balanced blend, without the dominance of cloves often encountered. Try the mixture as we make it, then adjust the spices to suit yourself. If you have an electric spice mill, by all means use it to prepare the ingredients—the flavor will be livelier than if you use preground spices.

Makes about 7 tablespoons (enough to fill a standard-sized spice jar)

**2 tablespoons freshly ground white pepper (2 heaping tablespoons
    peppercorns before grinding)**
**2 tablespoons freshly ground black pepper (2 heaping tablespoons
    peppercorns before grinding)**
4 teaspoons ground ginger
**4 teaspoons freshly grated nutmeg (about 1½ whole nutmegs before
    grating)**
**1 teaspoon ground cloves, preferably freshly ground (about 1 teaspoon
    before grinding)**

Blend the ground spices thoroughly. Store the mixture airtight.

SPICE PARISIENNE

Time was when jars so labeled could be found on most well-stocked spice shelves in stores, and here and there you may still be able to find this mixture. Spice Parisienne is a version of the blends originated by French chefs who regularly devised their own ready-mixed spices and herbs. No two experts of past ages had exactly the same formula, but the general idea was to marry the fragrant and the pungent. A good rule of thumb is to try this mix when you would ordinarily season with pepper, thyme, and bay leaves. The aromatic spices will add an extra dimension of flavor. Try a little, taste, then adjust the seasoning. Note that the blend is more intricate than Quatre Épices (page 197), which is much used in pâtés and sausage making.

Spice Parisienne is best (because freshest) when made with as many whole spices and herbs as possible, ground separately in a spice mill, then measured. However, it's still excellent when preground spices are used.

Makes about ½ cup

1 tablespoon salt
3 medium bay leaves
2 tablespoons freshly ground white pepper (2 heaping tablespoons peppercorns before grinding)
2 tablespoons freshly ground black pepper (2 heaping tablespoons peppercorns before grinding)
1 tablespoon freshly grated nutmeg (about 1 whole nutmeg before grating)
1 tablespoon ground cinnamon, preferably freshly ground (about 6 inches stick cinnamon before grinding)
1 ½ teaspoons ground ginger
1 tablespoon ground dried thyme, measured after grinding
1 ½ teaspoons ground mace (heaped 1½ teaspoons crumbled whole mace before grinding)
1 ½ teaspoons ground cloves, preferably freshly ground (about 1½ teaspoons before grinding)

Grind the salt and the bay leaves together, then blend them thoroughly with the remaining ground spices and herbs. Pack the mixture into small jars or bottles and close tightly.

FILÉ POWDER (Gumbo Filé)

Add filé powder to Louisiana-style gumbos to impart a delicate herbal flavor and a slightly mucilaginous texture. The powder is a gourmet-shop item, free for the gathering and drying of a few leaves to be found in woodlands in most of the eastern third of the country. For the raw material you need to identify the sassafras tree (botanically *Sassafras albidum, S. variifolium,* or *S. officinale*), which happens to be one of the easiest trees to identify, as it's the only tree we know that has leaves of three shapes on each plant. Some are oval, some have two large lobes, and some are mitten-shaped. To confirm the identity of your find, dig up a small root and sniff: sassafras will have the distinctive "root beer" aroma that makes the roots usable for sassafras tea. The bark is grey and only slightly textured, and the tree scatters seed so freely that young sassafras plants spring up yearly wherever there is a parent tree.

(continued)

1. Gather the leaves from sassafras trees of any size in the spring when they are fully unfolded but still tender. Don't wash them unless they are dusty. Strip them of any coarse stems and spread them in a single layer on a large, clean window screen, on an oven shelf you can spare for a few days, or on a frame over which cheesecloth or nylon net has been stretched. (You can also use a convection oven at very low heat, or a food dryer, if you have one.)

2. Put the leaves to dry in a warm, preferably dark place with good air circulation—don't try to dry them in the sun. When they are crisp, strip them from their stems and crumble them fine or powder them in a blender or a food processor.

3. Sieve the crumbled leaves and pack the filé powder into small jars with airtight covers. Don't add other herbs if you want the real thing.

NOTE: When you use filé powder for gumbos, be sure not to boil the food after the filé has been added (some recipes omit this direction); if gumbo containing filé is boiled, its texture becomes ropy.

CHINESE FIVE-SPICE POWDER

To be sure of a fresh blend of this spice mixture for Chinese cooking, mix your own. The recipe doesn't make a large quantity, as you will use only a little at a time. We recommend, again, using a spice mill to grind separately as many of the whole spices as possible; then grind the mixture again to blend it.

Makes about 3 tablespoons

1 tablespoon freshly ground Szechuan peppercorns (1 heaping tablespoon before grinding)
½ teaspoon ground cloves, preferably freshly ground (about ½ teaspoon before grinding)
1 tablespoon ground cinnamon, preferably freshly ground (about 6 inches stick cinnamon before grinding)
1 tablespoon freshly ground fennel seeds (1 heaping tablespoon before grinding)
6 whole star anise, ground

Mix the spices, then regrind them together until the mixture is very fine. Store in a jar with an airtight cover.

PICKLING SPICE

The recipe reproduced here comes courtesy of our knowledgeable friend Cecily Brownstone. Mixing your own pickling spice makes sense, especially if you don't favor the predominance of allspice and cloves encountered in many commercial mixtures. Cecily's spice is judiciously compounded of the aromatic, the pungent, and the peppery.

Makes about 2/3 cup

4 cinnamon sticks (each about 3 inches long)
1 piece dried gingerroot (1 inch long)
2 tablespoons mustard seeds
2 teaspoons whole allspice berries
2 tablespoons whole black peppercorns
2 teaspoons whole cloves
2 teaspoons dill seeds
2 teaspoons coriander seeds
2 teaspoons whole mace, crumbled medium fine
8 bay leaves, crumbled medium fine
1 small dried hot red pepper (1½ inches long), chopped or crumbled
    medium fine, seeds and all

Cecily's method is to wrap the cinnamon and gingerroot loosely in a piece of cloth and bash them with a hammer until well crumbled. She discards any stringy parts of the ginger, then mixes the cinnamon and ginger bits with the other ingredients.

TO STORE: Store the spice in an airtight jar and shake it to mix it well before using.

DRIED MUSHROOMS

Used for their concentrated flavor—not to replace fresh mushrooms when these are a key ingredient—dried mushrooms are convenient to have on hand and simple to prepare. They can be added, as is, to long-simmered foods; or, if you prefer, soak them for a few minutes in warm water before adding them to the pot. Use the flavorful soaking liquid, too, or save it for soup.

Thoroughly dried mushrooms can easily be powdered to make a highly concentrated flavoring (see below). In this form, the taste of a pound of mushrooms is embodied in a few tablespoons of aromatic powder.

1. Select unbruised mushrooms without exposed gills. Wipe caps clean with a damp cloth if they appear soiled, and cut off any discolored tips of stems.

2. With a sharp knife, thinly slice the mushrooms from cap through stem. Spread the slices in a single layer on a large cake rack (or racks) covered with cheesecloth. Place in a warm, dry spot—if the temperature doesn't go much over 100 degrees, an oven warmed by a pilot light is good; otherwise try an attic or any place on your premises where the right conditions exist. (Don't dry the mushrooms in the sun, however.) If you have a dehydrator or a convection oven, use it according to the manufacturer's instructions.

3. When the mushroom slices are crisp-dry, store them airtight in a jar. Check them after a day or so—if any sign of moisture appears in the container, remove the mushrooms and dry them further before returning them to storage. They will keep indefinitely if protected from dampness.

POWDERED DRIED MUSHROOMS

Reduce thoroughly dried mushroom slices to a fine powder in an electric blender, a spice mill, or a food processor. Store the powder airtight. Use sparingly in sauces, soups, stews, or gravies.

GARLIC SALT

A fresher-tasting garlic seasoning than most commercial products (but nothing like the fresh), to be used in any preparation calling for both garlic and salt. It's a good thing to make when the garlic harvest arrives in the market in the late summer or fall. The cloves are full of flavorsome juice then, and if you like you can make a supply that will last for up to a year.

Add the garlic powder to food conservatively until you are acquainted with its strength, and remember to reduce the salt you would ordinarily add to the dish. It's safe to assume that ¼ teaspoon of this garlic salt contains almost ¼ teaspoon of salt.

Makes about ⅔ cup

¾ cup coarse (kosher) salt
½ cup peeled garlic cloves

1. Pour the salt into the container of a blender or a food processor, cover the container, and start the blades.

2. Through the feed opening in the cover, add the garlic cloves in a steady stream. Process the salt and garlic until a paste forms, if necessary stopping the action and scraping down the sides of the container.

3. Cover a baking sheet with waxed paper and spread or scatter the paste on the paper. Dry the paste in a barely warm oven—an oven heated to only about 100 degrees by a pilot light is excellent. If yours stays at 140 degrees or below when set at "warm," it won't be too hot. If it's hotter than 140 degrees, prop the door open, or turn off the heat from time to time during drying so the garlic-impregnated salt can dry without acquiring a cooked taste. Stir the paste occasionally—it will be lumpy. (Warning: Your kitchen will be redolent of garlic while this goes on; but you'd be unlikely to use this recipe if you dislike the aroma.)

4. When the paste is thoroughly dry (1 to 3 hours), return it to the blender jar or food processor and grind it to a uniform powder. Store airtight at room temperature.

TARRAGON PRESERVED IN VINEGAR

When fresh tarragon is out of season, many expert cooks prefer tarragon leaves preserved in vinegar to the widely available dried tarragon. The acidity the leaves acquire from the vinegar is not objectionable when the tarragon is used in an herbed vinaigrette or a Béarnaise sauce, for example. The leaves may be rinsed and patted dry before use, if you wish.

Preserved tarragon makes an attractive gift, particularly if you take a moment to arrange the sprigs upright in the jar or bottle so they appear to be growing naturally.

As you use the tarragon, the liquid level will drop. Add more white wine vinegar when necessary in order to keep the leaves covered.

When they have all been used you'll have a delightful bonus—a bottle of well-flavored tarragon vinegar.

Fresh tarragon
White wine vinegar

1. Gather or buy fresh tarragon in early summer when its first growth is at its best, selecting bushy, unwilted stalks. If they seem dusty (but not otherwise), rinse the stalks quickly and dry them by rolling them loosely in a towel and leaving them for an hour or two, or whirl them in a salad dryer, then roll them gently in a towel if they are still damp. Let all surface moisture evaporate.

2. Scald jars (or fairly wide-mouthed bottles) and let them dry. Fill the jars *very* loosely with tarragon sprigs, tips upward, arranged attractively. Leave at least 1 inch of space above the tallest stalks.

3. Scald enough white wine vinegar to fill the jars almost to the top and pour it hot over the tarragon, making sure all the leaves are immersed. Leave the jars uncovered until the vinegar has cooled, then cover them closely. Metal lids should be lined with doubled or tripled plastic wrap to prevent their corroding. Store the tarragon at room temperature. It is ready for use at any time. When necessary, add more white wine vinegar (it is unnecessary to scald the vinegar you are adding) to keep the leaves well covered.

FROZEN HERBS

Certain herbs are so satisfactory when dried (whether by yourself or by a reputable commercial packer) that it makes no sense to freeze them —examples are thyme and rosemary. Other herbs lose character when dried, although exceptions are *some* of the few herbs sold freeze-dried.

Among the herbs worth freezing are parsley, both the flat-leaved (Italian) and the curly kind; chives; tarragon; dill; basil; and, if you grow them or can get them, summer savory and sweet marjoram. Either buy or gather herbs at the peak of their flavor—each has its best season— and store away many months' supply with very little effort.

PARSLEY

The flat-leaved or Italian parsley is our choice for flavor; it's at its best in fall. The curly kind, fine for garnishing and okay for flavor, is always with us. (You may want to freeze some of each.) Our waste-not, want-not suggestion: Strip the parsley leaves from the heavy stems, rinse the stems, and freeze them separately, closely wrapped and sealed, for seasoning those soups and stews in which a *bouquet garni* is indispensable. To prepare the leaves, rinse them, with only the smallest stems left on, and roll them up in a terrycloth towel until they're free of moisture. Then chop the parsley, either with a chef's knife on a board or (easier) in a food processor fitted with the steel blade. Make the particles as fine as you like. Pack into screwtop jars (packing firmly diminishes airspace, so helps keep in flavor), put on the cover, label, and pop into the freezer. When you need minced parsley, dig some out with a spoon. It thaws in an instant and looks and tastes surprisingly fresh.

CHIVES

Wash, sort, trim off any brown tips, and roll the spears up in a towel until they're free of moisture. Bunch the spears on a board, hold the bunch firmly together, and slice—don't chop—the chives into short lengths (this is the secret of keeping in the juice, hence the flavor). Pack the chives firmly into screwtop jars, put on the tops, label, and freeze. Thawed, these chives won't look fresh-cut, but they're satisfactory as a garnish for hot foods or in vinaigrettes or other sauces where their slightly wilted appearance won't be noticeable.

TARRAGON

If you grow this princely herb, by all means use some to make Tarragon Vinegar (page 187) and put some up (see Tarragon Preserved in Vinegar, page 203). To freeze it, rinse the sprigs, roll them up to dry in a towel, then lay them on sheets of foil in quantities you judge you're likely to use for an average recipe. Fold the foil over each batch into a flat packet, tape the seams, label, and freeze.

DILL

We've mentioned in the pickling section (see page 132) a way of freezing whole blossoming dill plants to be used later for the pickle crock. For fresh dill to be used in cooking, rinse, dry, mince, and pack dill as described for parsley (see above), using only the tender leaves.

BASIL

This tends to look pretty dreadful when frozen and thawed, but some basil flavor is there. We prefer to freeze basil in sprigs, as described for tarragon (see above); chopping it releases enough juice, we think, to deplete its flavor.

SUMMER SAVORY AND SWEET MARJORAM

We recommend the tarragon method (see above) for these, as they're most often used as sprigs, not in minced form, for seasoning.

Beverages

On Potables
Tomato Juice
Tomato Cocktail (Bloody Mary Base)
Cranberry Juice and Home-Style Cranberry Sauce:
  A Dual Recipe
Pear, Peach, Nectarine, or Apricot Nectar
Concord Grape Juice (Whole-Grape Method)
Rich Concord Grape Juice (Extraction Method)
Ginger Syrup for Home-Style Ginger Ale
Iced Tea Made with Cold Water
Spiced or Minted Tea and Spiced Coffee Mixtures
About Homemade Cordials
Lemon-Flavored Vodka
Caraway Liqueur ("Kümmel")
Orange Liqueur
Cherry Liqueur
Tangerine Liqueur
Anise Liqueur

On Potables

This is a group of recipes for drinkables that have little in common apart from the fact that they are not chewed or cut up before swallowing. What other similarities could you find between tomato juice and anise liqueur?

We do not provide any recipes for wines (which need a book to themselves), beer (ditto), or bottled and capped sodas (of which we generally disapprove and which require special equipment), or for hard liquors, which need distilling paraphernalia—and the law on your side.

We offer a small sampling of recipes from several genres (vegetable juices, fruit nectars, liqueurs) that are worth trying at home. If the liqueurs intrigue you, try infusing just about any herb or spice in alcohol (either brandy or vodka). Experiment with small amounts until you come up with a balance of taste that suits you. Incidentally, we hope that ginger lovers will be happy with a syrup that lets you make home-style ginger ale without the necessity of bottling.

TOMATO JUICE

For making your own thick, flavorful tomato juice, try to find (or grow) Italian-type pear or plum tomatoes. These are fleshy and contain few seeds and little surplus moisture. Other types of tomatoes (salad or slicing tomatoes) can be used, but their juice tends to be thinner.

This recipe, and the recipe for Tomato Cocktail following, are for the height of the tomato season, late summer or early fall, when (if) you can get fully vine-ripened tomatoes. Neither recipe is worth attempting with out-of-season tomatoes.

(*continued*)

Makes about 1 quart of juice from each 2 quarts of whole tomatoes

Fully ripened Italian-type tomatoes, without spoiled spots or bruises

For <u>each 2 quarts</u> of tomatoes:

½ to ¾ teaspoon salt, or to taste
  Strained lemon juice (optional; but see A Note on Canning Safety,
    below)
  Sugar (optional)

1. Wash the tomatoes well. Cut away green or yellow parts and remove white or green cores. Quarter the tomatoes and measure them into a stainless-steel or enameled kettle; you should have about 5 cups per 2 quarts of whole tomatoes. Bring the tomatoes to a boil, then simmer them until soft.

2. Work the tomatoes through the finest disc of a food mill. If the juice contains escaped seeds or is not smooth enough, sieve it.

3. If the sieved juice seems watery, let it stand until it settles, then ladle off the very thin liquid at the top. If it is thick enough after sieving, taste it and add salt and, if you like, a little lemon juice and sugar.

4. Return the juice to the rinsed-out kettle and bring it to a boil, then, following the Pointers on Preserving on pages 153–56, ladle into clean, hot quart or pint jars, leaving ¼ inch of headspace. Wipe the rims, put on two-piece lids, and fasten the screw bands.

5. Set the jars on a rack in a deep kettle half filled with boiling water. Fill the kettle with boiling water to cover the jars by at least 2 inches. Bring to a boil, cover, and boil hard (process) for 15 minutes for quarts, 10 minutes for pints.

6. Remove the jars from the boiling-water bath and cool.

A NOTE ON CANNING SAFETY: Tomatoes, because of their acid content, have in past years been considered safe to can in a boiling-water bath. However, in recent years hybridizers have developed "sub-acid" varieties that may be on the borderline of acid content where the safe canning of tomatoes or their juice is concerned. To be on the safe side, taste the juice before canning it. If it lacks tartness, be sure to add enough lemon juice to re-create the characteristic pleasant tomato sharpness.

TOMATO COCKTAIL (Bloody Mary Base)

Served straight and iced, or spiked with vodka to make a Bloody Mary, this spicy brew has the freshness of good vegetables and none of the strong flavoring additives found in many canned or bottled cocktail bases.

Makes about 1 quart of juice from each 2 quarts of whole tomatoes

Fully ripened Italian-type plum or pear tomatoes, without spoiled spots or bruises

For <u>each 2 quarts</u> of whole tomatoes:

½ **medium red or green sweet pepper, chopped**
½ **small onion, peeled and chopped**
½ **clove garlic, peeled and sliced**
½ **to 1 rib celery (depending on size), with leaves, chopped**
¼ **teaspoon whole black peppercorns**
 1 **small dried hot red pepper (about 1½ inches long) or a ½-inch slice of fresh hot pepper (use more if you like "hotter" juice, or add bottled hot pepper sauce to the finished juice, as described in the directions)**
½ **teaspoon coriander seeds or ¼ teaspoon ground coriander**
¼ **bay leaf**
 2 **or 3 small sprigs parsley**
 3 **or 4 fresh basil leaves or ¼ teaspoon crumbled dried basil**
¼ **teaspoon mustard seeds**
   Optional: ½ teaspoon sugar
½ **to ¾ teaspoon salt, or to taste**
   Strained fresh lemon or lime juice to taste (see note below)

 1. Wash the tomatoes well. Cut away any green or yellow parts and remove white or green cores. Quarter the tomatoes and measure them into a stainless-steel or enameled kettle; each 2 quarts of whole tomatoes should yield about 5 cups, cut up.
 2. Add to the tomatoes the sweet pepper, onion, garlic, celery, peppercorns, hot pepper (if used), coriander, bay leaf, parsley, basil, and mustard seeds. Bring to a boil, then simmer, stirring occasionally, until the vegetables are soft.
 3. Force the vegetables through the finest disc of a food mill. Sieve

the juice if it isn't smooth enough, or if any seeds have passed into it. If the juice seems too thin, let it settle, then skim off and discard the thin liquid on top.

4. Taste the juice for seasoning and add sugar, salt, pepper sauce (if you are including it), and strained lemon or lime juice to taste.

5. Return the juice to the rinsed-out kettle and bring it to a boil, then, following the Pointers on Preserving on pages 153–56, ladle it into clean, hot canning jars, leaving ¼ inch of headspace. Wipe the rims, put on two-piece lids, and fasten the screw bands.

6. Set the jars on a rack in a deep kettle half filled with boiling water. Add boiling water to cover the jars by at least 2 inches. Bring to a boil, cover, and boil hard (process) for 15 minutes for quarts, 10 minutes for pints.

7. Remove the jars from the boiling-water bath and cool.

NOTE: Because you want highly seasoned cocktail juice, you'll undoubtedly add enough lemon or lime juice to ensure that the juice is acid enough to be canned safely in a boiling-water bath. In any case, check the Note on Canning Safety that follows the recipe for Tomato Juice (page 210).

Cranberry Juice and Home-Style Cranberry Sauce: A Dual Recipe

There are a few reasons why this twofold recipe deserves your attention: First, it enables you to produce 5 cups of juice, very rapidly, from a small packet of berries (fresh cranberries keep virtually forever in the freezer). Second, making your own juice eliminates toting a heavy jug from the market. Third, homemade juice can be sweetened to taste. Fourth, after extracting the juice you will have the pulp, which needs only sugar and a few seconds' boiling to become a flavorful coarse-textured cranberry sauce. Fifth, the cost of the combined products is very low. And if all that isn't enough, cranberries abound in vitamin C, and are as healthful as all get out.

CRANBERRY JUICE

Makes about 5 cups

1 pound cranberries
5 cups water

Optional: 2 or 3 orange slices
Pinch of salt
½ cup sugar, or to taste

1. Wash the berries and put into a saucepan with the water, orange slices, and the salt. Cook over moderate heat until all berries pop, about 10 minutes.

2. Turn the berries, optional orange slices, and liquid into a cheese-cloth-lined sieve. Strain the juice, without pressing, and reserve the berry and orange pulp to make Home-Style Cranberry Sauce (see below).

3. Return the juice to the pot with the sugar and boil 2 or 3 minutes. Cool and chill.

TO CAN: If you'd like to can the juice, dissolve the sugar in the hot juice, ladle it into hot, clean quart or pint canning jars (leaving ¼ inch of headspace) and proceed as directed in the Pointers on Preserving on pages 153–56, using the boiling-water bath and processing for 10 minutes.

HOME-STYLE CRANBERRY SAUCE

Makes about 2 cups

Cooked cranberry and orange pulp remaining from Cranberry Juice
(see above)
¾ cup sugar
½ cup Cranberry Juice (see above)

1. Force the cranberry and orange pulp through the medium disc of a food mill into a saucepan.

2. Add the sugar and cranberry juice and boil for 30 seconds. Pour into a bowl or jar and press a sheet of plastic onto the surface of the sauce to prevent a skin from forming.

3. Refrigerate. The sauce will keep for several weeks.

PEAR, PEACH, NECTARINE, OR APRICOT NECTAR

When ripe, sweet-smelling summer fruits are abundant and inexpensive, you can easily put up a store of delicious fruit concentrates. These nectars, diluted about half-and-half with chilled water, will produce a more flavorful (and, if you like, less sweet) drink than those sold in cans.

You may also use the concentrates to make fresh-tasting fruit sherbets or ice creams all year round.

Makes about 4 pints

4 pounds ripe pears, peaches, nectarines, or apricots
4 cups water, approximately
  Pinch of salt
½ cup sugar, or to taste
¼ to ½ cup lemon juice, to taste

1. Wash, quarter, and core the fruit (or remove the pits); you should have 12 to 13 cups.

2. Combine the fruit and water in a large stainless-steel or enameled saucepan, using about 1¼ cups water for each 4 cups of fruit. Simmer, covered, until the fruit is soft. Let cool slightly.

3. Puree the fruit and juice in a food processor or blender, processing it in several batches; you should have 8 to 10 cups of puree.

4. Pour the puree through a fine sieve back into the pot. Add a pinch of salt, then ½ cup of sugar. Stir to dissolve the sugar, then taste and add more sugar as you wish. You should oversweeten somewhat, as the puree will be diluted when used as a drink. Add lemon juice to taste; use enough to give a pleasant tartness.

5. Stir the puree over moderate heat until the mixture simmers (about 180 degrees); do not boil it, lest the flavor be diminished.

6. Following the Pointers on Preserving on pages 253–56, pour the puree into 4 clean pint canning jars, leaving ½ inch of headspace. Wipe the rims, put on two-piece lids, and fasten the screw bands.

7. Set the jars on a rack in a deep kettle half full of boiling water.

Add boiling water to cover the lids by 2 inches or more. Bring to a boil, cover, and boil hard (process) for 15 minutes.

8. Remove the jars from the boiling-water bath and cool.

NOTE: Alternatively, the nectar may be frozen in straight-sided jars or plastic freezer containers.

TO USE: Chill the nectar (or thaw, if frozen) and mix about half-and-half with ice water.

CONCORD GRAPE JUICE (Whole-Grape Method)

An old-fashioned method for obtaining a great deal of juice from few grapes, with no work involved aside from the final processing. The result is a delicate, light grape juice. For a more concentrated brew, follow the recipe for Rich Concord Grape Juice (Extraction Method), which follows. If by good fortune wild grapes grow nearby and you find that they are a full-flavored kind, you can use them instead of the cultivated Concords.

Ripe Concord grapes
Sugar
Boiling water

1. Wash and stem the grapes. Put 1¼ to 1½ cups in each clean quart-size jar. Add ½ cup sugar to each and pour in boiling water to come within ½ inch of the rims.

2. Following the Pointers on Preserving on pages 253–56, cover the jars with two-piece lids and fasten the screw bands. Place the jars on a rack in a deep kettle half full of boiling water. Add boiling water to cover the lids by 2 inches.

3. Bring to a boil, cover, and boil hard (process) for 10 minutes.

4. Remove the jars from the boiling-water bath and let them cool. Store in a dark place for at least 2 weeks. Strain off the juice and serve it chilled.

RICH CONCORD GRAPE JUICE (Extraction Method)

Because this juice contains no added water, it is indeed rich, but it has a pleasant hint of tartness that keeps it from being cloying. It is concentrated enough to need dilution. Those with a well-developed sweet tooth can add sugar.

Juice prepared in this way can also be used to make grape jelly later, at your leisure; use a standard recipe calling for added pectin. Note that the grapes are not boiled during their initial heating, and the hot (*not boiling*) water bath used to process the juice in the jars is also kept below the boiling point. This low-temperature processing is the secret of the fresh taste of the juice.

Makes 1 pint per quart (about 1½ pounds) of stemmed grapes

Ripe Concord grapes
A little water

1. Wash ripe Concord grapes while still in their bunches, then remove from their stems and measure.

2. Crush the grapes thoroughly (or process in a food processor, using the plastic blade) and pour into a stainless-steel or enameled pot. Add about 3 tablespoons water per quart of grapes.

3. Heat, stirring frequently, to no more than 190 degrees (use a thermometer); cook at or below that temperature, stirring often, until the grapes are very soft, 10 to 15 minutes.

4. Ladle the grapes into a jelly bag or a sieve lined with 4 layers of cheesecloth. Let most of juice drip into a container; then twist the neck of the bag and press on it to extract as much juice as possible from the pulp.

5. Refrigerate the juice for 12 hours or slightly longer; this allows sediment to settle and helps prevent the formation of crystals of tartaric acid (perfectly harmless) in the juice.

6. Pour the juice off the sediment. Heat the juice to 200 degrees—don't let it get hotter—and fill clean, hot canning jars, allowing ¼ inch of headspace. Cover the jars with two-piece lids and fasten the screw bands. Put the jars on a rack in a deep kettle half-filled with simmering water, and add more simmering (190-degree) water to cover the jars by

at least 2 inches. Simmer for 30 minutes for either pints or quarts, keeping a thermometer in the hot-water bath to be sure the water does not go above 190 degrees.

7. Remove the jars from the simmering-water bath and cool.

GINGER SYRUP FOR HOME-STYLE GINGER ALE

Making and bottling real ginger ale or ginger beer is a lengthy procedure involving specialized equipment and hard-to-find ingredients, so we don't suggest a recipe. What you *can* make is a concentrated ginger syrup for mixing with club soda to produce an amazingly bright-tasting, vividly gingery quaff blended to suit your palate. As fresh gingerroot is now easily available in many supermarkets as well as in smaller stores with a Latin or Oriental clientele, and as the syrup keeps indefinitely, this is certainly worth concocting if you fancy ginger ale. Incidentally, although this is intended as a beverage base, a spoonful over vanilla ice cream is luscious.

Makes 1 1/2 to 2 cups

6 ounces fresh gingerroot, approximately
2 cups water
1 1/4 cups sugar

1. Peel and finely chop the ginger; you should have about 1 cup.
2. Bring the ginger to a boil with the water in an enameled or stainless-steel saucepan. Simmer for 5 minutes, then let stand for 12 to 24 hours, covered with a cloth.
3. Strain through a sieve lined with two layers of cheesecloth; squeeze the pulp in the cloth to extract all possible juice.
4. Return the juice to the saucepan, add sugar, and bring to a boil over moderate heat, stirring. Boil gently for 5 minutes, skimming off any froth.
5. Cool, strain into a bottle, and refrigerate.

TO USE: Use about 1 tablespoon of syrup mixed with 6 ounces of chilled soda water to make a gingery drink.

ICED TEA MADE WITH COLD WATER

Predictably delicious, unclouded iced tea has a permanent summer home on our refrigerator shelf. If you even just *sort* of follow these absurdly simple guidelines, you'll surely be captivated by the cool, clean brew that results. But you must start with tea leaves that are worth brewing in the first place. Tea should have a fascinating aroma. It does not last forever—either in your home canister or in the store. Take a good deep sniff before you infuse it; if it smells dusty or almost not-at-all, replace it.

Makes 1 quart

6 heaping teaspoons tea leaves or tea plus herbs or spices (see the
following recipe)
1 quart cold water

Combine the tea and water in a quart jar. Cap the jar and shake it, or stir the leaves with a spoon for a moment. Leave the jar in the refrigerator for at least 12 hours (it may be left for days this way, if you like). When you want some, strain the tea and sweeten it to taste with extra-fine sugar. Add lemon, lime, or orange slices or juice, or mint sprigs, as the tea flavor dictates.

SPICED OR MINTED TEA AND
SPICED COFFEE MIXTURES

Would you believe chocolate tea? Green apple tea? Mocha-mint tea? We wish it were a bad dream, but poor little innocent tea leaves are being packed daily into jazzy containers and suffocated with synthetic flavors that make the soda spectrum look pale. But you can make some decent mixed tea flavors, so if for some reason you don't like your tea straight, you needn't purchase the expensive (and often weary) mixtures that are so popular. Concoct your own house brands, using a small amount of whole, sweet spices with your black tea, and adding a bit of dried citrus peel, if you so fancy. Cinnamon, whole cloves, and allspice berries work well. Or add some dried peppermint or spearmint leaves to your tea when you brew it. Be sparing when you add *any* aromatics to your tea leaves, or none of the worthwhile real-tea flavor will get through the exotics.

A newcomer to supermarket shelves is coffee in fantasy flavors. We suggest the merest hint of spicing, accomplished by grinding a tiny scrap of cinnamon, an allspice berry, a clove, or a few cardamom seeds with your coffee beans. If you buy your coffee already ground, add one of the above—a bit more generously—when you prepare drip coffee.

About Homemade Cordials

Short of getting into the distilling business (of which the "revenooers" might take a dim view), you can't, alas, make the more intricate liqueurs at home. But you can produce some surprisingly full-flavored cordials by simple infusion methods.

We prefer cordials made with vodka, but we do not find that "all vodkas taste alike," as some claim. Some are raw enough to qualify as firewater. So use a smooth brand to make cordials; flavoring will not soften a harsh alcohol taste.

The cordials for which we give recipes are moderately sweetened. If after tasting you decide you prefer more sweetness, boil sugar and water, half and half, cool the syrup, and add it to suit your taste. Filtering your cordials isn't essential, but it makes for a clearer product. Use thin coffee-filter paper fitted into a funnel for filtering.

When you bottle cordials, choose a container of a size to leave little or no air space. If the bottle is only partly filled, flavor is apt to depart too soon.

LEMON-FLAVORED VODKA

Makes 1 quart

1 small lemon
1 quart vodka

Remove the thin outer peel from a small lemon in one long spiral; avoid the bitter white pith. Drop it into a quart of vodka and let stand at least 1 week, removing the peel when you think its job has been done. The lemon colors the vodka pale yellow and imparts a slight citrus sweetness and pungency.

TO USE: Serve the vodka chilled. If you wish, the vodka may be stored in the freezer.

CARAWAY LIQUEUR ("KÜMMEL")

This is a homey version of a favorite European cordial, kümmel. We find the warm, clean flavor of its spices make a liqueur that is among the least cloying of after-dinner nips.

Makes about 3½ cups

1 tablespoon caraway seeds
¼ teaspoon fennel seeds
¼ teaspoon cumin seeds
3 cups vodka
½ cup water
½ cup sugar

1. Add the caraway, fennel, and cumin seeds to the vodka in a bottle or jar, cover, and let stand for 1 to 3 weeks, shaking occasionally. When the flavor is strong enough, strain out the seeds.

2. Boil the water and sugar together for 2 or 3 minutes, skimming off any froth. Cool, then mix the syrup with the spice infusion.

3. Pour through a funnel lined with coffee-filter paper into a clean, dry bottle or jar and cover closely. Store indefinitely at room temperature.

ORANGE LIQUEUR

After the orange peel has flavored this cordial, don't throw it away. Save it in a jar in the refrigerator for adding to mixed drinks, or shred it into sauces calling for orange peel.

Makes about 1 quart

6 medium oranges
1 teaspoon coriander seeds, bruised
3 cups vodka
1 cup water
1 cup sugar

1. Strip the thin outer rind or zest (no white pith should adhere) from the oranges, using a swivel-bladed peeler. Spread the strips of rind on

a cake rack and let them dry completely. Dry until almost crisp, which will take 12 to 36 hours, depending on the humidity.

2. Combine the dried zest and the coriander seeds with the vodka in a jar, then cap and let steep for 8 days or more, shaking occasionally. Taste; when the flavor is pleasing, strain off the liquid. Save and use the peel as suggested above.

3. Bring the sugar and water to a boil and boil for 2 or 3 minutes, skimming if necessary. Let the syrup cool.

4. Stir the syrup into the orange infusion, then pour the cordial through a funnel lined with coffee-filter paper into a clean, dry bottle. Cap and store indefinitely at room temperature.

CHERRY LIQUEUR

A fruity cordial with the lovely hue of ruby port. The cherry flavor is rather soft-spoken, the kernel aroma a bit more intense. If you prefer a very mild bitter-almondy aroma, use only half the pits for the infusion.

If you can get sour cherries, use them and adjust the sweetening accordingly.

Makes about 2½ cups

2 cups pitted sweet cherries, pits reserved
2 cups vodka
1 cup unpitted sweet cherries, to be added after a week
½ cup water
½ cup sugar

1. Combine the pitted cherries and vodka in a clean jar to just fit. Wrap the reserved pits in a towel and crush them with a meat pounder or a cleaver. Add them to the jar, cap it, and shake.

2. Soak the cherries for about a week, shaking the jar a few times a day, or whenever convenient.

3. Strain the liqueur through a coffee filter, pressing down hard to extract all the liquid, and discard the cherries and kernels. Return the liqueur to the jar.

4. Prick the unpitted cherries all over with a needle and add to the liqueur. Cap and let stand another week or so, shaking a few times daily.

5. Strain the liqueur again through a coffee filter, this time without pressing on the fruit.

(continued)

6. Bring the water and sugar to a boil and boil for 2 or 3 minutes, then cool completely.

7. Add the syrup to the liqueur and mix well. Cap tightly before storing.

TANGERINE LIQUEUR

Not that we're against the advancement of horticultural science, but citrus breeders now market many hybrid fruits that *look* like tangerines but aren't. They're fine to eat, but the peel lacks the intense, exotic tangerine taste you want for this liqueur. So do a surreptitious scratch-and-sniff test of the skin before you bag your tangerines.

Makes about 2½ cups

6 tangerines
2 cups vodka
½ cup sugar
½ cup water

1. Remove the thin outer, orange-colored skin from the tangerines with a swivel-bladed peeler; avoid the white pith. Spread the peel on a baking sheet or a rack to dry out, which will take from 12 to 36 hours, depending upon the humidity.

2. Put the peel into a jar with the vodka. Let the peel steep for at least a week, shaking the jar daily. Taste now and then to see if the flavor is strong enough. Strain off the liquid, saving the peel for flavoring drinks and sauces.

3. Bring the sugar and water to a boil and boil for 2 or 3 minutes, skimming if necessary. Let the syrup cool.

4. Stir the syrup into the tangerine infusion. Pour the liqueur through a funnel lined with coffee-filter paper into a clean, dry bottle. Cap and store indefinitely at room temperature.

ANISE LIQUEUR

Among the cordials we've made, this one is perhaps closest in character to the genuine article—because of its simple flavoring—particularly when compared to the Spanish and Portuguese brands sampled.

Makes about 3¾ cups

3 cups vodka
3 tablespoons anise seeds
¾ cup sugar
½ cup water

1. In a clean jar with a tight lid, combine the vodka and anise seeds and let stand at room temperature for about 1 to 3 weeks, shaking occasionally. Taste; when the flavor is pleasing, strain the infusion.

2. Combine the sugar and water in a saucepan, bring to a boil, and boil for 2 or 3 minutes, skimming if necessary. Cool.

3. Combine the anise infusion and the syrup and pour through a funnel lined with coffee-filter paper into a clean, dry bottle or jar. Cover and store at room temperature.

Cookies
and Desserts

A Choice of Sweets
Shortbread
"Fig Newtons"
Ladyfingers
Chinese Almond Cookies
Granola Cookies
Pfeffernüsse
Graham Crackers
Zwieback
Almond Toast (Mandelbrot)
Crunchy Anise Toast
Toasted Anise Sponge Fingers
Lemon or Vanilla Wafers
Whole-Wheat Doughnuts
Pound Cake
Gingerbread and Ginger-Cookie Mix
Meringue Shells
Chestnut Dessert Puree
Lemon or Orange Curd
Pudding Mixes
   Chocolate Pudding Mix
   Vanilla Pudding Mix

A Choice of Sweets

As in the other chapters, we are including here recipes for foods that we think are delicious to begin with. Artificially flavored cupcakes (to name one food we *don't* want), filled with greasy-sandy "creme," do not inspire us to create homemade versions of same. On the other hand, real pfeffernüsse, anise toast, zwieback, and mandelbrot are worthy of attention. Obviously, so are real chocolate-chip cookies, fruit-flavored gelatins, and oatmeal cookies, but we think that enough reliable books already have good recipes for those. Adding to the array would only be frosting an already frosted cake.

SHORTBREAD

Properly pale, crumbly, and buttery—and only a moment's work. Because it is so simple to prepare, you can always have really fresh shortbread on hand. Although many cooks advise keeping the pastry for long periods of time, we think it is at its best for only a week. Store at room temperature, in an airtight tin.

Makes 1 pound, or 12 individual wedges

1 ½ sticks (12 tablespoons) unsalted butter, at room temperature
  ¼ cup plus 1½ tablespoons extra-fine granulated sugar, either purchased or made in a food processor (see page 295)
1 ½ cups all-purpose flour
  ¼ cup cornstarch
  ⅛ teaspoon salt

1. Preheat the oven to 325 degrees.
2. In the small bowl of an electric mixer, cream the butter until it is light. Add the ¼ cup sugar and beat until pale.
3. Combine the flour, cornstarch, and salt in a bowl, stirring to mix. With the mixer on low speed, dump the dry ingredients into the butter mixture. Beat just until the mixture forms small, crumbly particles. Do not try to make a smooth mass.

(continued)

4. Pour the crumbly mixture into a 9½-inch fluted tart pan that has a removable bottom and press down firmly to make an even surface. Press the tines of a fork around the edge to make a regular design, then sprinkle the surface with the remaining 1½ tablespoons sugar.

5. Cut the shortbread into 12 even wedges, using a very sharp, thin knife and cutting all the way through to the pan. With a skewer or some other rounded, pointed instrument, make several deep holes in each wedge.

6. Bake the shortbread for 30 to 35 minutes, or until it is just barely colored an ivory-beige. Do not let it brown.

7. Cool for 10 minutes. Remove the rim of the pan, but keep the bottom under the shortbread and cool it completely on a rack. When cooled, cut through the wedge markings again, divide into pieces, and store in an airtight tin.

"FIG NEWTONS"

For the child of any age who has wondered how the filling gets into a fig bar, here's one way that doesn't require a factory full of machinery. The sweet, figgy filling tunnels through tender, puffy pillows of cookie dough to produce a generously overstuffed version of a sweet that's been a favorite for generations.

Makes about 20

Dough:

5 tablespoons unsalted butter, at room temperature
2 tablespoons sour cream
⅔ cup (packed) dark brown sugar, sifted through a coarse sieve
2 eggs, at room temperature
1 teaspoon vanilla extract
2 cups all-purpose flour
2 teaspoons baking powder
½ teaspoon baking soda
¼ teaspoon ground cinnamon
½ teaspoon salt

Filling:

2 cups dried figs, preferably moist-pack black figs
1 ¾ cups water

⅓ cup sugar
2 teaspoons grated lemon rind
¼ teaspoon salt

1. In a small bowl, beat the butter and sour cream until light. Gradually add the brown sugar, beating until the mixture is very light and thick. Incorporate the eggs one at a time; beat in the vanilla.

2. Sift together the flour, baking powder, soda, cinnamon, and salt. Add to the creamed mixture, beating on low speed or by hand. Mix well and turn out on a sheet of floured plastic; wrap, then refrigerate for at least 2 hours.

3. Cut the heavy stems off the figs. Combine the figs and water in a heavy saucepan and simmer, covered, for 30 minutes, or until the fruit is soft. Add the sugar, lemon rind, and salt and simmer, covered, for 15 minutes longer. Press the mixture through the coarse disc of a food mill, then cool.

4. Preheat the oven to 350 degrees. Cover with parchment or lightly grease a large baking sheet.

5. Divide the chilled dough into thirds and refrigerate two parts. Roll the remaining piece on a well-floured board to form a rectangle about 5 × 11 inches.

6. Spread one-third of the fig filling slightly to one side of center, along the length of the dough, covering an area roughly 2 inches wide and 10 inches long and leaving a ½-inch pastry margin on the three sides of the filling away from the center. Mound the filling slightly in the center along its whole length, then moisten the exposed margin with water. Very gently, lift the uncovered pastry with a spatula and fold it over the filling. Press the upper pastry against the lower to seal it. Trim the edges and shape the roll into a neat, half-cylinder form about 11 inches long and 2 to 2½ inches wide. Place on the prepared baking sheet.

7. Repeat the filling operation with the remaining two-thirds of the dough and filling, then bake the three rolls for 25 minutes, or until they are slightly browned.

8. Cool the rolls somewhat on a rack, then trim off the ends and, with a sharp serrated knife, cut each one into slices about 1½ inches wide. Replace the slices on the rack. When the fig bars are completely cool, store them airtight.

LADYFINGERS

Serve versatile ladyfingers as a delicate accompaniment to tea, or with dessert wines or summer fruit compotes; or use them to line a charlotte mold. Slightly sweet, dry yet tender, these ladyfingers have only their name in common with the soft, spongy packaged variety.

Makes 20 to 22

  3 eggs, at room temperature
    Pinch of salt
 ⅛ teaspoon cream of tartar
 ½ cup sugar
  1 teaspoon vanilla extract
    Large pinch of grated nutmeg
 ⅛ teaspoon almond extract
 ½ cup less 1 tablespoon sifted all-purpose flour
  2 tablespoons cornstarch
 ½ cup confectioners' sugar (for sprinkling on top)

1. Preheat the oven to 300 degrees. Cover with parchment (or grease and flour) a large baking sheet (measuring at least 14 × 17 inches), or two smaller baking sheets.

2. Separate the eggs, putting the whites into a medium-sized bowl, the yolks into a small one. Beat the whites with an electric beater until foamy. Add salt and the cream of tartar and continue to beat until soft peaks form. Beat in ¼ cup of the sugar, a tablespoonful at a time, beating for 60 seconds at high speed after adding each spoonful.

3. Without washing the beaters, beat the egg yolks until lightened. Add the vanilla, nutmeg, almond extract, and the remaining sugar. Beat the mixture until very light and thick. Scrape it over the beaten whites and fold together gently.

4. Combine the flour and cornstarch in a small sieve and sprinkle gradually over the eggs, at the same time folding in with a rubber spatula. Fold thoroughly but gently so that the mixture is not deflated.

5. Fit a pastry bag with a ¾-inch plain tube and very delicately scoop half the batter into the bag. Pipe the batter slowly and carefully onto the prepared pan to form ladyfingers about 4 inches long and 1½ inches wide. Sieve the confectioners' sugar evenly over the lady-fingers.

6. Check the oven temperature to be sure it is correct. If using one

sheet, bake the biscuits in the upper third of the oven until they are pale gold, not brown, about 20 minutes. Turn off the oven and let them remain for 5 minutes. If you are using two pans, bake the ladyfingers on the middle and upper levels of the oven for 10 minutes, then turn the pans front to back and switch their shelf positions. Bake for another 5 to 8 minutes, or until the biscuits are pale gold. Turn off the heat and let them remain in the oven for 5 minutes.

7. If your pans are parchment-covered, slip the parchment and biscuits off the sheet and cool 5 minutes, then peel off the parchment and cool the biscuits on a rack. If you are using greased and floured pans, remove the ladyfingers gently with a spatula and place on a rack to cool. Store the cooled biscuits airtight. They will keep for up to 2 weeks.

CHINESE ALMOND COOKIES

A good Chinese almond cookie has a unique texture—dense, sandy, and crunchy. To possess that texture, the cookies must be very rich in shortening. Lard gives a distinctive flavor and crumbliness, so try it before substituting more usual fats. If you have never had the pleasure of a lard pastry, you might be happily surprised.

Makes about 32

½ cup lard, at room temperature
¼ cup solid vegetable shortening
⅔ cup granulated sugar
¼ cup (packed) light brown sugar, sifted through a coarse sieve
 2 eggs
 1 tablespoon almond extract (yes, this is correct!)
2 ½ cups all-purpose flour
 ¾ teaspoon baking soda
 1 teaspoon salt
 2 tablespoons water
 32 whole, blanched almonds or whole apricot pits (which are more traditional; available in health-food stores)

1. In a medium-sized bowl, cream together the lard, vegetable shortening, and sugars until very light and creamy. Beat in one of the eggs and the almond extract.

(continued)

2. Sift together the flour, baking soda, and salt.

3. Beating at low speed if using a mixer, add the flour mixture to the creamed mixture, about one-third at a time. Press the dough together with your hands to form two balls, which you will find to be very crumbly.

4. Place each ball on waxed paper and roll it into a cylinder about 8 inches long. Chill the wrapped dough for several hours, or even overnight.

5. Preheat the oven to 275 degrees. Beat the remaining egg with the 2 tablespoons water.

6. With a sharp serrated knife cut each cylinder into 16 equal slices. Place the rounds on a large, ungreased baking sheet. Brush the cookies with the egg and water mixture and press an almond (or apricot pit) into the center of each.

7. Bake the cookies in the center of the oven for 25 minutes, then raise the heat to 325 degrees and bake the cookies for 10 to 15 minutes longer, or until they are golden.

8. Transfer the cookies to a rack and let cool completely. Store airtight for up to several weeks.

GRANOLA COOKIES

Most appealing—in spite of their "health-food" connotations—these cinnamon- and orange-scented cookies deserve to be included in anyone's baking repertoire. This recipe was developed with our Granola (page 294), but you can use commercial granola if you crumble it thoroughly.

Makes about 4 dozen

        2 cups all-purpose flour
        ½ teaspoon baking soda
        1 teaspoon baking powder
        ½ teaspoon salt
        1 teaspoon ground cinnamon
    1 ½ sticks (12 tablespoons) unsalted butter, at room temperature
        ½ cup (packed) dark or light brown sugar
        ¼ cup granulated sugar

2 eggs
1 ½ teaspoons vanilla extract
½ teaspoon grated orange rind
1 ½ cups Granola (page 294)

1. Sift together into a bowl the flour, soda, baking powder, salt, and cinnamon.

2. Cream the butter until light, then gradually add the sugars and beat until fluffy. Beat in the eggs, one at a time; beat in the vanilla and orange rind.

3. With the electric mixer at its lowest speed (or by hand), add the flour gradually and blend in. Stir in the granola. Chill the dough in its bowl for at least 3 hours, or until firm.

4. Preheat the oven to 375 degrees. Cover with parchment (or grease and flour) a large cookie sheet (11 × 17 inches).

5. To form cookies, take scant tablespoonfuls of dough and roll between the palms of your hands to make balls. Place 24 balls, evenly spaced, on the cookie sheet and flatten each with the bottom of a glass that has been dipped in flour; cookies should be about 1½ to 2 inches in diameter.

6. Bake in the center of the preheated oven for 12 minutes, or until golden. Remove from the pan and cool on racks.

7. Meanwhile, if you have two cookie sheets, prepare the second panful of cookies and bake them as soon as the first panful is done. If the same pan is being reused, let it cool before putting any more of the dough on it. Store the cookies airtight. They will keep for up to 2 weeks.

PFEFFERNÜSSE

These hardy, spicy German Christmas cookies have been softened and simplified in their grocery-store form. You may still purchase the traditional "peppernuts" in some European-style bakeries, but they are available only during the Christmas season and at a pretty steep price. They keep virtually forever—as they are without shortening, but richly spiced—and, like gingerbread, they are welcome all year round. Be sure to let them mellow for several weeks after baking to lose their initial rock-hardness.

(*continued*)

Makes about 50

2 ⅓ cups all-purpose flour
 ¼ teaspoon salt
 ¼ teaspoon finely ground black pepper
 ¼ teaspoon ground cloves
 ¼ teaspoon grated nutmeg
 1 teaspoon ground cinnamon
 ½ teaspoon ground anise seeds
 ½ teaspoon ground cardamom
 ½ teaspoon baking soda
 2 eggs
 ¾ cup (packed) dark brown sugar
 ½ cup dark honey
 1 teaspoon lemon extract
 2 tablespoons very finely chopped Candied Lemon or Orange Peel
   (page 255) or candied citron, chopped with 1 extra tablespoon
   all-purpose flour
 2 to 3 tablespoons hot milk
 ¾ cup confectioners' sugar

1. Sift together the flour, salt, pepper, cloves, nutmeg, cinnamon, anise seeds, cardamom, and soda. Set aside.

2. Beat the eggs in an electric mixer for 3 minutes, or until very light. Beat in the sugar at high speed until mixture is fluffy. Beat in the honey and lemon extract.

3. Incorporate the dry ingredients gradually, together with the candied fruit, then wrap the dough in a sheet of flour-dusted plastic and chill it for at least 1 hour.

4. Flatten the dough on a lightly floured board and cut into 50 to 55 pieces. Form into balls and put onto floured waxed paper. Let stand for 24 hours at room temperature to harden.

5. Preheat the oven to 325 degrees. Cover with parchment (or grease and flour) two cookie sheets.

6. Combine the hot milk and confectioners' sugar to make an icing that spreads easily. Brush the icing over all exposed surfaces of the cookies.

7. Place the cookies about 1 to 1½ inches apart on the prepared cookie sheets and bake for 15 to 20 minutes, or until firm; they will be pale.

8. Cool the cookies on a rack.

TO STORE: Pack the pfeffernüsse airtight and let them mellow for 3 weeks or more. They will keep indefinitely but will be extremely hard at first. If you favor a more friable texture, put a piece of fresh apple into the container with the cookies.

GRAHAM CRACKERS

Many of us did not lose our love for graham crackers upon leaving kindergarten. Although some really good graham crackers are still to be found in the stores, we have noticed with regret the disappearance of honey from the ingredient list on most boxes. We like honey grahams, and we like crackers (cookies?) with a grainy texture and a full wheat-rye flavor.

It is appropriate to drink the classic accompaniment (milk or juice —for those boors unfamiliar with fine American culinary tradition) from a paper cup.

Makes 24 to 28

  1 cup all-purpose flour
¾ cup whole-wheat flour
½ cup rye flour, plus additional for rolling out the dough
  5 tablespoons sugar
½ teaspoon salt
½ teaspoon baking soda
  1 teaspoon baking powder
¼ teaspoon ground cinnamon
  3 tablespoons chilled unsalted butter, cut into small bits
¼ cup solid vegetable shortening
  2 tablespoons honey
  1 tablespoon molasses
¼ cup cold water
  1 teaspoon vanilla extract

1. Blend the all-purpose flour, whole-wheat flour, rye flour, sugar, salt, soda, baking powder, and cinnamon in a bowl. With a pastry blender or your fingertips, work in the butter and shortening until small, even particles are formed.

2. Mix together the honey, molasses, water, and vanilla extract in a small bowl. Sprinkle gradually into the dry ingredients, tossing with a

fork until the liquid is evenly incorporated. Press the dough together into a ball. It may be crumbly, but do not add water. Wrap in plastic and chill for several hours or overnight.

3. Preheat the oven to 350 degrees.

4. Halve the dough. Let soften about 15 minutes.

5. Sprinkle a sheet of waxed paper sparingly with rye flour, place one piece of the dough on top, and flatten it with a rolling pin. Sprinkle lightly with rye flour and top with another sheet of waxed paper. Roll out to form a rectangle roughly 7 × 15 inches, rolling slowly and with even pressure so the crumbly dough does not break.

6. Peel off the top sheet of waxed paper and prick the dough all over at ½- to 1-inch intervals, using a skewer, sharp-tined fork, or a puff-pastry pricker if you have one. Cut into approximately 2½-inch squares. Transfer the squares to a large, ungreased baking sheet with a spatula, placing them very close together—almost touching.

7. Repeat the process with the remaining piece of dough. Reroll and cut the scraps.

8. Bake the crackers in the middle level of the oven for about 15 minutes, or until they brown lightly on the edges.

9. Remove to a rack and let cool completely, then store airtight. Keep for at least 24 hours before serving

ZWIEBACK

Crunchy, toasty, gently nutmeg-scented, and very lightly sweetened, zwieback (the name means "twice-baked") is typical of the cookie-toasts of the rusk family. It is first baked in a loaf, then sliced and dried out in a warm oven.

Some of us have such a deep and abiding affection for these old-fashioned "baby biscuits" that we can't be objective about this recipe. Do remind yourself that zwieback is not just a wholesome biscuit to be gnawed by teething infants. These crisp toasts are marvelous with café-au-lait, or at teatime.

The yield of this recipe is large, but if you're sufficiently fond of them, you'll be glad to have an ample supply.

Makes 90 to 100

¼ cup warm (110-degree) water
½ cup plus 1 teaspoon sugar
 2 packages dry yeast
 2 cups milk

  1 stick (8 tablespoons) unsalted butter, or ½ stick (4 tablespoons)
     unsalted butter plus ¼ cup solid vegetable shortening
  1 teaspoon salt
  ¼ teaspoon ground cinnamon
  ⅛ teaspoon grated nutmeg
  ¼ teaspoon ground mace
  3 eggs, beaten
  1 cup light or medium rye flour
5 ½ to 6 cups unbleached all-purpose flour, or as needed
  4 to 6 tablespoons melted unsalted butter (for baking sheet and tops of
     loaves), approximately

1. Stir together the warm water, the 1 teaspoon sugar, and the yeast
in a small bowl. The mixture will rise to several times its original volume
while you continue.

2. In a saucepan, heat together the milk, ½ cup sugar, butter, and
salt just until the butter has melted. Cool to 100 degrees (or until the
mixture feels barely warm).

3. Combine the milk mixture and the yeast mixture in a large bowl.
Stir in the cinnamon, nutmeg, and mace, then beat in the eggs, then
the rye flour.

4. A cupful at a time, beat in as much as possible of the all-purpose flour. When the dough is too stiff to stir, turn it out onto a pastry surface dusted with flour and knead in the remaining flour, or as
much as necessary to make a smooth, elastic, medium dough, not
too stiff. Knead thoroughly, 5 to 10 minutes. Gather the dough into
a ball.

5. Lightly butter a large bowl and turn the ball of dough about in
it to coat all surfaces. Cover the bowl with plastic wrap and let the
dough rise until it has doubled in bulk, about 1½ hours.

6. Punch the dough down to expel air, cover it again, and let it rise
again until doubled, about 45 minutes.

7. Turn the dough out onto a floured pastry surface, knead it a few
strokes to expel air, and divide it into five equal parts. Form each part
of the dough into a smooth cylinder about 10 inches long, rolling the
pieces under the palms of your hands.

8. Lay the cylindrical loaves crosswise on a large, generously buttered baking sheet (about 11 × 17 inches), leaving 2 inches between
them and an inch of space at each end of the pan. Brush all surfaces of
the loaves with melted butter. Let loaves rise again in a warm place
until they have almost doubled in bulk.

9. While the loaves are rising, preheat the oven to 350 degrees.

(*continued*)

10. Bake the loaves in the center of the oven until they are firm and golden and test "done" when the bottoms are tapped—they will produce a slightly hollow sound. Remove them from the baking sheet and cool them on wire racks.

11. When the loaves are almost cool, reheat the oven to 200 degrees. Slice the cylinders slightly on the bias, into ½-inch slices, about 18 to a loaf. Lay the slices flat, close together, on baking sheets or cake racks and dry them in the preheated oven until they are dry throughout; then raise the oven temperature to 300 degrees and allow them to brown delicately, watching closely lest they overbrown.

12. Cool the zwieback on wire racks. Store the slices in airtight containers. They will keep almost indefinitely.

ALMOND TOAST (Mandelbrot)

A favorite European café nibble, this crunchy-dry, subtly nutty biscuit is at home with ice cream, dried fruit compotes, espresso, or a glass of light red wine.

Makes about 2 dozen

      1 cup whole, unblanched almonds
      2 cups sifted all-purpose flour
  2 ½ teaspoons baking powder
      ½ teaspoon salt
         Large pinch of grated nutmeg
      ¾ stick (6 tablespoons) unsalted butter, at room temperature
      ⅔ cup sugar
      1 teaspoon almond extract
      ½ teaspoon vanilla extract
      2 eggs

1. Preheat the oven to 300 degrees.

2. Spread the almonds on a baking sheet and roast them for 15 minutes, or until barely golden. Remove from the oven and turn the oven heat up to 375 degrees.

3. Sift together the flour, baking powder, salt, and nutmeg. Set aside.

4. In a mixing bowl, cream the butter until it is light. Gradually cream in the sugar until the mixture is light and fluffy. Add the almond

and vanilla extracts, then beat in the eggs, one at a time. Stir in the flour mixture (on lowest speed, if you are using a mixer). Mix in the almonds thoroughly.

5. Smooth foil over a baking sheet measuring at least 11 × 17 inches. Spoon two strips of batter crosswise onto the sheet, equidistant from each other and the ends of the sheet; they should measure about 9 inches in length and 3½ inches in width. Smooth them and even the sides with a flexible spatula dipped in cold water.

6. Bake the strips for 15 to 20 minutes, or until they are pale golden. Slide the foil off the sheet and place the strips on a rack to cool for 15 minutes, having first peeled off the foil.

7. While the strips are cooling, reset the oven heat to 300 degrees.

8. With a very sharp serrated knife, cut the almond toast carefully into slices ¾ inch wide and lay them flat, very close together, on the baking sheet.

9. Return the biscuits to the oven for 15 minutes, then turn them over and bake for 15 minutes longer, or until they are golden.

10. Cool the almond toast on a rack. Pack airtight; it will keep for a month.

CRUNCHY ANISE TOAST

Unlike the Toasted Anise Sponge Fingers (see the following recipe), these toast strips are like zwieback in shape and are rather substantial. To our way of thinking, this cookie is the consummate coffee companion, especially with a strong, dark French- or Italian-roast coffee.

Makes 4 dozen

2 ¼ cups sifted all-purpose flour
2 ½ teaspoons baking powder
 ½ teaspoon salt
 ¾ stick (6 tablespoons) unsalted butter, at room temperature
 ¾ cup sugar
1 ½ teaspoons anise extract
 2 teaspoons anise seeds
 2 eggs
 ¼ cup milk

1. Preheat the oven to 375 degrees. Cover a large baking sheet (14 × 17 inches) with foil.

(continued)

2. Sift together the flour, baking powder, and salt. Set aside.

3. Cream the butter in a mixing bowl. Add the sugar gradually and cream well. Beat in the anise extract and anise seeds, then the eggs, one at a time. Add the milk and beat briefly.

4. Mix in the dry ingredients (on low speed, if you are using a mixer) until the dough is too stiff to beat. Stir in the remainder by hand.

5. Spoon the dough onto the baking sheet to form three crosswise strips about 10 inches long and 2 inches wide. Smooth the top and sides of the dough with a flexible spatula dipped in cold water.

6. Bake for about 15 to 18 minutes, until light gold. Remove the strips from the sheet with a large spatula and cool on a rack, having removed the foil.

7. Reset the oven temperature to 300 degrees.

8. Using a thin serrated knife in a gently sawing motion, cut each strip into about 16 slices. Arrange the slices flat on the cookie sheet, close together, and bake them for 20 minutes. Turn the slices and bake for 15 minutes longer, or until they are golden.

9. Cool the toasts on a rack. Stored airtight, the toasts will keep for a month or so.

TOASTED ANISE SPONGE FINGERS

These biscuits have the same flavoring, anise (which one either adores or loathes) as crunchy Anise Toast (see the preceding recipe), but they are otherwise quite different. The sponge fingers are crumbly, light, and eggy. They should be served with very delicate desserts—possibly coffee, vanilla, or orange mousse or a Bavarian cream.

Makes about 4 dozen

    4 eggs plus 1 egg yolk
      Pinch of salt
⅔ cup sugar
    1 teaspoon vanilla extract
    1 cup all-purpose flour
    1 teaspoon baking powder
    1 tablespoon anise seeds, slightly crushed in a mortar or spice mill

1. Preheat the oven to 350 degrees.

2. In the large bowl of an electric mixer, beat the eggs, egg yolk, salt, sugar, and vanilla at high speed until very thick, fluffy, and light—like whipped cream (about 15 minutes).

3. Sift together the flour and baking powder, then sift a bit of the mixture at a time into the eggs, folding it in gently with a rubber spatula. When almost all of the flour has been added, fold in the anise seeds.

4. Line the bottom of an ungreased jelly-roll pan (10 × 15 inches) with waxed paper. Pour in the batter and smooth into a uniform layer.

5. Bake for 20 to 25 minutes, until the top is light brown and springs back when pressed lightly. Let cool in the pan for 5 minutes, then run a knife around the edge to loosen the cake and invert it onto a rack. Pull off the paper and let the cake cool.

6. Place on a cutting surface and halve lengthwise. Trim off the brown edges, then cut each piece in half crosswise. Cut each quarter crosswise into 12 strips, using a serrated knife.

7. Reheat the oven to 250 degrees.

8. Lay the slices on their sides, barely touching, on a very large baking sheet. Rebake for about 20 minutes, or until the slices are dry but not colored. Turn the slices over and rearrange them so that the center pieces are now near the edge of the pan. Bake for about 20 minutes longer, or until very slightly golden.

9. Cool on a rack. Store airtight. The biscuits will keep well for at least several weeks.

LEMON OR VANILLA WAFERS

We have happy childhood taste-memories of these most innocent of cookies, a permitted treat when we were very young. And we still maintain a certain fondness for the packaged hard-baked, golden wafers. Our recipe produces a crisp-edged, pale ivory disc with a tender center. Good enough for children, as well as adults.

Makes about 4½ dozen

¾ **cup sugar**
1 ½ **sticks (12 tablespoons) unsalted butter, at room temperature**
½ **teaspoon salt**
⅓ **cup egg whites (approximately 3, but varies with egg size)**
2 **teaspoons grated lemon rind** *or* 2 **teaspoons vanilla extract**
1 ⅓ **cups cake flour**

1. Preheat the oven to 375 degrees. Cover with parchment (or lightly grease) two large baking sheets (each 14 × 17 inches).

(continued)

2. Blend the sugar, butter, and salt in a bowl just until mixed. Gradually add the egg whites and incorporate well; add the lemon rind (or the vanilla). Sift in the cake flour (blending on low speed, if you use a mixer), and mix well.

3. Half-fill a pastry bag fitted with a plain ½-inch tube. Pipe flattened rounds about 1½ inches in diameter 2 inches apart on one of the prepared baking sheets; there should be about 28 cookies.

4. Bake for about 12 to 15 minutes, or until the cookies have a narrow brown rim and have turned a pale ivory.

5. While the cookies are baking, pipe the remaining half of the batter onto the second baking sheet. Remove the first batch from the oven, carefully transfer to a rack, and let cool.

6. Bake the second batch and cool. Store airtight.

WHOLE-WHEAT DOUGHNUTS

Although good recipes for homemade doughnuts will always produce an immeasurably better product than doughnut factories do, we have provided a recipe for only one variety to represent an American favorite that must now include a flavor roll call that numbers in the hundreds. Any number of fine cookbooks will give you tried and true recipes for at least several kinds. But rarely—if ever—will you run into a good recipe for our own personal preference, whole-wheat doughnuts.

Makes about 18

    1 egg
    ¼ cup (firmly packed) light brown sugar, sifted through a coarse sieve
    ¼ cup granulated sugar
    3 tablespoons unsalted butter, melted and cooled
    ½ teaspoon vanilla extract
1 ¼ cups all-purpose flour
    1 cup medium or fine whole-wheat flour (not the coarse kind)
    1 tablespoon baking powder
    ¼ teaspoon salt
    ¼ teaspoon ground mace
    ¼ cup unprocessed coarse bran
    ¾ to 1 cup milk, as needed
      Solid vegetable shortening (for frying the doughnuts)
    ½ cup sugar mixed with 2 teaspoons cinnamon (for coating the
      doughnuts)

1. Beat together the egg and the sugars until thick and light. Beat in the butter and vanilla.

2. Sift together the flours, baking powder, salt, and mace. Stir in the bran.

3. Add the flour mixture to the egg-sugar mixture, alternating it with the ¾ cup milk. Stir to combine the ingredients into a soft dough, adding as much more of the milk as necessary to achieve this. Mix just until the dough is the proper consistency; do not overbeat or the doughnuts will be tough. Form the dough into a rough rectangle, wrap in floured plastic, and refrigerate for at least 1 hour.

4. Over moderate heat, in a deep-fryer or kettle, begin heating enough solid vegetable shortening to make a depth of 3 inches.

5. Roll the dough out on a pastry cloth or floured board to a thickness of ⅜ to ½ inch. Cut with a 2½-inch doughnut cutter, or use a round plain cookie cutter and cut a center hole with a bottle cap or shot glass. (Keep the centers.) Continue cutting and rolling until the dough is all cut.

6. The temperature of the deep fat should be 375 degrees on a deep-frying thermometer. Drop a few doughnuts into it, leaving plenty of room for them to swell. (A good-sized deep-fryer will usually take about four at a time.) Keep an eye on the thermometer the whole time; if you let the fat get too hot, the doughnuts will be burned on the outside and raw inside. If the temperature is too low, the doughnuts will be greasy and soggy. Fry the doughnuts for about 2 minutes on each side —the cut-out centers will take less time to fry.

7. Remove the doughnuts with tongs to a rack covered with paper towels. Let them drain while you put in the next batch to fry.

8. Mix the coating of sugar and cinnamon in a paper bag. Drop in the drained doughnuts, shake the bag vigorously to coat them, and return them to the rack.

9. Continue in this way until all the doughnuts and centers are fried; eat within a day. If you wish to keep the doughnuts longer, let them cool completely, then wrap closely, seal, and freeze.

TO REHEAT: Place the doughnuts on a baking sheet in a preheated 350-degree oven for 15 minutes, uncovered. Eat warm. Freezing keeps the doughnuts very well; they do not get soggy, as you might expect.

POUND CAKE

The cellophane-wrapped cake slices that have been around forever on lunch counters and snack-food racks are the illegitimate heirs of a simple, noble pound cake with a fine grain and melting texture. Recipe herewith.

Makes 1 loaf cake

1 ½ sticks (12 tablespoons) unsalted butter, at room temperature
⅔ cup cake flour
¾ cup all-purpose flour
¼ teaspoon salt
¼ teaspoon ground mace
¼ cup liquid (either milk; orange juice plus 1 teaspoon grated orange
    rind; brandy; sherry; or dark rum)
 3 eggs, at room temperature
¾ cup granulated sugar
   Optional: Confectioners' sugar (for sprinkling on top)

1. Preheat the oven to 350 degrees. Grease and flour a 4- to 5-cup loaf pan.

2. Cream the butter till light and smooth; sift in the flours, salt, and mace, beating. Gradually add the liquid and beat well.

3. With clean beaters, beat the eggs and granulated sugar on high speed in the small bowl of an electric mixer until the mixture is tripled in volume, about 10 to 12 minutes.

4. With the mixer on lowest speed, add the egg mixture to the butter-flour mixture, about a quarter at a time, beating to just combine thoroughly; do not overmix.

5. Turn the batter into the prepared pan and bake in the center of the preheated oven for 1 hour, or until the cake tests "done"—a cake tester or a toothpick inserted into center will emerge dry.

6. Cool the cake in the pan for 10 minutes, then run a knife around the edges and remove the cake from the pan. Cool completely on a rack; wrap in plastic, and keep for 24 hours or more before serving. If you like, sift confectioners' sugar on top before serving.

GINGERBREAD AND GINGER-COOKIE MIX

Although most mixes somehow don't seem completely respectable to us, some of them are worth having on hand. By just being there in the cupboard, this particular mix can be comforting: you know you have the makings of an impromptu fresh-baked dessert or a supply of soft, glossy, warm-brown cookies for unexpected guests.

Try serving the old-fashioned, light-molasses gingerbread topped with some of your homemade Sour Cream (page 63), Crème Fraîche (page 62), or even Yogurt (page 64). If yours is a gingerbread-loving household, doubling the recipe for the mix may be a good idea.

Makes 5 cups of mix, enough for 2 pans of gingerbread
or about 8 dozen cookies

1 cup sugar
4 teaspoons ground coriander
3 ½ teaspoons baking powder
3 teaspoons ground ginger
2 teaspoons ground cinnamon
1 teaspoon salt
½ teaspoon baking soda
½ teaspoon ground cloves
4 cups sifted all-purpose flour

1. Measure all the ingredients except the flour into a large bowl and mix them with a whisk until the mixture is completely uniform.

2. Add the flour and mix again until no streaks of the spice mixture can be seen.

3. Divide the mix into two batches (2½ cups each) and store it airtight, at room temperature, in either plastic bags or jars.

GINGERBREAD

Makes 1 eight-inch-square cake

1 cup boiling water
¾ stick (6 tablespoons) unsalted butter, cut into small bits
¾ cup light unsulphured molasses
½ batch (2½ cups) Gingerbread and Ginger-Cookie Mix (see above)
1 egg plus 1 egg yolk

1. Preheat the oven to 350 degrees (325 degrees if you are using a glass baking pan). Butter and flour an 8 × 8-inch baking pan.

(continued)

2. Combine the boiling water, butter bits, and molasses. Stir until the butter has melted. Let cool to lukewarm.

3. Empty the mix into a bowl and stir in the lukewarm liquid. Beat the egg and the egg yolk until they are well mixed and stir them into the batter.

4. Scrape the batter into the prepared pan and bake for about 45 minutes, or until the top is springy when the center is pressed lightly or a cake tester emerges dry from the center.

5. Cool the gingerbread in the pan. Serve it warm or at room temperature.

GINGER COOKIES

Makes about 4 dozen 2¹/₂-inch cookies

½ stick (4 tablespoons) unsalted butter, melted and cooled
⅔ cup light unsulphured molasses
2 eggs, beaten just until well mixed
½ batch (2½ cups) Gingerbread and Ginger-Cookie Mix (see above)

1. Preheat the oven to 375 degrees. Butter two large cookie sheets (each 14 × 17 inches).

2. Mix the butter and the molasses thoroughly in a bowl, then mix in the beaten eggs. Stir in the mix, blending the dough just until the dry ingredients are well dampened.

3. Drop the dough by teaspoonfuls onto the baking sheets, leaving 2 inches between cookies. Bake the cookies in the preheated oven for 6 to 8 minutes, or until their centers are springy when pressed lightly with a finger.

4. Remove the cookies from the pans and cool them on racks. When the cookies are completely cool, store them airtight.

MERINGUE SHELLS

Make these when you have an abundance of leftover egg whites and a bit of time. Keep the shells on hand as an elegant base for a variety of desserts—filled with ice cream, fruits, Lemon or Orange Curd (page

249), or with Chestnut Dessert Puree (page 248) that has been lightened with cream or custard and topped with whipped Crème Fraîche (page 62).

Makes about 12 shells

    4 egg whites
 ¼ teaspoon cream of tartar
    Pinch of salt
 1 teaspoon vanilla extract
1 ⅓ cups confectioners' sugar

1. Preheat the oven to 200 degrees. Cover with parchment a large baking sheet (14 × 17 inches).

2. In the large bowl of an electric mixer, beat the whites until foamy. Add the cream of tartar and salt and beat for 30 seconds on high speed. Add the vanilla and beat for 30 seconds more. Add the confectioners' sugar, 2 to 3 tablespoons at a time, beating for at least 30 seconds after each addition.

3. Fill a pastry bag fitted with a plain ½- or ⅜-inch tube (or use a ½-inch star tube) with one-quarter of the mixture. Pipe six discs onto the parchment-covered baking sheet, making each about 3½ inches in diameter and ½ to ¾ inch thick. Fill the bag with another quarter of the mixture and pipe six more discs. To form a raised edge on each shell, put the remaining egg-white mixture into the bag and pipe a ring atop the perimeter of each round. Or use a star tube and make an edge of rosettes set closely together.

4. Bake the meringues for 2 hours and turn off the oven. Leave in the closed oven for several hours or overnight. Store in airtight containers. These keep for ages, as long as they are kept dry.

COFFEE-FLAVORED MERINGUE SHELLS

If you would like coffee-flavored shells to fill with Vanilla Ice Cream (page 70) and Dark Chocolate Sauce (page 160), replace the vanilla with 2 teaspoons of instant espresso powder dissolved in a teaspoon of water.

CHESTNUT DESSERT PUREE

Although there are decent sweetened chestnut purees available in the market, they do not compare in subtlety of texture or flavor with what you can make at home. There are certainly many other cookbooks with recipes for fine purees, but they are most often recipes that go on to turn the puree into some other dessert form. This recipe is for a chestnut puree that may be served as is, or combined with liquors, creams, custards, and the like to make more elaborate preparations—an all-purpose chestnut dessert base, in other words. It is also included here to remind you, in case you have forgotten, that these wonderful nuts, which have a relatively short season, freeze very well. Therefore, this recipe is for a quite large amount—because if you are going to spend the time to make the puree, you might as well make a worthwhile quantity.

Makes about 8 cups thick puree

4 pounds large, heavy chestnuts (watch out for worm holes)
4 cups water, more if necessary
3 cups sugar
1 vanilla bean, split
   Optional: milk or cream (to thin the puree)

1. Halve the chestnuts with a heavy knife or cleaver. Place them in a very large skillet or saucepan and add enough water to cover them. Boil for about 10 minutes, or until the shells can easily be removed.

2. Preheat the oven to 350 degrees.

3. Remove the chestnuts, a few at a time, from the water. Peel off the shells and husks, and place the nuts in a large, heavy saucepan. Add the water, sugar, and vanilla bean to the pan and stir to mix in the sugar. The liquid should just cover the chestnuts. (Add more water if it doesn't.)

4. Bake uncovered for 2 to 3 hours; the time will vary considerably, depending upon the dryness of the nuts. Stir the nuts every 30 minutes, adding water, if necessary, until they are very tender and the syrup is very thick.

5. Let the chestnuts cool completely in the syrup, then puree them in batches in a food processor, adding milk or cream if you want to have a thinner purée. Press the entire mixture through the fine disc of a food mill. Divide the puree among 1- or 2-cup freezer containers. Seal, date, and freeze.

LEMON OR ORANGE CURD

Although perhaps not familiar to some in the United States, this thick, eggy, tart-sweet spread or pastry filling has long been a favorite on tea tables all over the British Isles. Also known as lemon butter or lemon cheese, it can be found in markets alongside the imported jams and jellies. As it can be made economically in your own kitchen and it keeps admirably, make a supply and try using it on crisp toast, as a filling for layer cakes or cookie sandwiches, or in tiny tartlets.

Makes 1½ cups

  1 cup sugar
  ¾ stick (6 tablespoons) unsalted butter
  ⅓ cup fresh lemon juice or orange juice
  1 tablespoon finely grated lemon rind or orange rind
  3 eggs plus 1 egg yolk

1. In the top of a double boiler, combine the sugar, butter, juice, and rind. Stir over moderate direct heat until the sugar melts.

2. Beat together the eggs and the egg yolk and strain into the hot mixture, stirring constantly. Cook over barely simmering water for 15 to 20 minutes, stirring often, or until the mixture has thickened a good deal; it will become thicker when cool.

3. Pour into a jar or bowl, cover tightly with buttered waxed paper tied with a string, and chill immediately. The curd will keep for up to 3 weeks.

Pudding Mixes

Either you like pudding or you don't. If you do, you will probably be pleased to have on hand these remarkably inexpensive powders that, in addition to their superior natural flavors, have none of the chemical stabilizers found in packaged mixes. Our recipes for the finished puddings give you a rather soft, creamy consistency. If you prefer a stiffer pudding, reduce the liquid.

CHOCOLATE PUDDING MIX

Makes 4 one-cup batches, each enough for about 4 servings

2 ¼ cups instant dry milk
  1 cup sugar
  ½ cup cornstarch, measured without packing
  ⅔ cup unsweetened cocoa, measured and then sifted
  ¼ teaspoon salt

1. Combine all the ingredients and mix thoroughly (a whisk works well).
2. Divide into 1-cup batches in 4 plastic bags. If you have any mix left after dividing it (the exact yield depends on how much air has been whisked in), divide it among the bags. Store, tightly closed, at room temperature. The mix will keep for months if the bags are kept in a covered container.

CHOCOLATE PUDDING

Makes 4 servings

  1 batch (1 cup) Chocolate Pudding Mix (see above)
  1 cup water
  1 cup milk
  1 tablespoon unsalted butter
  ½ teaspoon vanilla extract

1. Put the mix in a heavy medium-sized saucepan, then gradually stir in the water and the milk. Bring to a boil over medium heat, stirring constantly. Simmer 1 minute, stirring vigorously and constantly.

2. Remove from the heat and stir in the butter and vanilla. Strain into four individual serving dishes, cover lightly with plastic, and chill.

MOCHA PUDDING

For a mocha pudding, use 1 cup strong coffee instead of the water.

VANILLA PUDDING MIX

Makes 4 batches, each enough for about 4 servings

3 cups instant dry milk
1 ½ cups sugar
1 ½ cups cornstarch, measured without packing
1 ½ teaspoons salt

1. Combine all the ingredients and mix them thoroughly with a whisk, being sure to blend well.
2. Divide the mix into 1-cup batches, pouring each into a small plastic bag. If any of the mix is left over (the exact amount you'll have after mixing depends upon how vigorously you have whisked), divide the remnant among the batches. Close the bags securely and store them in a closed container; the mix will keep for months.

VANILLA PUDDING

Makes 4 servings

1 batch (1 cup) Vanilla Pudding Mix (see above)
¾ cup milk
1 ¼ cups water
1 egg, beaten just to mix
1 teaspoon vanilla extract
1 tablespoon unsalted butter, cut into bits

1. Empty the mix into a medium-sized heavy saucepan and slowly whisk in the milk and the water.
2. Cook, stirring, over moderate heat until the pudding thickens and small bubbles show around the edges. Cook for 2 minutes longer, stirring constantly.
3. Remove from the heat. Add the vanilla to the beaten egg; whisk

into this about ½ cup of the hot pudding, stir, then add another ½ cup of pudding. Return this mixture to the saucepan and whisk until blended. Whisk in the butter bits.

4. Strain into four individual serving dishes, cover lightly with plastic, then chill.

Candies
and Confections

A Confection Selection
Candied Lemon, Orange, or Grapefruit Peel
Candied Pineapple
Candied Cherries
Candied Pear Slices
Crystallized Mint Leaves
Crystallized Violets
Apricot Leather
Apple Leather
Jelly Apples (Candy Apples)
Almond Paste
Almond Brittle
Almond Butter Crunch
Peanut Brittle
Sesame Crunch
Caramel Corn with Peanuts
Caramels
Marshmallows
Orange Jellies
Lollipops or Hard Candy Drops

A Confection Selection

There are a number of candies that can be made at home that we have left out (quite arbitrarily), as this book would have been oversweet-toothed if we had begun to represent a fair amount of what is commercially produced, since such a large proportion of "store-bought" is in candyland.

We have limited ourselves here to describing how to make candies that do not require special milling, molding, drying, or heat-controlling equipment. Unfortunately, that excludes the possibility of making jelly beans, gumdrops, really good candy bars, halvah, licorice, and a few other favorites. But we *have* been able to create a delectable array of candies, including Almond Butter Crunch (page 268), Marshmallows (page 273), Peanut Brittle (page 269), Caramels (page 272), and real-fruit Orange Jellies (page 274).

CANDIED LEMON, ORANGE, OR GRAPEFRUIT PEEL

Pungent citrus peels, softened by simmering in syrup, then dried with a thin, crisp coating of granulated sugar are just plain *wonderful,* if you ask us. We find that this fruity, bittersweet old-fashioned confection is one of the few that can hold its own with good, strong after-dinner coffee. And think how virtuous you'll feel when you transform otherwise wasted peels into such a delicacy.

Makes about 1 pound

    6 lemons, approximately, or 2 medium-large grapefruit or 4
        medium-large oranges, preferably navel oranges
1 ½ cups sugar
1 ½ cups water
    6 tablespoons light corn syrup
    Granulated regular or extra-fine sugar (for coating the candied peel),
        if extra-fine, either purchased or made in a food processor (see
        page 295)

(continued)

1. With a sharp knife, score the skin of the fruit (use only one kind to a batch) into quarters, then peel it off with your fingers, keeping the white pith attached to it.

2. Lay each quarter of skin on a cutting board and, with a heavy knife, cut on the bias into uniform strips from ⅛ to ¼ inch wide, according to preference; you should have 3 cups of strips.

3. Cover the peel with a generous amount of water in a saucepan and bring to a boil over medium heat. Boil for a minute, then drain in a colander, rinse, and repeat the boiling and rinsing twice (three boilings in all). Then cover with fresh water and simmer the peel for 20 minutes. Drain and set aside.

4. In the saucepan, make a syrup with the sugar, water, and corn syrup. Boil for about 2 minutes, then add the peel. Simmer briskly, stirring occasionally, until the syrup is considerably reduced, then watch constantly.

5. The point of decision: If you like fairly tender candied peel, cook the syrup down until perhaps 2 or 3 tablespoons are left, then drain the peel (the syrup can be saved for another use). For medium-firm candied peel, leave only a spoonful of syrup, then drain. For candy-like, crisp peel, cook, watching closely, until syrup is on the point of hardening and has almost vanished.

6. With a long fork arrange the peel—at whatever stage you have stopped the cooking—on a bed of sugar on a jelly-roll pan. Straighten the strips while hot if you like them symmetrical, or tumble them in the sugar if you prefer a kinky tangle. Sprinkle more sugar over the strips of peel and toss them occasionally as they cool.

7. When cool enough to handle, put the strips, separated, onto cake racks and let them dry. The consistency of the finished candy will depend partly on the point at which cooking stopped, but also on how long the strips are left to dry. They will keep indefinitely if candied "hard"; not quite as long if left flexible and translucent. This choice is yours. Store the candied peel in plastic bags or containers, closely covered.

CANDIED PINEAPPLE

Pineapple packed in its own juice can be used without compunction for candying; no need to start with the fresh fruit. When you have candied the pineapple chunks, save the syrup to use as a base for fruit punch.

Makes about 1½ pounds

2 cans (15 ounces each) pineapple chunks packed in juice
⅓ cup light corn syrup
2 cups sugar
   Extra-fine granulated sugar (for coating the pineapple), either
      purchased or made in a food processor (see page 295)

1. Drain pineapple well in a sieve, saving the juice.

2. Measure 1 cup of the juice into a wide enameled or stainless-steel skillet. Add the corn syrup and sugar and boil until the syrup spins a short thread (that is, when a little syrup tipped from a spoon over the pot forms a filament 2 or 3 inches long, instead of dripping from the spoon).

3. Add the pineapple chunks and cook at a simmer until the pineapple is translucent, up to 45 minutes. Remove from the heat and let stand 12 hours, or overnight.

4. Return the syrup and fruit to a boil, stirring once or twice. Boil for a minute or two, then set the pan aside to cool again.

5. If the syrup is very thick, remove the chunks of pineapple with a fork and place them on a cake rack covered with cheesecloth and let them start to dry. If the syrup is thin, remove the fruit to a bowl, boil the syrup again until it spins a short thread, return the fruit, and let it cool again. Remove the pineapple pieces to the rack.

6. Let the pineapple pieces dry in a warm, dry room or in an oven heated only by a pilot light. After they look glazed—a matter of several hours—remove them from the cloth and complete the drying on the wire rack.

7. When the chunks are almost dry, sprinkle them on all sides with extra-fine sugar. Continue to dry them until they are not at all moist but still pliant. Store the candied fruit in a closed cardboard box or a plastic storage container in layers separated by waxed paper. It will keep for months.

CANDIED CHERRIES

These firm candied cherries taste like fruit, not like chemicals, and are a natural garnet color, not the brilliant artificial cerise or crimson shade of the commercial product. They keep well—they're neither syrupy nor sticky—and can be used to enliven fruited cakes or puddings. Or you may serve them straight, as a sweetmeat. If you want to double the recipe, be sure your pan will hold the fruit in a single layer. If it won't, use two pans.

Makes 1 half-pint jar

1 cup stemmed and pitted fresh, ripe cherries
   Water to cover
2 cups sugar
⅓ cup light corn syrup

1. Put the cherries in a single layer in a shallow stainless-steel or enameled pan. Add water just to cover them, then simmer until the fruit is barely tender. Drain thoroughly, reserving the juice.

2. Rinse and dry the skillet and measure into it 1 cup of the cherry cooking water; add the sugar and corn syrup. Boil, covered, for 2 or 3 minutes. Uncover, add the drained cherries, and simmer gently, turning the cherries a few times with a large spoon, just until the fruit becomes translucent.

3. Shake the pan occasionally as the cherries cool, then cover. Let the cherries stand in the syrup for 12 hours or overnight. (This rest permits the syrup to permeate the fruit.)

4. Bring the cherries to a full boil and cook for about 3 minutes, shaking the pan back and forth constantly, until the syrup is thick.

5. Cover a large cake rack with cheesecloth. Lift the cherries from the syrup with a fork and place them, well apart, on the rack to drain for several hours, or until they look slightly dry. (Save the flavorful syrup for another use.) Store the cherries at room temperature in a sterilized jar with a sterilized, airtight lid. They will keep for at least 6 months.

CANDIED PEAR SLICES

Pears might not be the first fruit that leaps to mind when one thinks of candying, but the process intensifies their delicate flavor and turns their flesh rosy-amber. As with other candied fruits, the leftover candying syrup should be saved for sweetening other fruits or in a drink.

Makes about 1½ pounds

4 cups peeled, cored, and sliced firm-ripe pears, cut into six segments each (about 2½ pounds before preparation)
2 cups water
1 tablespoon lemon juice
⅓ cup light corn syrup
2 cups sugar
   Extra-fine granulated sugar (for coating the fruit), either purchased or made in a food processor (see page 295)

1. As you prepare the pear segments, drop them into the mixed water and lemon juice in a wide stainless-steel or enameled skillet or pan. Simmer just until fruit is tender, then drain carefully, reserving the liquid.

2. Measure 1 cup of the cooking liquid and mix it in the wide pan with the corn syrup and the sugar. Boil until the syrup spins a short thread (that is, when a bit of syrup tipped from a spoon over the pan will form a filament 2 to 3 inches long, instead of dripping from the spoon). Add the pears and cook at a simmer until the slices are translucent. Remove from the heat and shake the pan occasionally as the fruit cools, then cover. Let stand overnight in the syrup.

3. Drain the syrup off the fruit and boil it again until it forms a short thread. Return the pears to the pan and bring to a boil, then set the pan aside and let the fruit cool, shaking the pan occasionally. The syrup should be quite thick by now. If not, remove the fruit and reboil the syrup until it spins a short thread. Return the fruit and let it cool in the syrup.

4. Lift the pear slices with a fork onto a cake rack covered with cheesecloth. Let them dry in a turned-off oven heated only by a pilot light, or in another warm, dry spot, until they are no longer moist but still pliant. After several hours, drying can be speeded up by moving the slices onto another, uncovered wire rack.

5. When the slices are almost dry, sprinkle them on both sides with extra-fine sugar, which will speed the drying somewhat. Complete the drying. Store the candied pears in a closed plastic or cardboard box in layers separated by waxed paper. They will keep for many months.

CRYSTALLIZED MINT LEAVES

For this confection you need fresh-picked leaves, ideally gathered several hours after a rain shower, when they are freshly washed but not moist. Any of the good garden mints may be candied. We especially like peppermint leaves—smaller than most kinds—but spearmint, apple mint, and bergamot or orange mint are all flavorful when preserved this way.

Freshly picked mint leaves
1 egg white, at room temperature
Few drops of water, if needed
Extra-fine granulated sugar, either purchased or made in a food processor (see page 295)

1. Pull or clip each mint leaf from the stalk, leaving, if possible, a short stem on the leaf (some kinds of mint grow almost directly from the main stalk).

2. With a fork, beat the egg white in a saucer until it is spreadable (a few drops of water may be added if the white seems very viscous). Have at hand a plate on which to "paint" the leaves, a plate of extra-fine sugar, and a cake rack, covered with waxed paper.

3. Using a small paint brush, cover every surface of a leaf with the egg white in as thin a layer as possible (tweezers will help in holding the leaf). As you coat each leaf, lay it on the sugar and sprinkle more sugar over it until it is evenly coated. Lift it to the cake rack and continue until all the leaves are coated.

4. Set the rack of leaves in a warm, dry place, such as an oven heated by a pilot light. When the leaves are superficially dry (they'll still be moist inside), transfer them to an uncovered rack and continue to dry them, if necessary for several days, until no moisture shows when a crisp leaf is broken open. Store in layers, separated with waxed paper, in a cardboard box. Kept dry, the leaves will keep for many months.

CRYSTALLIZED VIOLETS

Any kind of violets, wild or from the garden, may be candied, but scented ones (if you can find them—violet scent is going the way of the fragrant rose) will taste the best. Any will be beautiful to look at, whether on a plate of confections or used as decorations on small cakes.

> **Freshly picked violets, with their stems left on**
> **1 egg white, at room temperature**
> **Few drops of water, if needed**
> **Extra-fine granulated sugar, either purchased or made in a food**
> **processor (see page 295)**

1. Unless violets are dusty—unlikely in the fresh springtime—don't wash them. Leave the stems on for the time being (you'll clip them off later). Assemble a saucer on which to paint the flowers and one for the egg white, a small paint brush, a thin skewer or a cake tester, a plate for the sugar, and a cake rack covered with waxed paper.

2. Beat the egg white in a saucer until foamy, if necessary adding a few drops of water to make it more spreadable.

3. Holding a violet by its stem, dip it into the egg white, then lay the flower on your "painting" saucer and carefully spread the egg white on every surface with the small brush, using the skewer to open up the petals. Then transfer the flower to the plate of sugar and, again using the skewer to hold the petals open, sprinkle every surface with sugar, making sure none is missed. Arrange the flower on the cake rack, using the skewer to put the petals in a natural position and sprinkling on a little more sugar if you disturb the surface. Clip the stem off with scissors. Continue until all the flowers are coated.

4. Set the rack in a warm, dry place, such as an oven heated by a pilot light, to let the flowers dry. When they are partially dry, transfer them to an uncovered cake rack and continue to dry them, if necessary for several days, until they are dry throughout (check a specimen to be sure that the green base of the bloom and the heart of the flower are completely without moisture). Store in layers, the flowers separated and covered by soft paper, in a cardboard box. They will keep indefinitely if stored in a dry place.

APRICOT LEATHER

Preserving fruit by this ancient method yields a fragrant, nutritious confection that has never gone out of style. Although generally considered a children's snack in this country, glowing, translucent apricot leather is appreciated by all family members in Middle Eastern homes. Fresh apricots are usually difficult to obtain in prime condition in the United States and are enormously expensive, so we have used the flavorful dried fruit.

If you own a dehydrator or a convection oven, by all means use either one (following manufacturer's instructions) to speed up the drying process.

Makes 1 sheet

½ pound dried apricots, preferably Turkish (but any kind will do)
1 cup water
**2 to 6 tablespoons light corn syrup, depending upon the sweetness of
    the fruit**
2 tablespoons lemon juice
1 drop almond extract

1. Combine the apricots and water in a heavy saucepan and bring to a boil over moderate heat. Lower the heat, cover, and cook at a bare simmer for about 30 minutes, or until the apricots are soft and have absorbed nearly all the water.

2. Press the fruit through the medium disc of a food mill and return it to the saucepan. Add the corn syrup, beginning with 2 tablespoons, and the lemon juice. (The necessary sweetening varies considerably from one batch of fruit to another, so taste for the right amount.)

3. Stir over moderate heat for 4 or 5 minutes, or until the mixture is a thick mass that pulls away from the sides of the pot when it is stirred. Add the almond extract.

4. Line a 10 × 15-inch baking sheet with plastic wrap, folding the ends of the wrap under the ends of the pan and securing them with tape. Gently spread the paste over the plastic, as thinly and evenly as possible. This is a rather slow, sticky job; with patience you will have an almost translucent sheet.

5. Put the pan in an oven heated only by a pilot light. (If you have no pilot, turn on the oven briefly at its lowest setting, turn it off, then place the pan in the warmed oven; repeat the warming occasionally.) Let the paste dry for 2 or 3 days, until it is almost entirely dried through.

6. When the apricot leather is almost totally dry, remove it from the oven, peel it carefully from the plastic, flip it over, and let it dry a few more hours, or until smooth to the touch, with no damp spots. Then lay it on a fresh sheet of plastic and roll it up together with the plastic; close the ends and store. The leather will keep for months.

NOTE: Put a sign on the oven door to warn yourself to remove the leather when you heat the oven for other uses. Return the leather to continue drying only when the oven has cooled off to barely warm.

APPLE LEATHER

The apple, a cold-weather cousin of the exotic, warmth-loving apricot, makes an equally delicious fruit leather. Preparing the fruit pulp in this way intensifies the flavor and aroma—imagine the sweet fragrance of lightly spiced apple pie concentrated in a thin, shiny strip.

Although we have given a recipe for a single panful, it's reasonable, because of the long drying time, to make a double amount if you have two pans. It is also reasonable to use a convection oven or dehydrator, if you have either, to facilitate the drying procedure.

Makes 1 sheet

2 ½ pounds baking apples
  2 to 3 tablespoons apple juice (or water)
  ⅓ to ⅔ cup light corn syrup, to taste
    Ground cinnamon or ground coriander to taste (optional)

1. Quarter and core the apples and chop them roughly. Cook the apples and juice (or water) in a large, heavy pot, covered, over moderately low heat for 20 to 30 minutes, or until the apples are soft, stirring occasionally.

2. Press the fruit through the medium disc of a food mill. Return the pulp to the pot with ⅓ cup of the corn syrup. Stir over moderate heat for about 30 minutes, until the mass is thick and sticky and leaves the

sides of the pan when stirred; the time will vary according to the moisture content of the apples. As the mixture cooks, taste for sweetness and add more corn syrup as desired. Add cinnamon or coriander to taste, if you wish.

3. Line an 11 × 17-inch baking sheet with plastic wrap, folding the ends of the wrap under the ends of the pan and sealing them in place with tape. Spread the apple mixture over the pan in as smooth and thin a layer as possible, using a spatula.

4. Put the pan in an oven heated by a pilot light. (If you have no pilot light, turn on the oven briefly at its lowest setting, turn it off, then place pan in the warmed oven; repeat the warming occasionally.) Leave the leather in the oven for 2 or 3 days, or until no longer sticky. Peel the leather from the plastic, flip the sheet over, and let the underside dry in the oven for a few hours longer. The leather should be smooth, pliant, but not damp.

5. Lay the leather on a sheet of fresh plastic wrap, roll it up together with the plastic, and close the ends. If properly dried, the leather will keep for months.

NOTE: While you're drying the apple leather, put a sign on the oven door, or a label on the oven control, reminding yourself that the oven isn't empty. Remove the pan before heating the oven for other uses, and let the oven cool down to barely warm before you continue the drying.

JELLY APPLES (Candy Apples)

One of those sweets of childhood that signifies a special occasion to us —like candy canes, or half chocolate–half vanilla ice-cream cups. If you know any experimental candy-apple eaters (most tend to be conservative), you might try the surprisingly delicious combination of flavors that we prefer—anise-flavored candy coating over tiny Golden Delicious or Granny Smith apples.

Makes about 12 apples, plus lollipops

2 cups sugar
½ cup light corn syrup
⅔ cup water

2 teaspoons fruit-flavored extract or 1½ teaspoons spice or herb
    extract (anise, mint, cinnamon, etc.)
  Optional: Food coloring
12 very small apples, at room temperature, with sticks or skewers stuck
    into the stem ends

1. Combine the sugar, corn syrup, and water in the top part of a double boiler and stir over moderate direct heat until the syrup is clear and boiling. Wash down the sides of the pot with a wet brush to remove any crystals.

2. Boil the syrup briskly, without stirring, until it reaches 250 to 260 degrees on a candy-jelly thermometer. Lower the flame and boil the syrup gently until it registers 300 degrees on the thermometer. Remove the pot from the heat and stir in the flavoring and coloring you have chosen.

3. Set the syrup over gently simmering water and spread out a large sheet of aluminum foil.

4. Quickly dip an apple into the syrup, leaving uncandied an area about 2 inches in diameter around the stem. Place the apple on the foil and repeat the process with the next apple. When the syrup gets too low to dip the apples, drop spoonfuls on the sheet of foil to make lollipops (which are the same recipe).

NOTE: Be sure you don't touch the syrup at any time. It burns treacherously.

ALMOND PASTE

There is enormous confusion about the differences between what we call "almond paste" and what some confectioners call "marzipan," and manuals on candy aren't much help. Some would call our recipe one for marzipan, others would say, as we do, that it's almond paste. By whatever name, you can use the paste made by this recipe in pastry and cake fillings, as well as to make small candy shapes that you can tint, if you like, using a small brush and food coloring.

The advantage of this paste over most of the versions available in shops is the absence of certain inexpensive fillers and excessive bitter almond extract that compromise the delicacy of the flavor. Those with nineteenth-century leanings might prefer rose water to the almond extract in the recipe. Well wrapped and refrigerated, the paste will keep for many months.

Makes about 14 ounces

½ pound whole, blanched almonds
  2 tablespoons water (for processing the almonds)
  1 cup sugar
½ cup water (for the syrup)
  2 tablespoons light corn syrup
¼ teaspoon almond extract, or more to taste

1. Preheat the oven to 250 degrees and spread the blanched almonds on a baking sheet. Bake them, stirring them frequently, until they are heated through but not browned.

2. While the almonds are still hot, put them into the container of a blender or a food processor and grind them as fine as possible, adding the 2 tablespoons water gradually and stopping and scraping down the sides of the container occasionally. When you pinch a bit and feel no coarse grain, the nuts are fine enough.

3. In a small saucepan, combine the sugar, ½ cup water, and corn syrup. Boil without stirring until the syrup reaches 235 degrees on a candy-jelly thermometer. Remove from the heat and stir in the flavoring.

4. Start the blender or food processor and add the hot syrup in a thin stream through the feeder opening in the cover. Continue to process until the mixture is uniform.

5. Cool the almond paste and pack it into a jar, or wrap it in plastic, and allow it to ripen in the refrigerator for a week or more before using it.

NOTE: If it is necessary to soften the almond paste after storage, heat it, wrapped in foil, in a steamer over boiling water, or place it, unwrapped, in the upper part of a double boiler over boiling water, just until it is pliable enough to use.

ALMOND BRITTLE

An abundance of nuts bound together in a sheet by the merest slick of transparent amber brittle. The chopped almonds modify the hardness of the candy, while the whole nuts are left unblanched to contribute a fuller almond flavor.

Makes about 1¼ pounds

1 ¾ cups whole, unblanched almonds
1 ⅓ cups blanched, chopped almonds
 ¾ cup (packed) light brown sugar
 ⅔ cup light corn syrup
 ¼ cup water
 ¼ teaspoon salt
 1 tablespoon unsalted butter
 ½ teaspoon vanilla extract
 ¼ teaspoon almond extract

1. Preheat the oven to 325 degrees.

2. Place the whole and chopped almonds on a jelly-roll pan and toast them for 15 minutes in the oven, tossing and stirring them occasionally. Turn off the heat and leave the nuts in the oven. They must be warm when added to the syrup.

3. In a heavy 1½-quart saucepan, stir together the brown sugar, light corn syrup, water, and salt. Swirl over high heat until the sugar dissolves, washing down the sides of the pan with a wet brush to remove any sugar crystals. Boil to 290 degrees on a candy-jelly thermometer, without stirring.

4. Meanwhile, butter a large baking sheet and a metal spatula.

5. When the syrup is ready, remove from the heat and stir in the hot nuts, then the butter, vanilla, and almond extract.

6. Pour the candy onto the baking sheet and press it out as flat as possible with the spatula. Let cool.

7. Remove the brittle from the pan and break into serving pieces. Pack airtight and store it for 24 hours before serving to let the flavor improve. It will keep for many weeks.

ALMOND BUTTER CRUNCH

One of the world's great candies when impeccably fresh—a state you can assure by making your own, starting with whole, unblanched almonds. (Remember to store your supply of almonds—or any other nuts —in the freezer.)

This rich, buttery-chocolaty-nutty confection deserves to be served with after-dinner coffee, as a dessert in its own right.

Makes about 1¾ pounds

¾ cup whole, unblanched almonds
1 ½ cups finely chopped, unblanched almonds
1 ¼ cups sugar
⅓ cup light corn syrup
⅓ cup water
 1 stick (8 tablespoons) unsalted butter
 1 stick (8 tablespoons) margarine
½ teaspoon salt
¼ teaspoon baking soda
 4 ounces dark sweet chocolate
 2 ounces (2 squares) unsweetened baking chocolate
 1 teaspoon tasteless vegetable oil

1. Preheat the oven to 300 degrees.
2. Toast the whole almonds on a baking sheet, and the chopped almonds in a baking pan, until each batch is barely colored—about 10 minutes for the chopped nuts and 20 minutes for the whole ones. Cool the whole almonds for 10 minutes, then chop them coarsely. Return to the baking sheet in the turned-off oven to keep warm. Cool the finely chopped nuts.
3. In a heavy pan, combine the sugar, corn syrup, and water and bring to a boil over medium heat, stirring. Cover and simmer for 2 minutes. Add the butter and margarine and stir until melted. Boil over moderate heat, stirring occasionally, until a candy-jelly thermometer reads 240 degrees. Continue to cook, stirring constantly, until the thermometer reads 300 degrees.
4. While the candy is cooking, butter a baking sheet and warm it slightly; butter a metal spatula.
5. Remove the candy mixture from the heat and add the salt, soda, and the warm chopped almonds; stir. Pour onto the slightly warmed,

buttered baking sheet and spread out ¼ inch thick with the buttered metal spatula, keeping to a rectangular shape. Set the pan on a cake rack and let the candy cool slightly, until it is somewhat set but still warm and pliable.

6. Using a large knife or a cleaver, score the candy into 1½ × 2-inch pieces. Immediately go back over the scorings, cutting through the candy and moving the pieces slightly apart, one row at a time, first in one direction, then the other. Let the candy cool completely.

7. In a double boiler over simmering water, melt the chocolate with the oil. Stir to blend, then cool to 85 degrees.

8. Push the candy pieces back together as closely as possible. Pour the chocolate over the reassembled sheet of candy, spreading it evenly with the back of a pancake turner. Cover the chocolate with the finely chopped almonds, pressing them in.

9. Let the chocolate set; if the process seems slow, you may want to separate the pieces (it doesn't matter if some chocolate has run underneath to coat the bottoms) and place them on cake racks for several hours, covered with paper towels. Pack the candy in layers, separated by plastic or waxed paper, in an airtight container in the refrigerator or freezer.

PEANUT BRITTLE

The real thing. Glassy-thin, salty-sweet, a thick layer of small peanuts encased in a crackly amber brittle. Use raw peanuts, which are available in all health-food stores, as roasted ones would become overbrowned while cooking in the candy mixture.

Makes about 1¾ pounds

1 ½ cups sugar
  1 cup light corn syrup
  ½ cup water
  3 tablespoons unsalted butter
2 ¼ cups raw, shelled, and skinless peanuts (the smaller the better—
     Spanish peanuts are fine if you can get them)
  ¾ teaspoon salt
  ¼ teaspoon baking soda
  ¾ teaspoon vanilla extract

1. In a heavy saucepan, combine the sugar, corn syrup, and water and bring to a boil over moderate heat, stirring. Wash down any crystals

on the sides of the pan with a brush dipped in water.

2. Add the butter and cook over moderately high heat, without stirring, until a candy-jelly thermometer registers 250 degrees. Add the nuts and cook, stirring, until the mixture reaches 300 degrees.

3. While the candy is cooking, butter a cookie sheet and a metal spatula.

4. Remove the candy from the heat. Stir in the salt, soda, and vanilla, then spread the candy as thin as possible on the cookie sheet, using the spatula. Cool the sheet of candy for a few minutes, then turn it over on the cookie sheet with the spatula.

5. Stretch the candy with your hands (wear gloves, if necessary), pulling firmly in all directions until it has at least doubled in area and halved in thickness. Start by stretching the edges first, as they cool and become brittle first, and work toward the center. Don't mind holes—the candy will be broken up anyway.

6. Cool the candy completely, then break it into pieces. Store airtight. It will keep for months.

SESAME CRUNCH

Small, thin rectangles; golden, brittle, shiny, and nutritious—as candies go.

Makes about 1¾ pounds

  2 cups hulled sesame seeds
1 ¼ cups sugar
  ½ cup light corn syrup
  ¼ cup water
  2 tablespoons unsalted butter
  ¼ cup honey
  ⅛ teaspoon salt
  ⅛ teaspoon vanilla extract

1. Preheat the oven to 300 degrees.

2. Spread the sesame seeds on a jelly-roll pan and bake for about 5 minutes, or until seeds are a cream-beige, stirring a few times. (Do not overbake, as the seeds will continue to brown later in the syrup.)

3. In a heavy 3-quart saucepan, combine the seeds, sugar, corn syrup, water, butter, honey, and salt. Bring to a full boil over moderate

heat, stirring constantly. Boil without stirring until a candy-jelly thermometer in the syrup reads 295 degrees.

4. While the candy is cooking, butter a baking sheet and a metal spatula.

5. Remove the pan from the heat and stir in the vanilla. Pour the candy onto the prepared sheet and very quickly spread it with the spatula to an even thickness of about 1/8 to 1/4 inch.

6. With a sharp, heavy knife, score the brittle into 1-inch squares. Let it cool completely.

7. Lift the sheet of candy from the pan and break it into pieces. Store in an airtight container with sheets of waxed paper between the layers. Sesame crunch will keep for weeks.

CARAMEL CORN WITH PEANUTS

Good crunchy peanuts and corn, a crisp molasses-flavored glaze, and you have a version of one of America's favorite nibbles. Homemade, it's never stale, and has as many peanuts as your heart desires.

Makes about 6 to 7 cups

2 quarts (8 cups) freshly popped corn
1/2 cup raw, shelled, and skinless peanuts, preferably the small Spanish ones
1/4 cup (firmly packed) light brown sugar
3 tablespoons unsalted butter
1/4 cup light corn syrup
1/4 cup light molasses
1/2 teaspoon salt
1/4 teaspoon vanilla extract
1/4 teaspoon baking soda

1. Preheat the oven to 250 degrees.

2. Spread the popcorn in a large, well-buttered roasting pan. Sprinkle the peanuts on top and set the pan aside.

3. In a heavy saucepan, combine the sugar, butter, corn syrup, molasses, and salt. Stir over moderate heat until the mixture boils. Continue boiling gently, without stirring, until a candy-jelly thermometer in the syrup reads 250 degrees. Remove from the heat and stir in the vanilla and baking soda.

4. Pour the syrup over the popcorn and peanuts and rapidly mix with a spatula to coat the pieces evenly.

5. Bake the caramel corn in the preheated oven for 1 hour, stirring occasionally, then cool the candy in the pan.

6. Slip the cooled candy out of the pan with a spatula and break into fairly large chunks. Store airtight for up to about a week.

CARAMELS

If the voluptuous-masochistic pleasure of coping with caramels is one of your vices, you—and your teeth—might as well contend with the genuine article.

Makes 1 1/4 pounds

1 cup sugar
1 cup light corn syrup
2 tablespoons water
1/2 stick (4 tablespoons) unsalted butter
3/4 cup evaporated milk, scalded
1 teaspoon vanilla extract
1/4 teaspoon salt

1. In a heavy saucepan, combine the sugar, corn syrup, and water. Stir over moderate heat until the mixture boils and becomes clear. Wash down the sugar crystals on the sides of the pan with a wet brush.

2. Boil the syrup over high heat until its temperature reaches 250 degrees on a candy-jelly thermometer. Stir in the butter, a tablespoon at a time. Turn the heat down to moderate and add the evaporated milk gradually—in about six parts—boiling and stirring constantly until each addition is thoroughly incorporated.

3. Continue boiling the syrup, stirring often, until the thermometer registers 245 degrees (the temperature will have dropped with the addition of the milk); this usually takes about 10 minutes. Remove from the heat and stir in the vanilla and salt. Cool for 2 minutes.

4. Lightly grease a baking sheet. Pour the caramel mixture onto the sheet, placed on a rack. As the candy begins to cool down—in about 5 minutes—form it into a 7-inch square with a buttered spatula or your hands. Cool until firm throughout, about an hour.

5. Place the candy on a board and cut it into eight strips, using a sharp, serrated knife and cutting with a rapid sawing motion (cut in any other fashion, the caramels will stick together). Separate the strips as you cut them. Cut each strip into eight pieces, again separating the pieces as you cut them apart.

6. Immediately wrap each square in plastic or waxed paper. Pack airtight; the caramels will keep for months.

MARSHMALLOWS

Among the oldest living citizens are some who claim to recall marshmallows that tasted like marshmallows—tender, vanilla-scented pillows that melted in the mouth. If you have an electric mixer, such marshmallows are ridiculously easy to re-create and marvelously cheap.

Makes 3 dozen

⅟₄ cup cornstarch
⅓ cup confectioners' sugar or, preferably, powdered Vanilla Sugar
    (page 296)
 1 envelope unflavored gelatin
⅓ cup water
⅔ cup granulated sugar
⅟₂ cup light corn syrup
    Pinch of salt
 1 teaspoon vanilla extract

1. Sift the cornstarch and confectioners' (or powdered vanilla) sugar into a bowl. Lightly grease an 8 × 8-inch square baking pan and sprinkle 1 tablespoon of the cornstarch and sugar mixture into it. Tilt the pan in all directions to coat the sides as well as the bottom. Leave any excess in the pan.

2. Sprinkle the gelatin into the water in a small saucepan and let soak for 5 minutes. Add the granulated sugar and stir over moderately low heat until the gelatin and sugar dissolve.

3. In the large bowl of an electric mixer, combine the gelatin mixture, corn syrup, salt, and vanilla and beat for 15 minutes on high speed, until peaks form.

4. Spread the fluffy mixture in the prepared pan and smooth the top. Leave for 2 hours, or until set.

5. With a wet knife, cut the marshmallow mixture into quarters and

loosen around the edges. Sprinkle the remaining cornstarch and sugar mixture on a baking sheet and invert the marshmallow blocks onto it. Cut each quarter into nine pieces and roll each one in the starch and sugar.

6. Place the marshmallows on a cake rack covered with paper towels and let them stand overnight to dry the surface slightly. Store airtight; the marshmallows will keep for a month.

ORANGE JELLIES

Modern cooks may quail at the notion of boiling a gelatin mixture actively for a considerable time, but in this recipe it works beautifully. Intrigued by a recipe in a gelatin pamphlet from the early part of the century, we tried the unorthodox method we found therein and adapted it for the making of an old favorite.

These sugar-sanded jellies, made with fresh citrus juice and rind, are particularly light and fresh tasting, sparkling clear and of a tender, not bouncy, consistency. And they keep very well, given a chance.

Makes about 1 1/4 pounds

2 cups sugar
3 envelopes unflavored gelatin
1/2 cup water
1/4 cup strained lemon juice
1/2 cup strained orange juice
 Pinch of salt
1 1/2 tablespoons grated orange rind
1 1/2 teaspoons grated lemon rind
 Extra-fine granulated sugar (for coating the candies), either purchased or made in a food processor (see page 295)

1. In a heavy saucepan, stir together the granulated sugar, gelatin, and water. Set the pan over medium heat and bring to a boil, stirring constantly. Boil for 15 to 20 minutes, or until the mixture spins a short thread (that is, when a little syrup poured from the spatula forms a filament 2 or 3 inches long instead of dripping from the spoon). Remove from the heat.

2. Add the lemon juice, orange juice, and salt to the hot sugar mixture. Let it cool.

3. Add the grated orange and lemon rinds, then pour the mixture

into a 9 × 5-inch loaf pan that has been rinsed with cold water. Let stand until very firm, 4 hours or more.

4. Run a blunt knife, dipped into water, around the sides of the pan. Invert a baking sheet over the pan and, holding the two together, turn out the candy.

5. Using a serrated knife dipped in cold water, cut the candy into cubes. Separate the pieces and sieve extra-fine sugar over them, then roll the cubes in the sugar to coat them generously.

6. Arrange the sugar-coated jellies on a cake rack, cover with a cloth, and allow the sugar coating to dry for several hours. (The time needed will depend on the humidity; it may be as much as 8 to 12 hours.) Store in a cardboard box or on a sheet of cardboard enclosed in a paper bag. The candies will keep well for several weeks.

LOLLIPOPS OR HARD CANDY DROPS

Shiny, smooth, and hard—not brittle, so they won't break into shards. If you happen to like hard candy grownup-style, make small drops without sticks. Lollipop sticks are sold by suppliers of confectionery ingredients (see Mail-Order Sources of Supplies, page 309). The same suppliers also have more powerful flavorings available than the ones sold in the market. They give a more intense taste, if you prefer, and should be used in small doses.

Makes about 3 dozen 2-inch pops or 6 dozen drops

⅔ cup water
½ cup light corn syrup
2 cups sugar
2 teaspoons vinegar
2 teaspoons fruit-flavored extract, or 1½ teaspoons spice or herb extract (anise, mint, cinnamon, etc.)
Food coloring (optional)

1. Combine the water, corn syrup, sugar, and vinegar in the top part of a double boiler. Cook over moderate direct heat, stirring until the syrup is clear and boiling. Cover the pot and let it bubble gently for 3 minutes.

2. Uncover the pot and keep the syrup at a rolling boil until its temperature reaches 260 degrees on a candy-jelly thermometer. Turn

down the heat slightly and boil the syrup gently until the temperature reaches 300 degrees.

3. While the syrup is cooking, heat water to simmering in the bottom part of the double boiler.

4. When the syrup reaches 300 degrees, remove it from the heat and stir in the flavoring extract and optional food coloring.

5. Set the pot of syrup over the simmering water. Carefully spoon teaspoonsful of the mixture (or tablespoonsful, depending upon the size you wish) onto a very lightly greased cookie sheet or a smooth, flat sheet of aluminum foil (not greased) laid on an absolutely flat working surface. (If it's not flat the syrup will make distorted shapes, not rounds.) Press a stick into the hot candy as you pour out each lollipop.

6. Let the lollipops cool until hard, about 30 minutes, then pull them gently off the baking sheet. Or, if you are using foil, pull the foil off the pops. Place the lollipops or candy drops, not touching, in an airtight container with waxed paper between the layers. They will keep almost indefinitely if protected entirely from moisture.

Omnium-Gatherum

. . . Or What Have We Here?
Sprouting
Mung-Bean Sprouts
Soybean Sprouts
Alfalfa Sprouts
Bean Curd
Sauerkraut
Grape Leaves (Vine Leaves) in Brine
Pumpkin Seeds, Salted and Roasted
Salted Roasted Almonds
Shredded Coconut
Salted Coconut Chips
Peanut Butter (and Variations)
Tahini (Sesame Paste)
Dried Sweet Corn
Granola
Extra-fine Granulated Sugar and Confectioners' Sugar
Vanilla Sugar (Granulated or Powdered)
Vanilla Extract
Lemon Extract
Noodling
Egg Noodles
Green (Spinach) Noodles
Whole-Wheat Noodles
Buckwheat Noodles
Egg "Spaghetti" or "Lasagne"

... Or What Have We Here?

This chapter is a raggle-taggle, bob-tailed, snaggle-toothed critter composed of what we couldn't bear to leave out—things that found no proper place in any of the preceding chapters.

Sprouting

It's possible that a few benighted souls in the United States have not heard of the tremendously high nutritive value, delicious flavor, and unbelievably low cost of sprouted beans and other seeds. It is a shame that many have relegated sprouts to the realm of "health food," considered to be good for the body but dull for the taste buds. They lend crisp texture and a fresh, earthy taste to mixed greens; Sprouts provide a springy cushion upon which to arrange foods; and the larger, crunchy sprouts are wonderful when blanched and tossed in a salad, or stir-fried in the Chinese fashion.

Almost any seed can be sprouted, from such exotics as fenugreek and sesame to the hearty lentil and soybean. We've chosen three useful, all-purpose sprouts to represent this category, but you can experiment at whim with all kinds of seeds. The general principles and procedures apply to all.

EQUIPMENT

A quart jar covered with nylon mesh or several layers of cheesecloth held in place with a screw band (or a stout rubber band) makes a good sprouter if it is kept out of the light (as should be any untinted transparent container). Some sprouting devices made of clear plastic have, in our experience, produced rather dark and tough sprouts because of the light admitted when the manufacturer's instructions were followed; we've noticed that the maker has recently begun to tint the plastic. For sprouting a moderate quantity of seeds—enough for 2 to 3 cups of sprouts—a quart jar is large enough. Need more sprouts? Use another jar; don't put more than ¼ cup of seeds in a single jar.

MUNG-BEAN SPROUTS

These are "the" sprouts, the ones you'll get when you ask for "bean sprouts," fresh or canned. They're middling in size, in between the horsey soy and the ephemeral alfalfa. They find their way into the Chinese cuisine on every level, from the simplest snack through salads to exquisite banquet dishes for which their roots (perfectly edible, if not symmetrical) are nipped off for added elegance.

Incidentally, "cellophane noodles," also known as "powdered silk," "long rice," "bean threads," "sliver noodles," and "pea-starch noodles," among other names, are made from mung beans—which are actually peas.

Makes 2 to 3 cups

¼ cup mung beans (available at most supermarkets and all health-food stores)
  Water as needed

1. Pick the beans over carefully, removing any broken ones. Rinse them, then soak overnight in tepid water to cover by about 2 inches. By morning they will have swelled to triple the original measure.

2. Drain the beans completely, put them into the sprouter, and put on the mesh cover. Set the container upright (or lay it on its side) in a dark spot—in a cupboard, or under an upturned pot or bowl on the counter.

3. At least twice each day (better three or four times), fill the container with cold water (if the weather is warm) or tepid water (in cold weather) and rinse the beans well. Drain them completely before returning the sprouter to its dark place. Always rinse the beans the first thing each morning; the other rinsings can be at convenient times.

4. After 3 to 5 days (sometimes sooner), the beans should have produced sprouts from 1½ to 2 inches long, the size we like them (although they can be used when smaller). The leaves may be quite developed or rudimentary, depending upon the time that has elapsed.

5. Empty the sprouts into a shallow pan and flood it with water to

float off the light hulls (which are rather tough) into the sink. Discard any seeds that haven't sprouted. If you wish to let the leaves of the sprouts turn green (many consider that this adds to their nutritiousness), leave the ready-to-eat sprouts in a sunny spot for a few hours in a closed jar (to protect them from drying).

6. Refrigerate, well drained, in a plastic bag. If any water accumulates in the bag at any point, rinse the sprouts and drain them thoroughly. They will keep, refrigerated, for up to 5 days.

SOYBEAN SPROUTS

Soybeans are among the earth's most nutritious foods, and even more so sprouted than when dry. As they are considerably larger than mung beans, they require a bit more hovering over to prevent spoilage. Be sure to pick out and remove any split or decaying seeds you may spy while rinsing them.

Makes about 2 cups

**¼ cup dried soybeans, preferably yellow-hulled and of the most recent
    crop (ask your supplier)
Water as needed**

1. Pick the beans over carefully, removing any broken ones. Rinse them, then soak overnight in tepid water to cover by about 2 inches. They will swell considerably.

2. Drain the beans completely and put them into the sprouter and put on its mesh cover. Set the jar upright (or lay it on its side) in a dark cupboard or under an upturned pot or bowl on the counter.

3. At least four times a day, fill the jar with cool water (in warm weather) or tepid water (in cold weather), rinse the seeds well, then drain them completely before returning the jar to its dark spot. Always be sure to rinse the beans first thing in the morning; rinsings during the day needn't be at fixed intervals.

4. The sprouts are ready to use as soon as they are ¼ inch long (in 3 to 5 days), but you may prefer to let them grow to as much as 1½ inches. If you do, continue to rinse and drain on the same schedule.

5. Empty the sprouts into a shallow pan and flood it with water to float off the hulls into the sink. Remove any unsprouted beans. If you want to "green up" the leaves of the sprouts, place the sprouts in a

closed jar (to prevent drying out) in a sunny spot for a few hours.

6. Refrigerate the sprouts, well drained, in a plastic bag. If any water accumulates in the bag at any time, rinse and drain the sprouts very thoroughly again and return to the refrigerator. They will keep for up to 5 days.

TO USE: Serve soy sprouts cooked, but never overcooked. They should be subjected to heat just long enough to lose their raw flavor, but never their crispness.

ALFALFA SPROUTS

Tiniest of sprouts, and many sprout fanciers say the best. Delicate, tendril-like, with a fleeting mossy undertaste. They need less attention than some other sprouts and cost a fraction of the price of the store-bought ones. Use them raw in salads and sandwiches.

Makes about 2 cups

¼ cup alfalfa seeds
  Water as needed

1. Soak the seeds for 4 to 5 hours in tepid water to cover (these seeds are very small, and it's important not to oversoak).

2. Drain the seeds completely and put them into the sprouting jar; put on the net cover. Set the jar upright or lay it on its side in a dark cupboard or under an upturned pot or bowl on the counter.

3. Twice or three times a day, fill the container with cold water (in warm weather) or tepid water (in cold weather) and drain all of it out. Return the jar to its dark spot. Repeat, always being sure to rinse the sprouts first thing in the morning and then at various times during the day for 2 or 3 days, or until the spouts are about 1 inch long and ready to eat.

4. Rinse and drain the sprouts again and remove any unsprouted seeds you can spot. If you wish, let the leaves become green by setting the sprouts, in a covered jar, in a sunny spot for a few hours.

5. Refrigerate the sprouts, well drained, in a plastic bag. If water accumulates in the bag at any point, rinse and drain the sprouts thoroughly before returning them, in a plastic bag, to the refrigerator. They will keep for about a week.

BEAN CURD

Professionally made fresh bean curd is almost always good and also inexpensive, but it isn't available everywhere. Make your own bean curd only if you can't find it for sale.

After considerable experimentation, we have come up with a reliable way to make smooth and toothsome bean curd. The raw materials —dried soybeans from the supermarket or a health-food store, and Epsom salts from the druggist—are widely available, and the chief item of equipment needed—a blender—is in almost every kitchen.

Made our way, bean curd, or *tofu* (Japanese) or *dow fu* (Chinese), has the rather firm texture preferred for most Chinese dishes. If you want softer bean curd in the Japanese style, weight and drain it just to the point where it will hold together.

Makes about 2 pounds

1 pound (2 cups) dried soybeans
Cold water
2 teaspoons Epsom salts (magnesium sulphate), dissolved in 1 cup cold
    water
Water as needed

1. Soak the soybeans overnight, or for about 12 hours, in 5 cups of cold water. Drain the soybeans and rinse; you will have about 7 cups.

2. Into the jar of a blender, put 1 cup of beans and 2 cups of cold water. Process the beans at high speed, covered, until the mixture is velvet-smooth. Empty the jar into a large bowl and repeat with batches of the remaining soybeans and water until all have been pureed.

3. Set a large colander over a pot and line it with a sheet of dampened cheesecloth. Pour about one-third of the puree into the colander. Twist the ends of the cloth together and press and squeeze the contents to extract the "milk." The pulp—the lees—will become pasty and yield no more milk. Discard the pulp and repeat the extraction with another batch; you should have about 12 cups of liquid.

4. Heat the soy milk over moderate heat, stirring often. Bring it to a full boil, then reduce the heat and simmer, stirring, for 2 minutes. Set the pot off the heat.

5. Line two 8-inch-square ceramic or glass baking dishes with two layers of dampened cheesecloth measuring about 14 × 18 inches.

(continued)

6. Stir into the hot soy milk the solution of Epsom salts and water. The mixture will curdle alarmingly, but don't be alarmed(!). Pour it into the lined baking dishes, fold the surplus cheesecloth loosely over the top, and allow the mixture to cool.

7. With a large pancake turner, pat down the top of the bean curd to firm it somewhat; liquid will rise to the surface. Holding the cheesecloth firmly, lift the cloth and its contents onto a flat surface. Wrap the block of soft curd as closely as possible in the cloth. Put each block onto the bottom of the inverted baking dish you used for a mold (set this on a drainboard or in a big baking pan to catch drips) and weight it with another baking dish or other large, flat utensil.

8. Let the liquid drain from the curd, gradually adding weight (such as cans of food) to the covering pan until you have about 2 pounds' weight at work firming each sheet of the curd.

9. When the curd seems to have nearly stopped draining, make the cloth wrapping snug and square up the sides if they need it. If the curd is a bit soft, allow it to drain longer with the weight back in place. When it is as firm as you like it—in 2 to 6 hours—remove the weights and cloth and cut the curd into 2-inch squares. Carefully lift the pieces into a storage container (use a pancake turner) and cover them gently with cold water.

TO STORE: Store the bean curd in the refrigerator, uncovered, changing the water every other day. It will keep for at least a week.

SAUERKRAUT

Fresh sauerkraut is a revelation in taste and texture if you have experienced only the canned kind, which is (through no fault of its own) too soft and too acid. Making your own crisp, pale-gold kraut is quite feasible as soon as "winter" cabbage—the kind with firm, white heads —is in the market. (Don't use green, early-maturing kinds.)

Traditional methods call for covering the salted cabbage with a cloth and a sterile board, plus weights, to keep the brine above the level of the cabbage as it ferments. But some unsung genius has discovered that water enclosed in a heavy plastic bag may be used instead to keep out air and to weight the cabbage, eliminating the need for the cloth, board, and tedious scalding procedure. House temperature—from the mid-60s to a maximum of 72 degrees—is ideal for fermenting cabbage at the correct rate.

Makes about 3 quarts

6 pounds firm, white "winter" cabbage, approximately
2 ounces fine white pickling salt or coarse (kosher) salt, more if needed
  Water, if needed

1. Remove any green or blemished leaves from the cabbage and quarter the head(s). Cut out the cores. Weigh out 5 pounds (set aside any surplus for another use).

2. Using the shredding blade of a mandoline, a "slaw cutter," or a sharp knife on a board, shred the cabbage into the thinnest and longest strands possible.

3. If you're using the coarse salt, process it in a blender or food processor until very fine.

4. In a large bowl, mix the cabbage very thoroughly with the salt, using your hands or a wooden spoon. Let stand about 15 minutes, until the cabbage has wilted and juices have started to run.

5. Pack the cabbage into a clean 1-gallon crock or jar, pressing it down firmly with your hands, an old-fashioned wooden potato masher, or the bottom of a jar. Keep pressing and packing until the juice comes above the surface of the cabbage, but don't be energetic enough to crush it.

6. Enclose a large, strong plastic bag (of the kind meant to be used with food) inside another of the same size and pour a quart or so of cold water into the inner bag. Set the doubled bag on top of the cabbage and add enough more water to the inner bag to expand it and weight the cabbage sufficiently to prevent any air from reaching the surface. Twist the necks of the bags together and fasten them with a wire twist.

7. Set the crock in a spot where the temperature won't exceed 72 degrees (too much warmth can cause spoilage). Check the crock daily (warning: it will be odoriferous for a few days). When fermentation is well under way, bubbles will appear. If at any point there isn't a covering of brine, add a little extra brine in the proportions of 2 teaspoons of coarse salt to a cupful of water. Fermentation will be complete in from 8 or 9 days to several weeks, depending on the temperature of the environment and how tart you like your kraut. When the flavor pleases you, it's done. Store the sauerkraut in jars, covered, in the refrigerator, where it will keep for months, or can it, as follows:

(continued)

Following the Pointers on Preserving on pages 153–56, fill clean, hot canning jars with sauerkraut and juice that has been heated just to simmering (about 190 degrees), leaving ½ inch of headspace. Cover with two-piece lids and fasten the screw bands. Set the jars on a rack in a deep kettle half filled with boiling water and add more boiling water to cover the caps by 2 inches. Process at a boil for 15 minutes for pints, 20 minutes for quarts. Cool the jars and store in a cool, preferably dark, place.

GRAPE LEAVES (VINE LEAVES) IN BRINE

If either wild or cultivated grapes grow nearby (the variety doesn't matter), you may preserve a supply of leaves for later use in Middle Eastern dishes. The process is simple and the price is almost nil— compare the cost of a jar of brined leaves from a delicacies shop. The leaves will keep, stored in a cool spot, at least until next season's new leaves appear on the vines.

An alternative to brining, if you want to store grape leaves for only up to 6 months or so, is to wrap the rolled-up stacks of leaves snugly in freezer-weight plastic wrap, seal them airtight with tape, and store them in the deep-freeze. They are ready to use as soon as they have thawed.

> **Grape leaves, either wild or garden variety**
> **Water as needed**
> **Coarse (kosher) salt as needed**

1. Gather the grape leaves in mid-June, or as soon as they are full-sized but still a tender, fairly light green. Clip off the stems and rinse the leaves.

2. Bring a large pot of water to a boil, drop in the leaves, a dozen or so at a time, and leave them in the water just until it boils again. Remove the leaves and plunge them into cold water. When they are cold, drain them, then shake off all surplus water; or pat the leaves dry with a towel.

3. Stack the leaves in piles of six and roll each stack up from a long side, not the stem end or the tip. Tie each roll with string.

4. Estimate the number of jars needed (a quart jar will hold about six rolls, depending on the size of the leaves: or use pint jars, if you prefer smaller batches). Prepare the brine, allowing at least 1 cup for

each quart jar. Boil together water and pure coarse salt (kosher salt or pickling salt, whichever you have) in the proportions of 1/4 cup of salt per quart of water. Boil the brine for 5 minutes and keep it hot.

5. Fit the rolls of grape leaves into clean, hot quart or pint canning jars, adjusting them by bending back the tips of the rolls so that they will fit beneath the shoulder of the jar.

6. Following the Pointers on Preserving on pages 153–56, fill the jars with the hot brine almost to overflowing. Run the blade of a table knife into the jars, close to the glass, to expel any air bubbles. Cover the jars with two-piece lids and fasten the screw bands. Place on a rack in a large kettle containing enough boiling water to come halfway up the jars. Add boiling water to cover the lids by 2 inches or more, cover the pot, bring to a boil, and boil hard (process) for 15 minutes for quarts, 10 minutes for pints.

7. Cool the jars and store in a cool, preferably dark, cupboard.

TO USE: Untie the rolls, drain the leaves, and rinse them quickly in cold water; drain again and proceed with your recipe calling for grape leaves.

PUMPKIN SEEDS, SALTED AND ROASTED

Don't waste the pumpkin seeds when you're making jack-o'-lanterns or pies. Instead, salt and toast them for nutritious snacks. If there are any child laborers on hand, let them slosh through the fibers in pursuit of the slippery seeds; it's the smooshiest orgy since mud pies.

Makes 2 cups

1 quart water
2 tablespoons salt
2 cups pumpkin seeds
1 tablespoon unsalted butter

1. Preheat the oven to 350 degrees.

2. Bring the water and salt to a boil. Add the seeds and boil for 10 minutes (or for 15 if they are large and horsey). Drain them well.

3. Combine the seeds and butter in a roasting pan or dish and toss until the butter is melted and the seeds evenly coated.

(continued)

4. Roast for 25 to 30 minutes, or until the seeds are crisp and golden, stirring and tossing often.

5. Cool the seeds and pack them airtight.

SALTED ROASTED ALMONDS

These delicious home-roasted nuts are much crisper and drier than their store-bought cousins. Nor do they have the oily texture and flavor that often obfuscate the delicate, natural taste of roasted nuts. You can salt them to taste, which is no small advantage for those of us who find commercial nuts more than slightly oversalted.

Makes 1½ pounds

1 egg white
1 ½ pounds whole, unblanched almonds
4 to 5 teaspoons coarse (kosher) salt

1. Preheat the oven to 275 degrees.

2. Beat the egg white until frothy. Place the nuts in a sieve and add the beaten white. Toss and stir the nuts to coat them evenly.

3. Pour the nuts onto an oiled baking sheet and sprinkle them with the salt, tossing to coat them evenly. Bake for 30 minutes, or until they are golden, shaking them often and breaking them apart with a spatula.

4. Turn off the oven and let the nuts remain another 30 minutes, until thoroughly crisp and dry.

5. Cool the nuts.

TO STORE: The nuts will keep indefinitely if stored airtight in the refrigerator or the freezer.

CURRIED OR CHILI-FLAVORED ALMONDS

For lightly spiced nuts, follow the directions above for Salted Roasted Almonds, but add about ¾ teaspoon Curry Powder (page 196) or Chili Powder (page 197) to the salt (about 1½ teaspoons) for each ½ pound nuts. Toast, cool, and store as for Salted Roasted Almonds. These freeze well for 3 to 4 months, or keep well in the refrigerator for 2 or 3 weeks.

SHREDDED COCONUT

Makes about 3 cups

Unsweetened fresh coconut is hard to come by and extremely expensive, as you have discovered if you have ever needed it for curries or for making coconut milk or cream. As it freezes well, retaining its character and texture, there is no reason to be without the real stuff.

1. Pick a medium-sized coconut, one that makes a splashy sound when shaken. Puncture two of the "eyes" in one end with a screwdriver and a mallet. Drain off, chill, and drink the coconut water, which has a light, refreshing sweetness.

2. Preheat the oven to 325 degrees.

3. Bake the whole coconut for 15 to 20 minutes on the shelf of the preheated oven. Remove, crack the shell with taps of a hammer, and pull the pieces of meat free. Remove the brown skin from the pieces with a swivel-bladed peeler, then chop or grate the meat in a food processor or by hand. Package airtight and freeze. Do not refrigerate; the coconut will spoil quickly.

SALTED COCONUT CHIPS

A remarkably simple, tasty, and nourishing snack food, fairly high-priced in the shops but very inexpensive to make, these are thin, crispy crescents with lightly browned edges and a rich coconut flavor. Coconut chips you make at home aren't likely to be around long enough to develop the predominantly oily character of some packaged chips.

The chips go well with Malaysian, Indonesian, Ceylonese, and Caribbean foods, as well as with Indian dishes. You might also try them as a garnish for crisply fried fish or for plain-cooked vegetables such as cauliflower, beans, or peas.

Makes 4 to 5 cups

1 medium fresh coconut (shake it to be sure it has liquid inside)
Fine salt as needed

1. Puncture the coconut through two of the "eyes," using a screwdriver and a hammer. Drain out the liquid.
2. Preheat the oven to 325 degrees.
3. Bake the whole coconut for 15 to 20 minutes on the shelf of the preheated oven. Crack the shell with taps of a hammer and pull the pieces of meat free. Leave the oven on, or preheat an electric skillet set at 350 degrees.
4. Using a swivel-bladed peeler, remove the brown skin. Use the peeler to shave the coconut into thin crosswise crescents.
5. Spread the coconut shavings in a single layer on a baking sheet and toast in the oven, turning often with a pancake turner; or toast in the preheated electric skillet, turning often.
6. When the coconut chips begin to turn a pale cream color, sprinkle with fine salt and continue toasting until light gold and crisp.
7. Cool the chips. Store airtight in the refrigerator or freezer. They will keep for 2 weeks refrigerated, for several months in the freezer.

TO REHEAT: Before serving, refresh the chips briefly in a warm (250- to 300-degree) oven.

CURRIED COCONUT CHIPS

Prepare and toast the coconut chips through step 4 of the recipe above. Mix about ¼ teaspoon Curry Powder (page 196) and fine salt to taste with each cupful of chips. Toast and taste; add more curry powder and salt, if needed. Store like the salted chips.

NOTE: Previously salted chips may also be spiced: simply mix them with curry powder and rewarm gently on a baking sheet in a 200-degree oven for 20 to 30 minutes, turning often.

PEANUT BUTTER

Making peanut butter has become a national pastime. In case you haven't happened upon one of the many recipes that abound in health-food and appliance cookbooks, use this one.

You may simply pour a can of salted roasted nuts into your blender or food-processor container and whirl away. Or you may use raw nuts and toast them before grinding, as we prefer. They are cheaper, apt to be fresher than most roasted nuts bought in bulk, and you can control the degree of toastiness, saltiness, and sweetness, as well as the consistency of the peanut butter.

Makes about 1¾ cups

1 pound raw, shelled peanuts (weight after shelling)
½ to 1 teaspoon salt
½ to 1 teaspoon sugar
2 tablespoons peanut oil

1. Preheat the oven to 300 degrees.
2. Spread the nuts in a jelly-roll or roasting pan and bake them for 20 minutes, shaking the pan now and then; they should be *light* gold.
3. Cool the peanuts, then proceed in either of the following ways:

FOR CREAMY PEANUT BUTTER: Put half the nuts in the container of a food processor (or jar of a blender) with half of the salt, sugar, and oil. Process to a creamy consistency (stopping the action and scraping down the sides of the container often with a spatula), then empty the peanut butter into a bowl and repeat with the remaining nuts, salt, sugar, and oil.

FOR CHUNKY PEANUT BUTTER: Use the processor to chop about one-third of the nuts coarsely; set aside, then process the remaining nuts, salt, sugar, and oil to a creamy consistency. Stir together with the chopped nuts. Or use a blender as follows: Do half of the nuts at a time and scrape down the sides of the container and scrape under the blades several times. Process to as crunchy a texture as you wish. It's not necessary to chop part of the nuts first for blender chunky peanut butter.

TO STORE: Store the peanut butter in a covered jar in the refrigerator, where it will keep for about 2 weeks (for this reason do not make more than a 10 days' supply).

(continued)

ALMOND, CASHEW, OR FILBERT BUTTER

Use the recipe for Peanut Butter (see above), but substitute almonds, cashews, or filberts; a combination of almonds and filberts is especially good. After roasting filberts, rub off as much of the husks as possible after toasting the nuts. And, of course, don't overbrown any of the nuts; filberts should be toasted just until they crack their skins.

TAHINI (Sesame Paste)

Tahini, or sesame-seed paste, figures in innumerable Middle Eastern recipes and is available through specialty food stores. However, if you lack a source for the authentic article (usually sold canned), you can make an acceptable version at home, using the recipe that follows. Professionally made tahini is smoother and creamier than your product will be, but if you make it yourself you can produce exactly the amount you need, as you need it. You can freeze any surplus, but we like it best made fresh.

Be sure to buy *hulled* white sesame seeds—the unhulled seeds make an unpalatable paste. Because sesame seeds are rich in oil, they become rancid easily, so taste them to be sure they are fresh. Store your fresh stock of seeds in the freezer.

Makes about 7/8 cup

1 cup hulled white sesame seeds
4 to 6 tablespoons cold water, as needed

1. Preheat the oven to 250 degrees.
2. Spread the sesame seeds in a jelly-roll pan and toast them in the preheated oven, stirring often, until light gold, not browned.
3. Scrape the seeds into the container of a blender (or a food processor fitted with the steel blade) and grind them, gradually adding the water (start with no more than 2 tablespoons) and scraping down the sides of the container as necessary. Process until the paste is very smooth. Use immediately, or store in the freezer in a closely capped straight-sided glass jar, where it will keep for many weeks.

DRIED SWEET CORN

This is an old-fashioned treat that is enjoying new appreciation from a generation to which it is a novelty. It is presently being bought at a brisk rate by mail order from country stores, but it's simple and satisfying to prepare your own supply if you live in sweet-corn country. Don't under any circumstances bother with "store-bought" fresh corn—it must be fresh picked and sweet enough to be served as corn on the cob if your dried corn is to be good.

An average ear of corn will yield about ½ cup of kernels, which when dried will amount to about ⅙ cup. Figure how much corn you can dry at one time by considering your oven shelf space—the kernels must be spread only about two deep on shallow pans. Drying will take from 4 to 8 hours, and can be interrupted for a few hours after the corn is partly dry—just turn the oven off, leaving the corn in it, and resume drying when convenient. If you have a convection oven or dehydrator, use it following the manufacturer's instructions.

We learned this modern method of preparing an old-time delicacy from Jane Moulton, a well-known Midwestern food writer who is especially interested in American food. The drying process takes time but little work. The dried corn will keep for a year if it is stored absolutely airtight.

1. Select and husk fresh, sweet corn, the younger and sweeter the better.

2. Bring 1 inch of water to a boil in a large pot. A dozen ears at a time, add the corn to the boiling water. Cover the pot and steam-blanch the corn for 3 minutes after the water boils again. Remove the corn and let it cool slightly while you blanch the next batch, assuming that you're doing more than a dozen ears.

3. Preheat the oven to barely warm (150 degrees or less).

4. Working over a jelly-roll pan, cut the corn from the cobs with a sharp serrated knife. Use the back of the blade to press out any "cream" remaining after the tops of the kernels have been cut off; add the cream to the cut corn.

5. Spread the kernels over the pan no more than two kernels deep and place in the barely warm oven. (Use a thermometer—if the oven tends to become warmer than 150 degrees, prop the door open, or turn

it off occasionally.) Stir the corn frequently (a pancake turner does the job well), spreading it out after each stirring. If you are drying two or more pans of corn, switch shelf positions every few hours. The drying time will depend on the heat of the oven, the depth of the kernels on the pans, and the size of the kernels; allow from 4 to 8 hours. The corn is dry enough when the kernels are pale caramel-colored, much shrunken, and decidedly hard.

6. Let the corn cool on the pans, then store it in jars with airtight lids. To be sure that the corn is completely dry (it won't keep well if it harbors any trace of moisture), check the jars after 2 days. If there is any sign of dampness on the inside of the jars, return the corn to the pans and the oven (kept at 150 degrees or less) and dry it further.

TO COOK: We like Jane Moulton's short method for preparing the corn, which has a wonderful deep-summer flavor.

Combine the dried corn with four times its volume of water in a saucepan and bring it to a boil. (Half a cup of dried corn will provide three to four moderate servings.) Cover the corn and simmer it until it has the texture you like. Cooking time varies: it may be as short as 10 minutes or as long as an hour, depending on the corn. Season the corn with salt and butter, adding cream or pepper if you like.

GRANOLA

A granola for granola lovers, who, judging from the proliferation of brands available, must be increasing their ranks at a frightening rate. This is a toasty, baked version, because we don't happen to like raw cereals. But by all means, don't stop at this if you're a granola fiend: experiment with all manner of nuts, seeds, and spices, keeping roughly to these proportions. Have granola with milk or on yogurt, or use it to bake Granola Cookies (page 232), breads, cakes, or candies.

Makes 6 cups

2 ½ cups quick-cooking oatmeal
  1 cup Shredded Coconut (page 289; or use unsweetened coconut
    from a health-food store)
  ⅓ cup untoasted sunflower seeds
  ¼ cup hulled sesame seeds
  ½ stick (4 tablespoons) unsalted margarine (or use salted margarine and
    do not add additional salt)
  ¼ cup (packed) dark brown sugar

¼ cup honey
½ teaspoon salt
1 ½ teaspoons vanilla extract
½ cup toasted wheat germ
½ cup raisins

1. Preheat the oven to 300 degrees.

2. Spread the oatmeal, coconut, sunflower seeds, and sesame seeds in a large, lightly buttered roasting pan or ovenproof dish (about 11 × 17 inches is best, although a smaller pan will do). Bake for about 20 minutes, tossing several times.

3. Meanwhile, combine in a small saucepan the margarine, brown sugar, honey, and salt and bring to a simmer, stirring. Add the vanilla off the heat.

4. Reset the oven control at 350 degrees, then add the wheat germ to the toasted mixture. Dribble the sugar-honey syrup over the granola, tossing with a fork to coat the dry mixture evenly.

5. Return the pan to the oven and bake for 5 or 6 minutes longer. Add the raisins, toss to distribute, and press the granola down firmly into an even layer. Bake 5 minutes or so longer, or until the granola is golden.

6. Remove from the oven and let cool slightly. Slip a flexible spatula under the granola to break it into large pieces. Let cool completely and store airtight.

EXTRA-FINE GRANULATED SUGAR AND CONFECTIONERS' SUGAR

It happens in the best of families that a staple ingredient runs short— or turns out to be missing—after you have begun preparing something, and there's just no substitute for the missing link. If what you lack is confectioners' (or powdered) sugar, or extra-fine sugar for a special purpose, the day is saved if you own a food processor.

Simply fit the bowl with the steel blade and process ordinary granulated sugar until it is as fine as you wish. It may take some time, but less time and aggravation than a trip to the grocery store would involve, especially if you're at your country house, ten miles from town. There. That's the recipe.

VANILLA SUGAR (Granulated or Powdered)

Because of its fragrance, vanilla sugar seems sweeter than unflavored sugar, either granulated or powdered. Use granulated vanilla sugar sparingly to enhance the flavor of sliced fruits; and use it, too, in place of regular sugar in delicate pastries and desserts. Sprinkle a snowfall of powdered vanilla sugar over crêpes, sponge cake, Ladyfingers (page 230), or Pound Cake (page 244). It is also particularly good for making icings.

Simply bury one, two, or even more vanilla beans in a jar of sugar and cover it with a tight lid. If you want the beans to flavor the sugar more quickly, cut them lengthwise with kitchen shears. Do this over the container of sugar so the tiny seeds—source of much of the flavor—will land where they belong.

Fine-quality vanilla beans will aromatize for many months, so it's feasible to add more sugar as you use your supply. When the beans are quite dry, they can still be used to flavor custards or syrups before being discarded; or powder them in a spice mill and use the mild vanilla "dust" as a flavoring.

The slight dampness of vanilla beans may cause powdered sugar to lump, but this is no problem if you sift it before using it.

VANILLA EXTRACT

This is an extract of moderate strength, not as concentrated as commercially produced vanilla extract, which usually includes glycerine and a sweetener and sometimes other additives. You'll probably find you will want to increase the measurement when using this extract, perhaps even doubling the quantity.

Vanilla beans
Vodka

1. Cut vanilla beans into quarters, then split the sections lengthwise with kitchen scissors. Drop the pieces into a small, clean, dry bottle that has a tight cap.

2. Add 1 ounce (2 tablespoons) of vodka per vanilla bean, shake well,

and set the bottle in a spot where you'll see it and remember to shake it often. The extract will be ready in about 4 weeks; an occasional sniff will help you judge its state.

3. Filter your extract into a clean bottle through a funnel lined with coffee-filter paper. (For super-vanilla, pour the extract onto a fresh batch of beans in another bottle.) Store tightly capped.

NOTE: The used beans can be recycled: add them to syrup when poaching fruit, or put them into a jar of sugar to yield up their remaining aroma to Vanilla Sugar (page 295).

LEMON EXTRACT

An appealingly fresh lemon extract, smoother and mellower than commercial kinds, the flavor of which comes mainly from lemon oil rather than fresh peel. As the flavor of homemade extract is less intense, double the quantity called for in recipes. Thrift note: When you're going to squeeze a lemon, first strip off the rind and add it to your extract bottle.

Lemons
Vodka

1. Choose bright lemons with plenty of oil in their skins (squeeze one to see if oil pops from the pores). Using a swivel-bladed peeler, strip off the skin in narrow pieces that will pass easily through the neck of a bottle, or in wider strips if you are making the extract in a jar. Fill your container loosely about half full of the thinly peeled rind. Top with vodka almost to the brim and cover the bottle or jar. Let stand at room temperature.

2. Shake the bottle daily, or whenever you pass by the spot where it's sitting. Sniff the extract once in a while to judge its progress. After about 2 weeks most lemons will have yielded up most of their essence. Discard the rind and replace it with a fresh batch. Let the extract stand as before, shaking it daily. Sniff occasionally and when the extract smells good, it's ready.

3. For a clear extract, filter the liquid through a funnel lined with coffee-filter paper into a second bottle. Cap and store at room temperature.

Noodling

Pasta fanciers are convinced that only hand-rolled noodles can achieve perfect texture, and they may well be right. We confess to a preference for the convenience of pasta machines, either hand-operated or electric. These machines knead the dough, roll it to the thickness (or thinness) you decide upon, then cut the noodles.

Freshly made noodles are very tender and quick-cooking. If you want a firmer texture, try using bread flour—if you can find it—or use 1 part gluten flour to 6 parts all-purpose flour in our recipes that don't call for gluten flour. Best of all is semolina flour—the professionals' choice—which is almost impossible to find at retail.

MIXING THE DOUGH

Using a Food Processor.   We have tried all the principal ways of mixing pasta dough, and by far the easiest is the food-processor method. It is incredibly simple: you put the dry ingredients into the processor container, fitted with the steel blade, and run the machine briefly to mix them. Then in go the eggs and any liquid called for, and the processor is run just until the mixture becomes a well-defined ball of kneaded dough circling around atop the blade.

Using an Electric Mixer.   What about electric mixers? Most household models won't handle a dough as stiff as that for pasta. A heavy-duty machine equipped with a dough hook will mix and knead the dough, however; about 10 minutes' mixing and kneading with the hook should do the job.

Mixing by Hand.   Either a mixing bowl or a mixing slab will do for making pasta dough by hand. First the flour goes into the bowl or onto the board and a crater is scooped out in its center. Into the depression go salt, eggs, and any other ingredients called for. With your fingers or a spatula, work from the center outwards, first mixing the moist ingredients and then gradually incorporating the flour. If the mixture is too dry to make a ball of dough you may have to sprinkle in a few drops of water; if it is too moist, dust on more flour. Knead by hand on a floured board until the dough is smooth and elastic—unless you have a pasta machine. In that case, you let the machine do the kneading.

ROLLING AND CUTTING NOODLES

Using a Pasta Machine. Divide the dough into portions of a good handful each and work with one part at a time, keeping the other portions covered with plastic wrap or an inverted bowl so they won't dry out.

Set the pasta rollers as far apart as possible, at the "kneading" opening. Flatten your piece of dough and dust a little flour on each side, then feed it through the machine. If the edges are ragged, fold the sides of the strip to the center and run it through again, repeating the folding (if necessary for smooth edges) and the rolling until the dough looks satiny and feels smooth. Then set the rollers closer together and roll the dough thinner. Continue to thin out the dough, resetting the machine notch by notch, until you reach the thickness you want. Lay the sheet of dough on a cloth to dry slightly while you knead and roll out the remaining dough.

Change to the cutting rollers and, starting with your first-rolled strip of dough, cut noodles. If the noodles are not cleanly separated, the dough is too damp; let the sheets dry a while longer before cutting them. Gather the strands as they are cut and either spread them out flat on a cloth-covered table, hang them over a rod between two chair backs, or tumble them with a dusting of flour on a cloth-covered table. Let them dry for about half an hour before cooking them; or, if they are to be stored, let them dry until crisp, then package them carefully and store them at room temperature.

Rolling and Cutting Noodles by Hand. After the dough has been kneaded, divide it into portions as described for machine-rolled noodles. Flour a big pastry board and a noodle pin, if you have one; otherwise use an ordinary rolling pin. Roll one portion of dough out from the center in every direction, stretching it often with your hands from time to time, until you can see through it. Dust with flour when necessary to prevent stickiness. When the sheet is thin enough, dust it again and set it aside for a few minutes to dry slightly, not to the point of brittleness. Roll the remaining portions of dough in the same way.

To hand-cut noodles, either accordion-pleat each sheet of dough into a neat stack about 2 inches wide, or roll it up into a cylinder. Use a very sharp serrated knife to cut noodles of the width you prefer. Shake the noodles out onto a floured cloth and proceed to dry partly or completely and/or freeze.

(continued)

FREEZING FRESH NOODLES

After pasta has dried a bit—just enough so the noodles won't stick to each other—it freezes very successfully in plastic bags and keeps almost indefinitely. Fine noodles tend to break less if they are dried in very loose coils, formed around your hand, of a few strands each.

COOKING HOMEMADE NOODLES

For up to a pound (dried weight) of noodles, boil 6 or 7 quarts of water and salt it generously after it boils. When it boils again, sprinkle in the pasta, stir occasionally with a long fork, and watch the pot—the pasta will be done very quickly. Dried pasta will take slightly longer to cook than fresh, but it requires less cooking time than the store-bought. Test a strand every half-minute or so by biting. Stop the cooking by pouring in 2 cups of cold water the instant the pasta is done to your taste.

For removing pasta from water, we prefer to use tongs or a spaghetti lifter instead of draining it in a colander. Put it into a warmed bowl and add butter, seasonings, or sauce.

EGG NOODLES

Makes about 1 pound fresh weight, 12 to 14 ounces dried weight

3 eggs
1 tablespoon olive oil
1 teaspoon salt
1 to 2 tablespoons water, as needed
2 cups all-purpose flour, or as needed, plus additional for kneading and
**   rolling the dough**

1. Lightly beat together the eggs, oil, salt, and 1 tablespoon of the water.

2. Mix the liquid into the flour to form a pasta dough, following the general instructions on page 298. If necessary, add a little more water, a few drops at a time, while mixing the dough; the exact amount needed will depend upon the moisture content of your flour.

3. Knead, roll out, and cut the dough by hand or by machine, following the general instructions.

TO COOK: Follow the general instructions above.

GREEN (SPINACH) NOODLES

Makes about 1¾ pounds fresh weight, about 20 ounces dried weight

**1 package (10 ounces) frozen spinach, thawed, or 1 cup (packed) fresh
  spinach that has been blanched, cooled in ice water, and drained
  A little water, if needed
2 eggs
1 ½ teaspoons salt
⅛ teaspoon grated nutmeg
3 cups all-purpose flour, or as needed, plus additional for rolling the
  noodles**

1. Puree the thawed frozen spinach or the blanched fresh spinach, using a blender (do the spinach in two batches, with a little water added to each) or a food processor fitted with the steel blade. Pour the puree into a very fine sieve (or a colander lined with cheesecloth) and let all the liquid drain; you should have a scant cup of firm puree.

2. To make the noodles, beat together the spinach puree, eggs, salt, and nutmeg and proceed to mix with the flour; knead, roll, and cut the dough as described in the general instructions on page 298.

TO COOK: Follow the general instructions on page 300.

WHOLE-WHEAT NOODLES

Makes about 1½ pounds fresh weight, 14 to 15 ounces dried weight

**2 cups whole-wheat flour
½ cup gluten flour plus ½ cup all-purpose flour, or (if available) 1 cup
  bread flour, plus additional for kneading and rolling the dough
4 eggs, lightly beaten
2 teaspoons salt
3 tablespoons water, if needed**

1. Combine the flours.

2. Mix the eggs and salt, then mix with the flours; knead, roll, and cut the dough, by hand or by machine, as described in the general instructions on page 298. If necessary, add a little water during the

mixing, a few drops at a time; the exact amount of water needed will depend on the moisture content of the various flours.

TO COOK: Follow the general instructions on page 300.

BUCKWHEAT NOODLES

Buckwheat flour is very low in gluten, so dough made from it tends to lack cohesion and elasticity; hence the inclusion of gluten flour. You must, knead this dough very thoroughly, by whatever method you choose, to "develop" the gluten. The noodles will be darker and grainier than imported Oriental buckwheat noodles, with a more pronounced buckwheat flavor.

Makes about 1 pound fresh weight, about 10 to 12 ounces dried weight

1 cup buckwheat flour
½ cup gluten flour
½ cup all-purpose flour, plus additional for kneading and rolling the dough
2 eggs
1 teaspoon salt
2 tablespoons water, or as needed

1. Mix the buckwheat, gluten, and all-purpose flours.
2. Beat the eggs lightly with the salt and 1½ tablespoons of the water and mix the dough as described in the general instructions on page 298.
3. Knead this dough *very* thoroughly, then roll and cut narrow noodles as directed.

TO COOK: Follow the general instructions on page 300.

EGG "SPAGHETTI" OR "LASAGNE"

Spaghetti should have bite. We like it firm enough to maintain its identity when sauced. If you cannot buy the fine imported Italian pastas, make our dough—the addition of gluten flour in the recipe produces a very firm, chewy spaghetti, while the eggs add flavor. When you use this dough to make lasagne, the pasta will remain firm during the baking, which is why we prefer it to the dough for egg noodles.

Makes about 3/4 pound fresh weight, about 8 to 10 ounces dried weight

1 ¼ cups all-purpose flour
¼ cup gluten flour
1 teaspoon salt
2 large eggs beaten with 1 tablespoon water

1. Combine the flours and salt, then mix with the eggs and water to make a dough and knead it, following the general instructions on page 298.

2. Cut the dough into three pieces. Cover with plastic and let stand for a few minutes.

3. For spaghetti, roll each piece of dough to medium thickness, either by hand or by machine, then cut into narrow widths. To cook, follow the general directions on page 300.

4. For lasagne, roll slightly thicker sheets of dough, then cut into strips about 3 inches wide and as long as the baking dish dictates. Cover with a towel and cook, according to the requirements of your recipe, within 1 hour.

A Note on Equipment

You probably own most if not all of the equipment needed for cooking your way through *Better Than Store-Bought*. As definitions of basic equipment most certainly vary from one house to another, here's our list of kitchen appliances and utensils that we find indispensable. We assume that your kitchen has a full complement of spoons, pots, pans, baking sheets, and the like.

An instant-reading food thermometer, the quickest and most accurate way to check food temperatures below 220 degrees.

A candy-jelly thermometer, without which making candies and jellies is virtually impossible.

Kitchen scales, preferably capable of weighing amounts from a few ounces to at least 10 pounds; beam-balance scales are generally more accurate than spring-balance types.

A food processor is required for several recipes in the book. When a blender will do as well, we have indicated that.

An electric blender, if you don't have a processor, will be useful.

A small electric spice or coffee grinder, reserved for milling spices only.

A meat grinder or a *multipurpose kitchen machine,* with the necessary attachments for stuffing sausages as well as grinding meat.

A few pieces of *fine-gauge nylon curtain netting* large enough to double-line a colander; more durable, much easier to handle and to clean for re-use than cheesecloth, which you can of course substitute.

Baking parchment, which promotes even, attractive coloring of the undersurfaces of cookies and other baked goods; and, most important, it prevents sticking.

An oblong steel pastry scraper or, instead, a large, stiff-bladed *putty knife*; for mixing dough and cleaning pastry surfaces.

Natural-bristle pastry brushes—or *paint brushes*—in various sizes and
widths.

Single-edged razor blades for slashing unbaked loaves; or, if you can
find one, a *baker's lame*—literally "blade" in French.

Nylon or stainless-steel strainers, in various sizes and degrees of fineness of mesh. These won't affect the flavor or color of certain delicate or acid preparations.

Mail·Order
Sources of Supplies

HERBS AND SPICES

Aphrodisia Products, Inc.
28 Carmine Street
New York, NY 10014

Bay Colony Spices, c/o IMI
401 Wood Street (12th floor)
Pittsburgh, PA 15222

Colonial Kitchens of Georgetown
Georgetown, DC 20007

Deer Valley Farm
R.D. 1
Guilford, NY 13780

Eden Foods
4601 Platt Road
Ann Arbor, MI 48104

Estus
2186 San Pasqual Street
Pasadena, CA 91107

Green Mountain Herbs
P.O. Box 2369
Boulder, CO 80302

Greensleeves, Ltd.
7 Stone Road
Brookfield, VT 05036

Hilltop Herb Farm
P.O. Box 866
Cleveland, TX 77327

Magic Garden Herb Co.
P.O. Box 332
Fairfax, CA 94930

Meadowbrook Herb Garden
Wyoming, RI 02898

Nature's Herb Co.
281 Ellis Street
San Francisco, CA 94102

Northwestern Coffee Mills
217 North Broadway
Milwaukee, WI 53202

Paprikás Weiss
1546 Second Avenue
New York, NY 10028

Rocky Hollow Herb Farm
Sussex, NJ 07461

H. Roth & Son
1577 First Avenue
New York, NY 10028

Specialty Spice Shop
2757 152nd Avenue N.E.
Redmond, WA 98052

The Spice Market
94 Reade Street
New York, NY 10013

The Spice Corner
Dept. G-127
904 South 9th Street
Philadelphia, PA 19147

The United Society of Shakers
Sabbathday Lake
Poland Spring, ME 04274

Yankee Tea Trader
P.O. Box 747
Escondido, CA 92025

FLOURS AND GRAINS

Arrowhead Mills
Box 866
Hereford, TX 79045

Better Foods Foundation, Inc.*
300 North Washington Street
Greencastle, PA 17225

The Birkett Mills
P.O. Box 440-A
Penn Yan, NY 14527

Brownsville Mills
Brownsville, NB 68321

Byrd Mill Co.
P.O. Box 5167
Richmond, VA 23220

Deer Valley Farm
R.D. 1
Guilford, NY 13780

Dutch School
22 North 7th Street
Akron, PA 17501

Erewhon Trading Co.
8454 Steller Drive
Culver City, CA 90230

General Nutrition Corporation
921 Penn Avenue
Pittsburgh, PA 15222

Great Valley Mills
Quakertown, PA 18951

Jaffe Bros.
P.O. Box 636
Valley Center, CA 92082

Nature Plus
125 First Avenue
New York, NY 10003

Old Town Mill Store*
4315 Mail Street
Union Gap, WA 98903

Paprikás Weiss
1546 Second Avenue
New York, NY 10028

H. Roth & Son
1577 First Avenue
New York, NY 10028

The Vermont Country Store
Weston, VT 05161

Walnut Acres
Penns Creek, PA. 17862

Wheatex Milling Co., Inc.*
1508 First Street
Marysville, WA 98270

Whole Grain Sales
Route 2
Waunakee, WI 53597

MISCELLANEOUS

SAUSAGE CASINGS

H. Roth & Son
1577 First Avenue
New York, NY 10028

Sedro Industries
P.O. Box 8009
Rochester, NY 14606

The Standard Casing Co., Inc.
121 Spring Street
New York, NY 10012

Tatarowicz's
390 Broadway
Bayonne, NJ 07002

*Gluten flour is available from these sources, as well as from many local health-food stores.

LOLLIPOP STICKS AND MUFFIN RINGS

Maid of Scandinavia Company
3244 Raleigh Avenue
Minneapolis, MN 55416

RENNET TABLETS (DESSERT TYPE)

For information about local or mail-order sources, if you can't find rennet at drug or grocery stores, write Consumer Service Department, Salada Foods., Inc., 235 Porter Street, Battle Creek, MI 49016.

TABLE OF METRIC EQUIVALENTS
(Weight and Volume)

Weight (common units)

1 ounce	28.35 grams
1 pound	453.59 grams
1 gram	0.035 ounces
1 kilogram	2.21 pounds

Volume (common units)

1 cup	16 tablespoons
	8 fluid ounces
	236.6 milliliters
1 tablespoon	3 teaspoons
	0.5 fluid ounce
	14.8 milliliters
1 teaspoon	4.9 milliliters
1 liter	1,000 milliliters
	1.06 quarts
1 bushel	4 pecks
1 peck	8 quarts
1 gallon	4 quarts
1 quart	2 pints
1 pint	2 cups
	473.2 milliliters

Index

Index